Oliver Parry

LAZY
DAZE

JIM DAVIS

RAVETTE PUBLISHING

This edition first published by Ravette Publishing 2004.

Printed and bound for Ravette Publishing Limited
Unit 3, Tristar Centre
Star Road, Partridge Green
West Sussex RH13 8RA

by Gutenberg Press Ltd, Malta.

ISBN: 1 84161 208 1

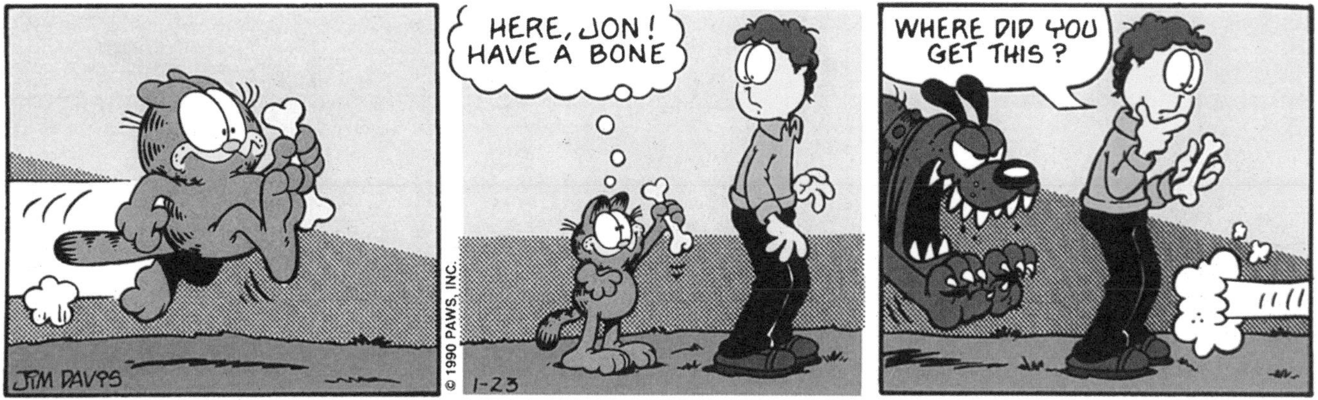

JIM DAVIS
HERE, JON! HAVE A BONE
© 1990 PAWS, INC.
1-23
WHERE DID YOU GET THIS?

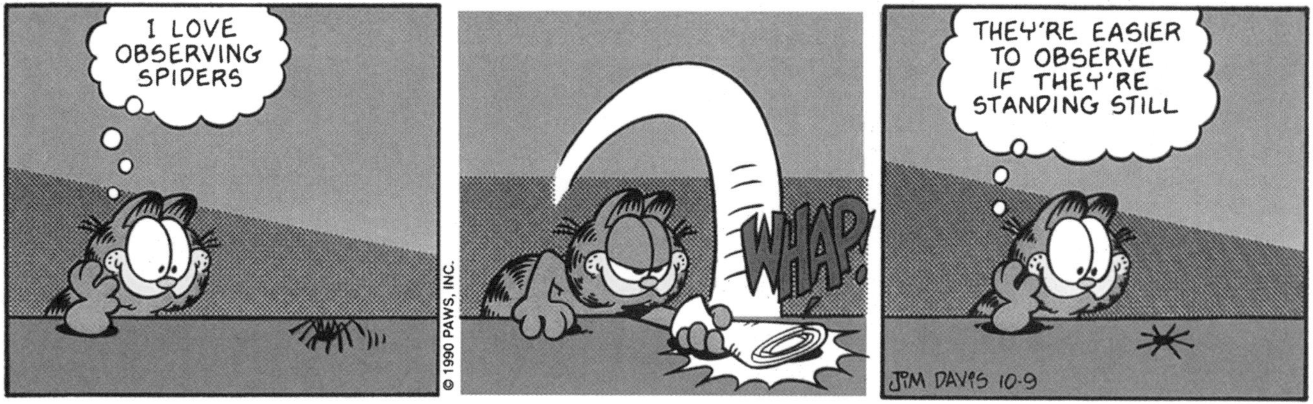

I LOVE OBSERVING SPIDERS
© 1990 PAWS, INC.
WHAP!
THEY'RE EASIER TO OBSERVE IF THEY'RE STANDING STILL
JIM DAVIS 10-9

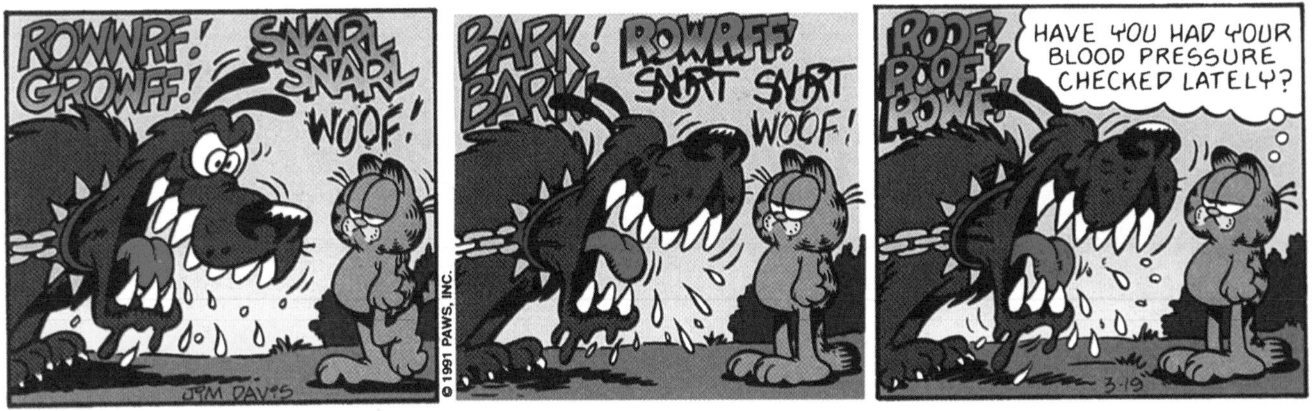
ROWWRF! GROWFF!
SNARL SNARL
WOOF!
JIM DAVIS
© 1991 PAWS, INC.
BARK! BARK!
ROWRFF!
SNRT SNRT
WOOF!
ROOF! ROOF! ROWF!
HAVE YOU HAD YOUR BLOOD PRESSURE CHECKED LATELY?
3-19

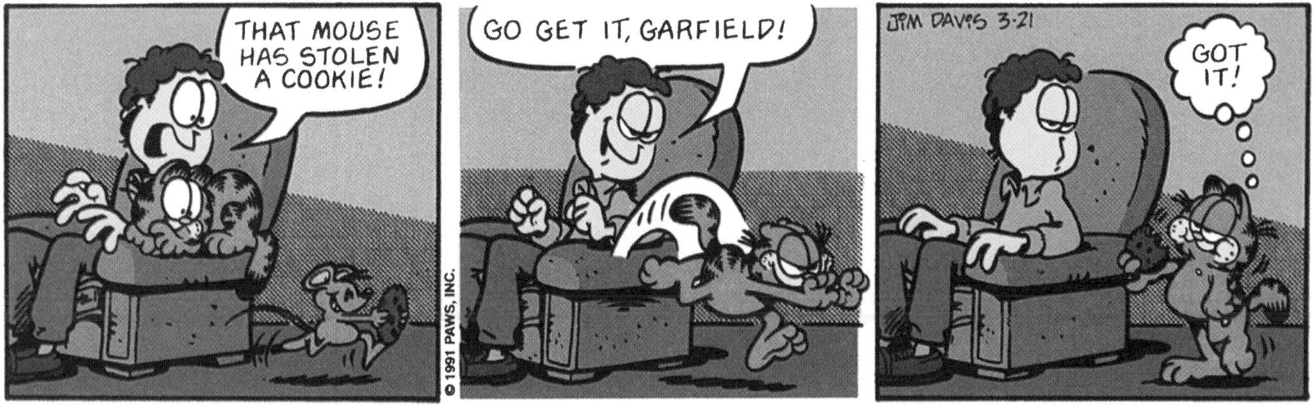
THAT MOUSE HAS STOLEN A COOKIE!
© 1991 PAWS, INC.
GO GET IT, GARFIELD!
JIM DAVIS 3-21
GOT IT!

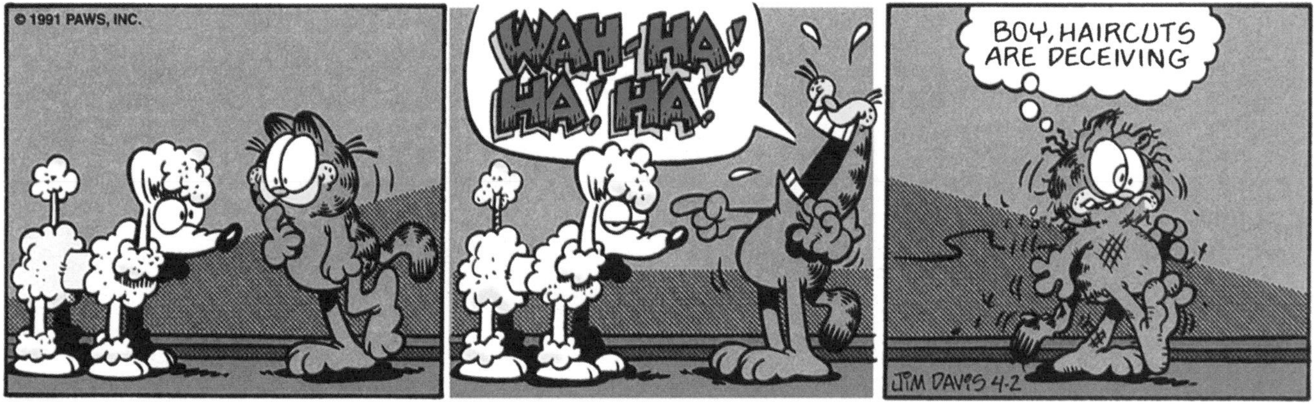
© 1991 PAWS, INC.
WAH-HA! HA! HA!
BOY, HAIRCUTS ARE DECEIVING
JIM DAVIS 4-2

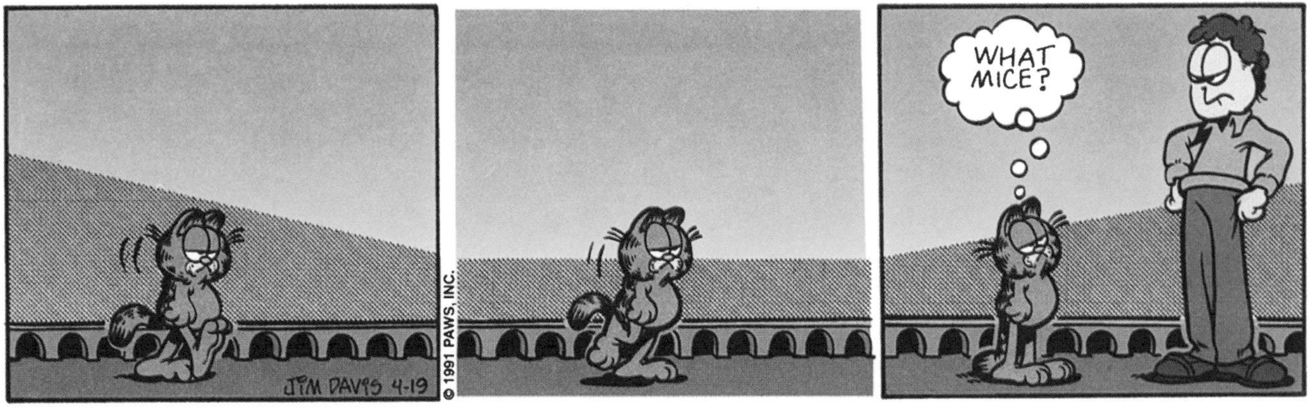
JIM DAVIS 4-19
© 1991 PAWS, INC.
WHAT MICE?

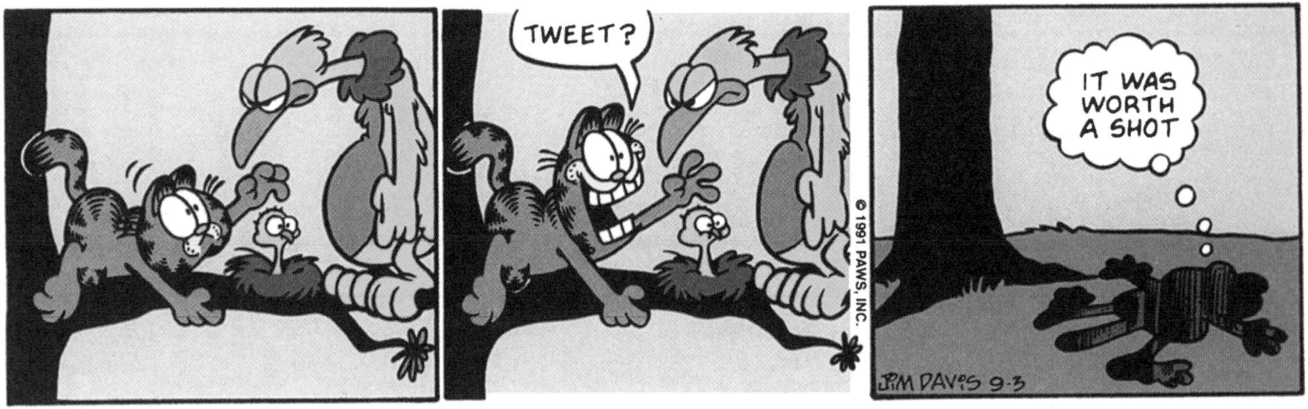
TWEET?
© 1991 PAWS, INC.
IT WAS WORTH A SHOT
JIM DAVIS 9-3

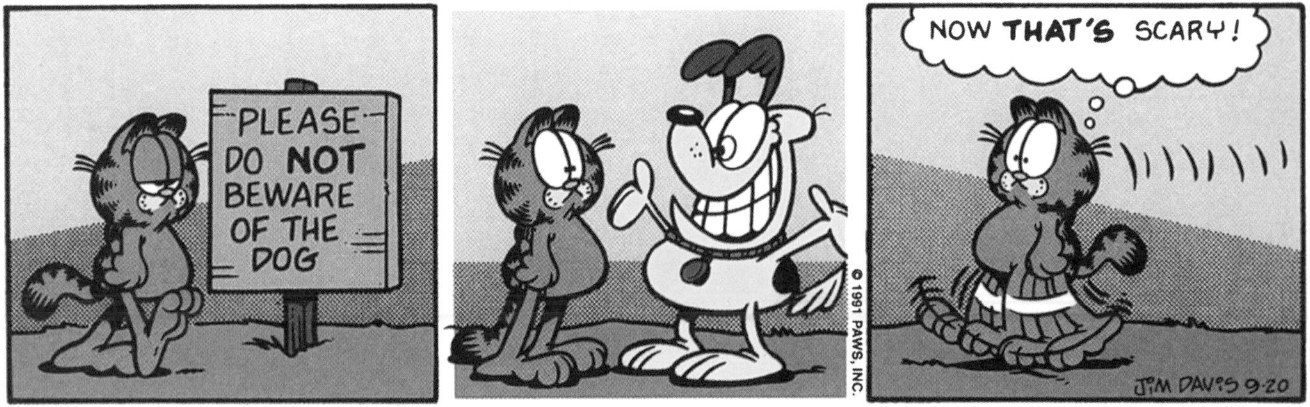
PLEASE DO NOT BEWARE OF THE DOG
© 1991 PAWS, INC.
NOW THAT'S SCARY!
JIM DAVIS 9-20

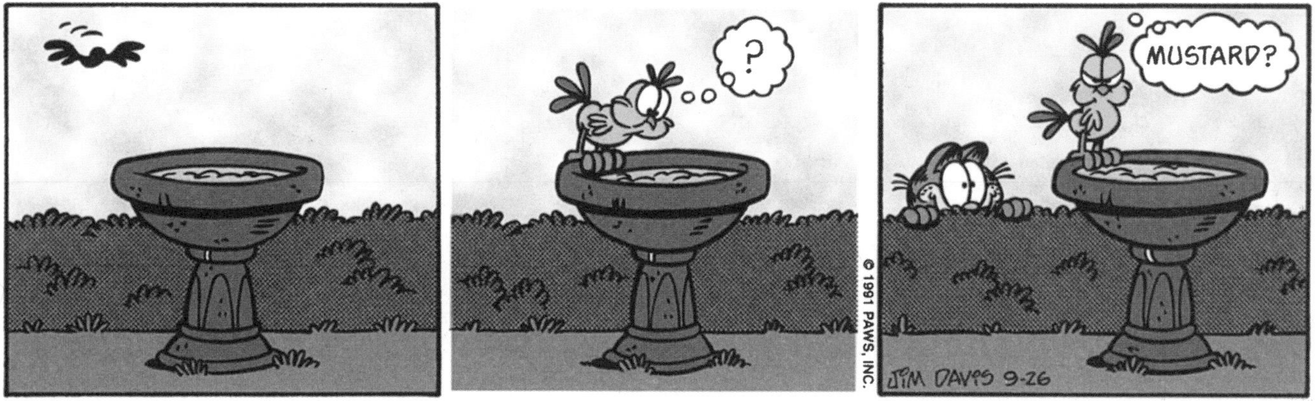
?
MUSTARD?
© 1991 PAWS, INC.
JIM DAVIS 9-26

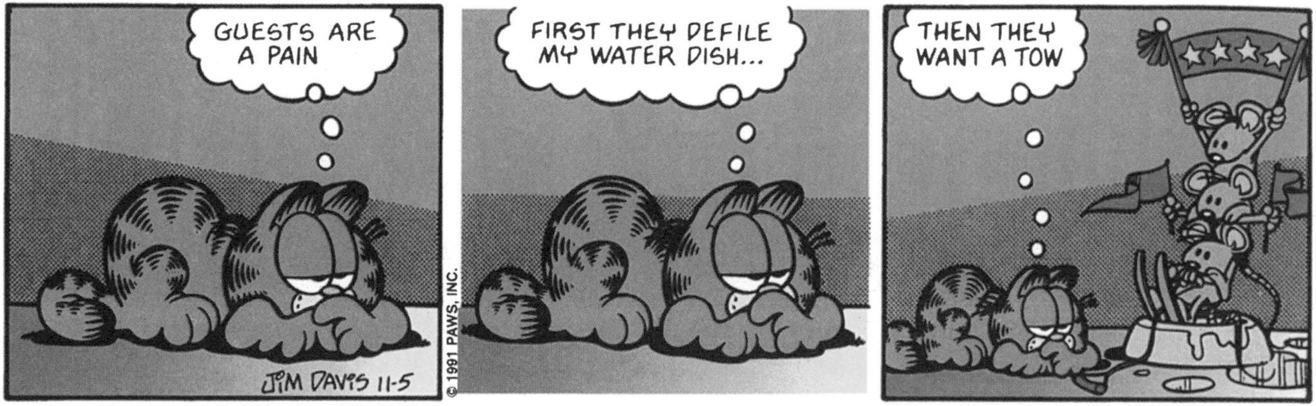
GUESTS ARE A PAIN
JIM DAVIS 11-5
© 1991 PAWS, INC.
FIRST THEY DEFILE MY WATER DISH...
THEN THEY WANT A TOW

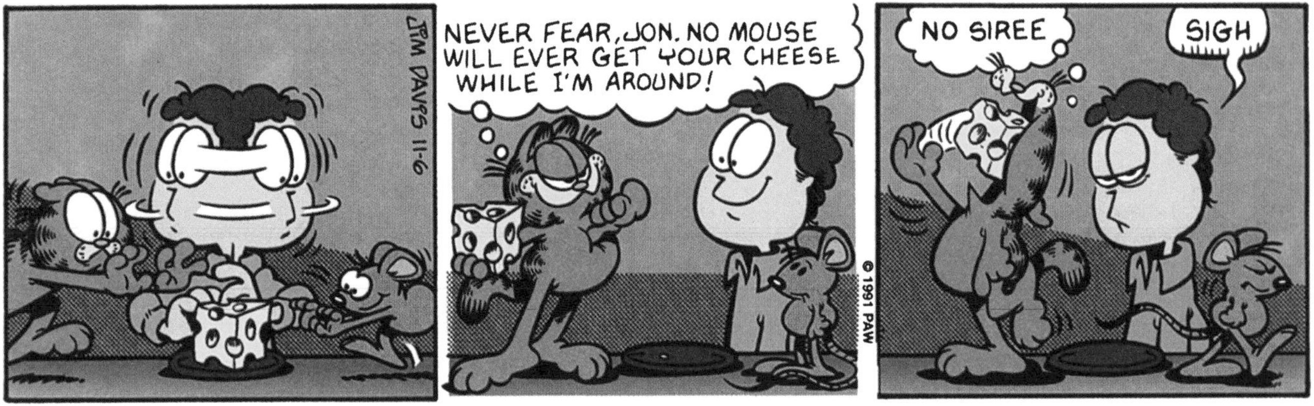
JIM DAVIS 11-6
NEVER FEAR, JON. NO MOUSE WILL EVER GET YOUR CHEESE WHILE I'M AROUND!
© 1991 PAW
NO SIREE
SIGH

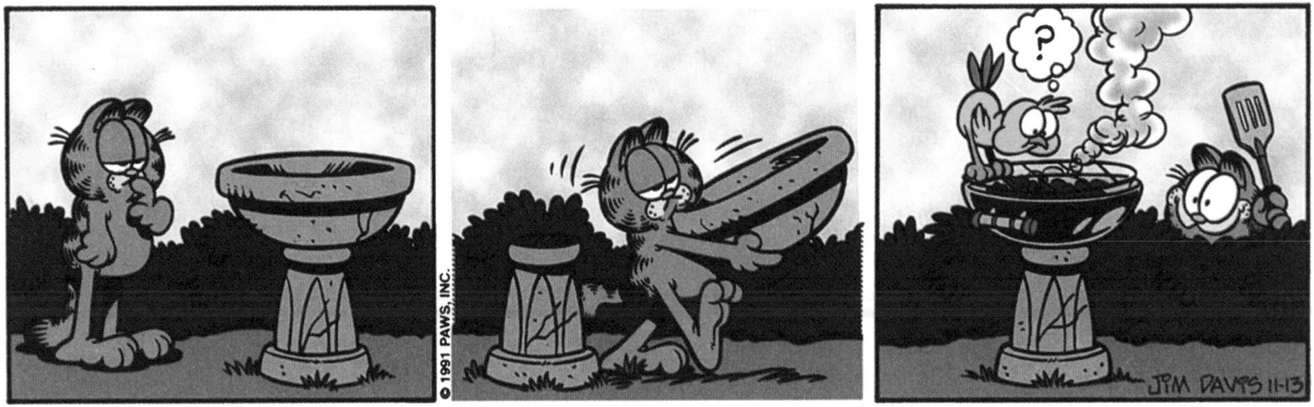
© 1991 PAWS, INC.
?
JIM DAVIS 11-13

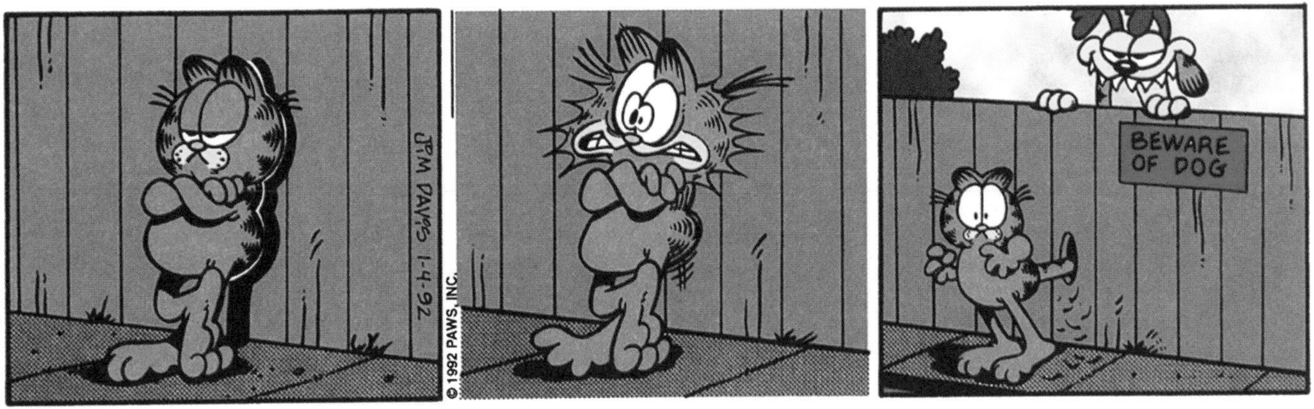
JIM DAVIS 1-4-92
© 1992 PAWS, INC.
BEWARE OF DOG

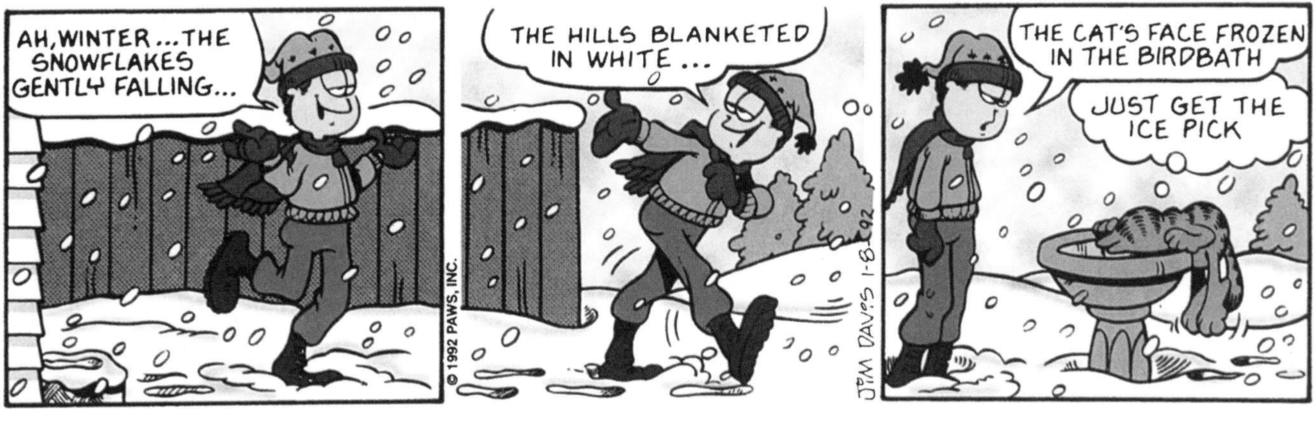
AH, WINTER ... THE SNOWFLAKES GENTLY FALLING...
© 1992 PAWS, INC.
THE HILLS BLANKETED IN WHITE ...
JIM DAVIS 1-8-92
THE CAT'S FACE FROZEN IN THE BIRDBATH
JUST GET THE ICE PICK

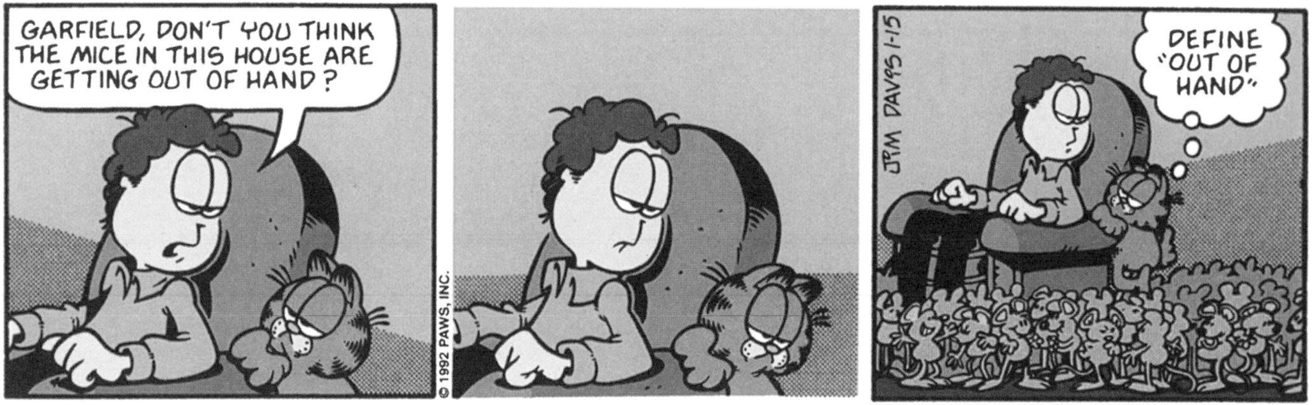
GARFIELD, DON'T YOU THINK THE MICE IN THIS HOUSE ARE GETTING OUT OF HAND?
© 1992 PAWS, INC.
JIM DAVIS 1-15
DEFINE "OUT OF HAND"

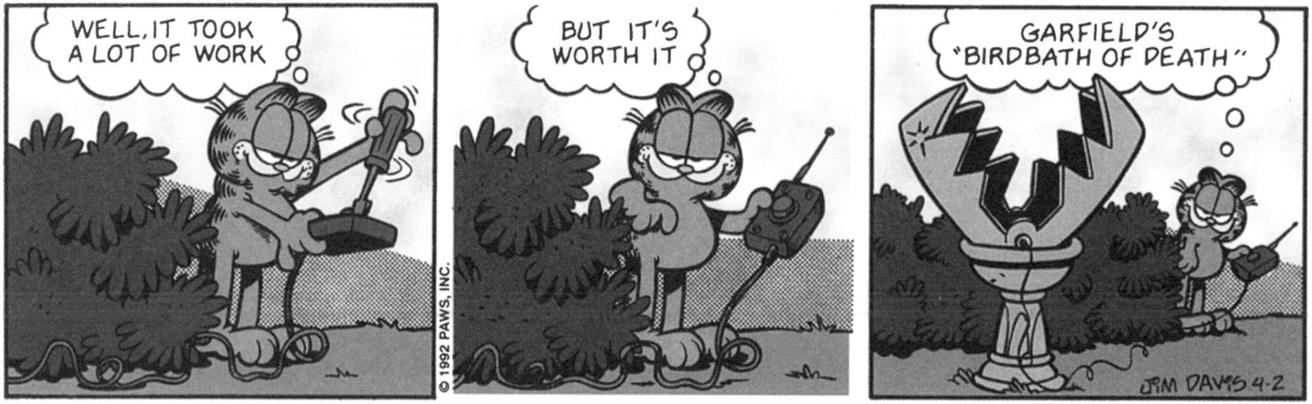
WELL, IT TOOK A LOT OF WORK
© 1992 PAWS, INC.
BUT IT'S WORTH IT
GARFIELD'S "BIRDBATH OF DEATH"
JIM DAVIS 4-2

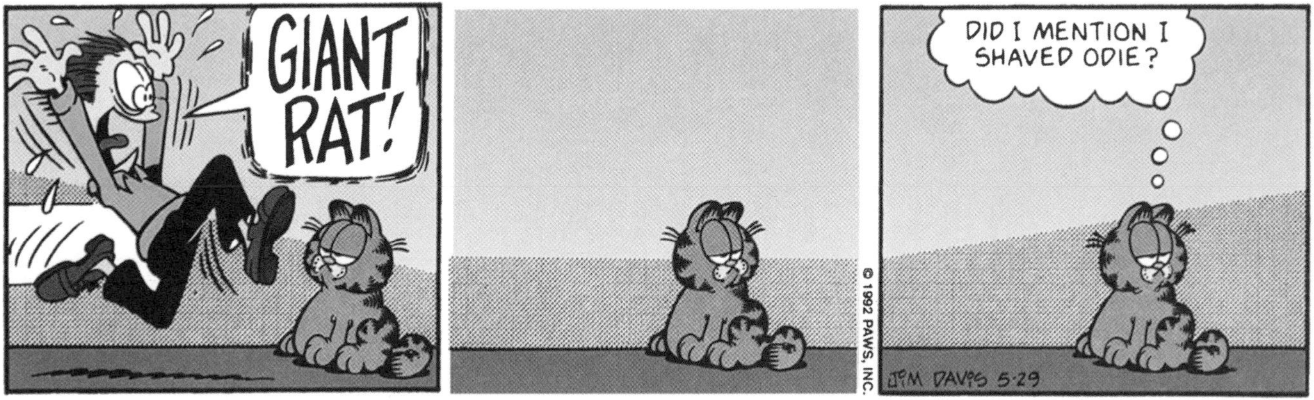
GIANT RAT!
DID I MENTION I SHAVED ODIE?
© 1992 PAWS, INC.
JIM DAVIS 5-29

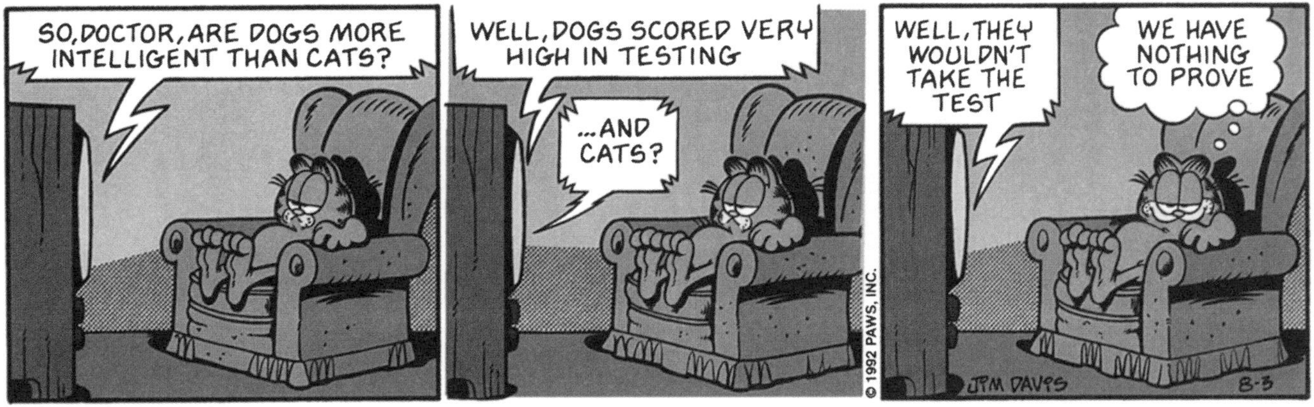
SO, DOCTOR, ARE DOGS MORE INTELLIGENT THAN CATS?
WELL, DOGS SCORED VERY HIGH IN TESTING
...AND CATS?
WELL, THEY WOULDN'T TAKE THE TEST
WE HAVE NOTHING TO PROVE
© 1992 PAWS, INC.
JIM DAVIS
8-3

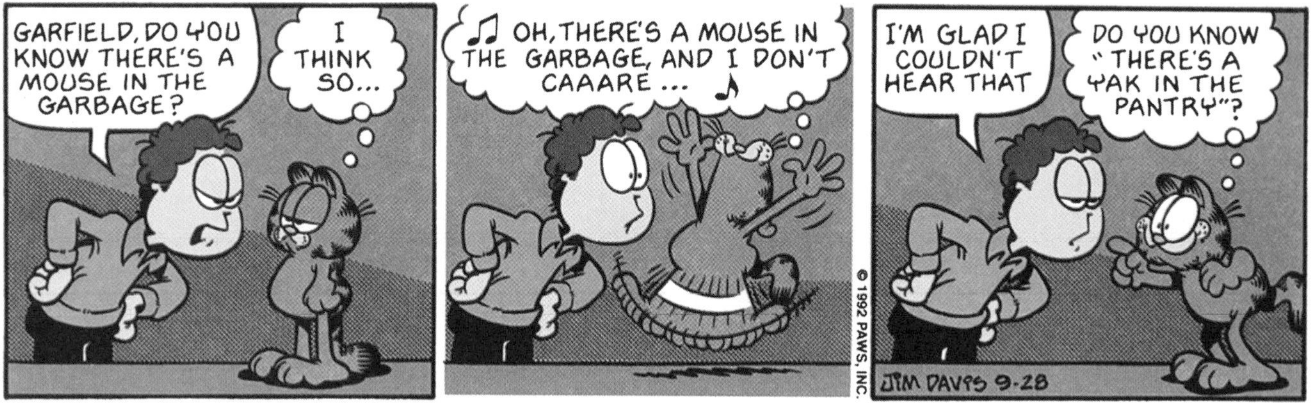
GARFIELD, DO YOU KNOW THERE'S A MOUSE IN THE GARBAGE?
I THINK SO...
♫ OH, THERE'S A MOUSE IN THE GARBAGE, AND I DON'T CAAARE ... ♪
© 1992 PAWS, INC.
I'M GLAD I COULDN'T HEAR THAT
DO YOU KNOW "THERE'S A YAK IN THE PANTRY"?
JIM DAVIS 9-28

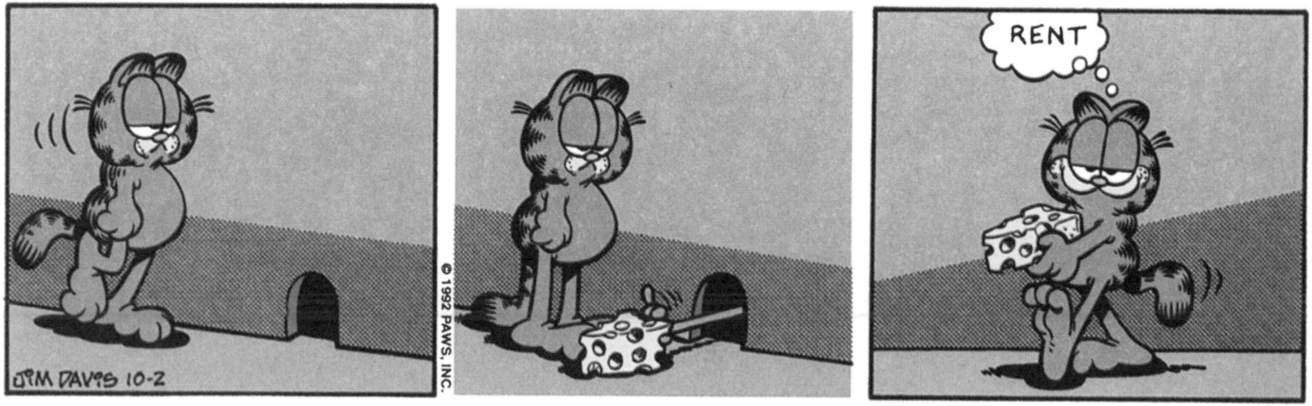
JIM DAVIS 10-2
© 1992 PAWS, INC.
RENT

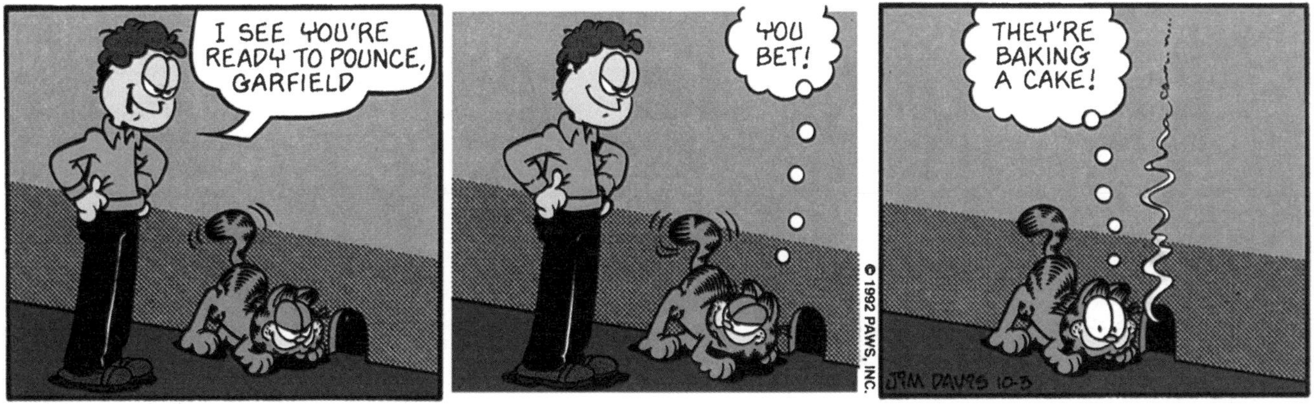
I SEE YOU'RE READY TO POUNCE, GARFIELD
YOU BET!
© 1992 PAWS, INC.
THEY'RE BAKING A CAKE!
JIM DAVIS 10-3

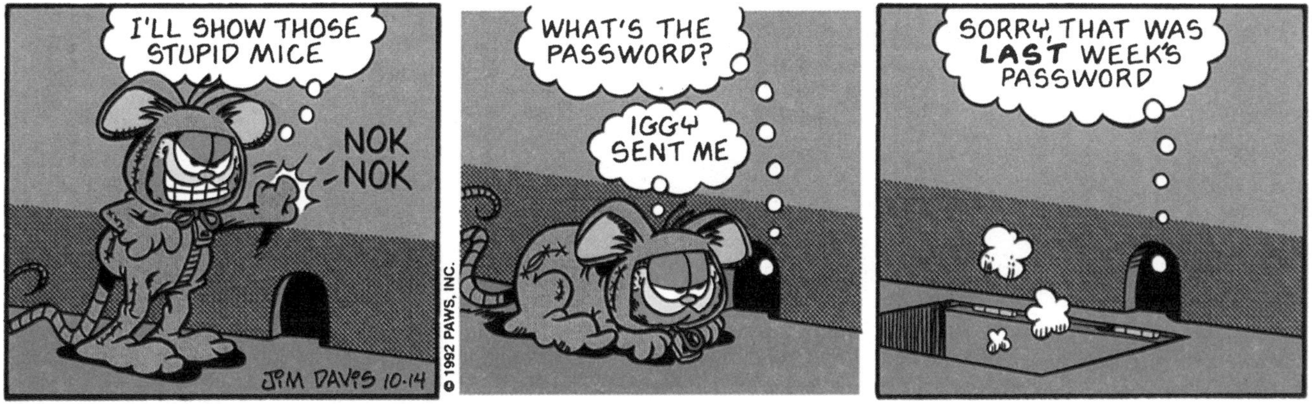
I'LL SHOW THOSE STUPID MICE
NOK NOK
JIM DAVIS 10-14
© 1992 PAWS, INC.
WHAT'S THE PASSWORD?
IGGY SENT ME
SORRY, THAT WAS **LAST** WEEK'S PASSWORD

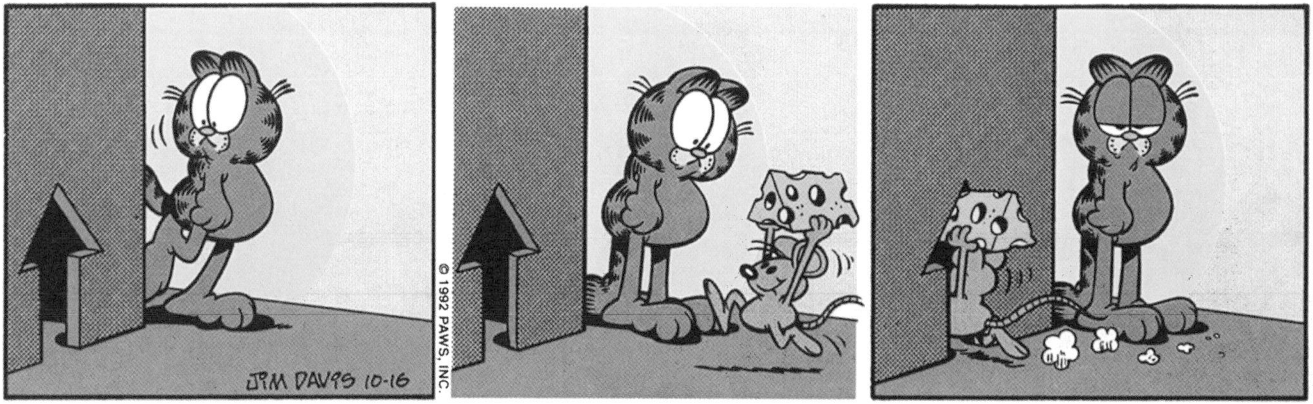
JIM DAVIS 10-16
© 1992 PAWS, INC.

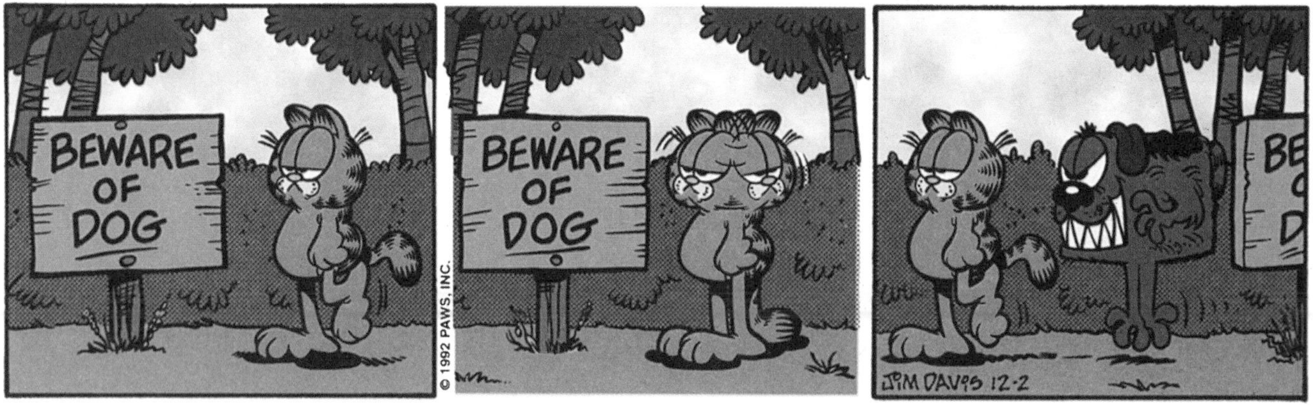
BEWARE OF DOG
© 1992 PAWS, INC.
BEWARE OF DOG
JIM DAVIS 12-2

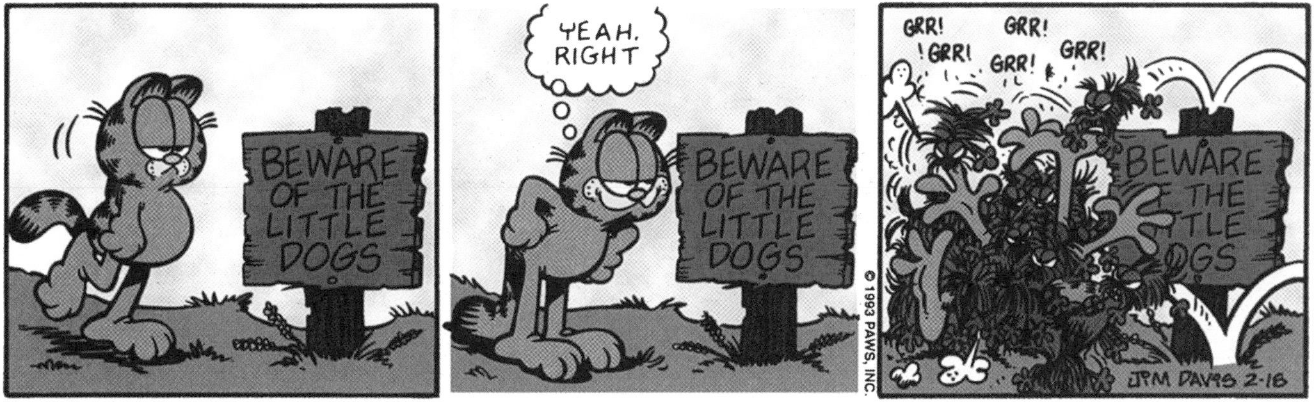
BEWARE OF THE LITTLE DOGS
YEAH, RIGHT
© 1993 PAWS, INC.
GRR! GRR! GRR! GRR! GRR!
JIM DAVIS 2-18

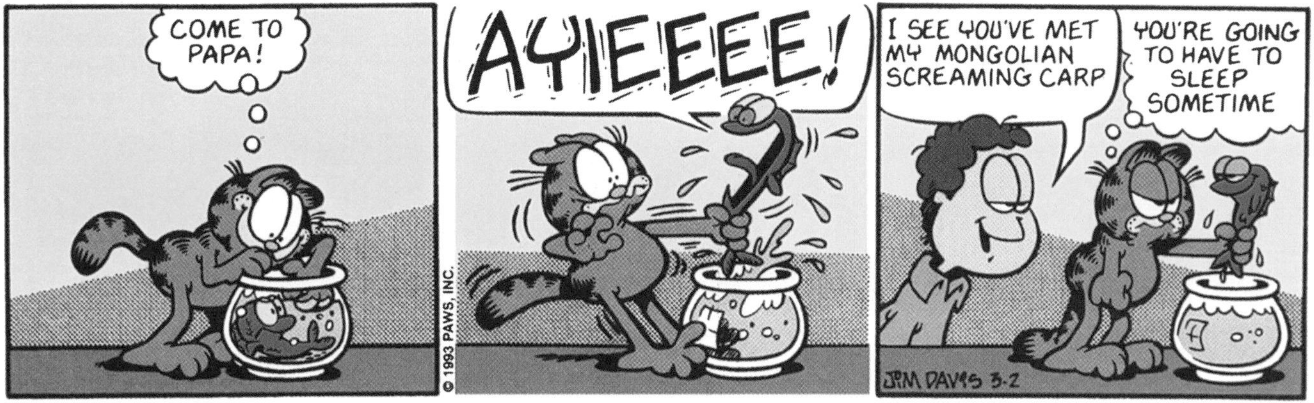
COME TO PAPA!
© 1993 PAWS, INC.
AYIEEEEE!
I SEE YOU'VE MET MY MONGOLIAN SCREAMING CARP
YOU'RE GOING TO HAVE TO SLEEP SOMETIME
JIM DAVIS 3-2

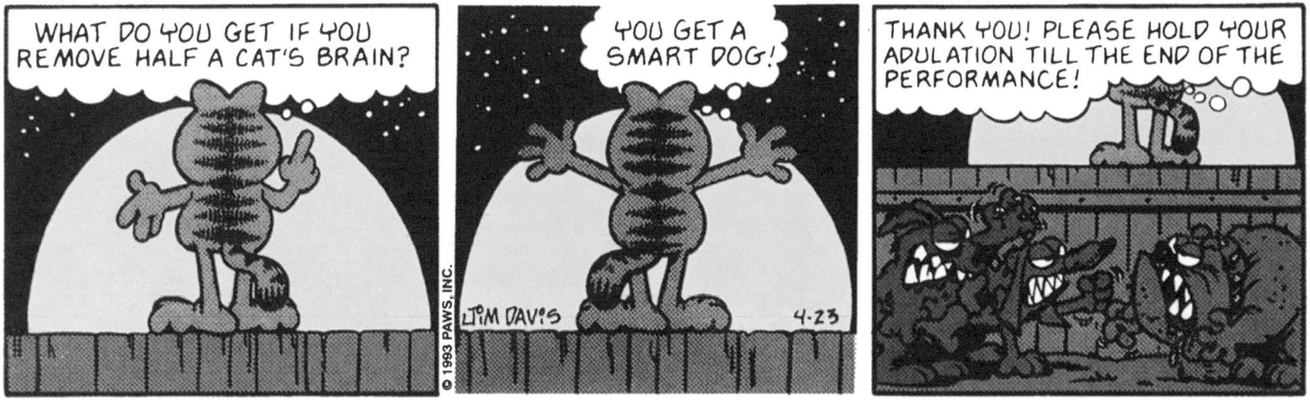
WHAT DO YOU GET IF YOU REMOVE HALF A CAT'S BRAIN?
YOU GET A SMART DOG!
JIM DAVIS 4-23
© 1993 PAWS, INC.
THANK YOU! PLEASE HOLD YOUR ADULATION TILL THE END OF THE PERFORMANCE!

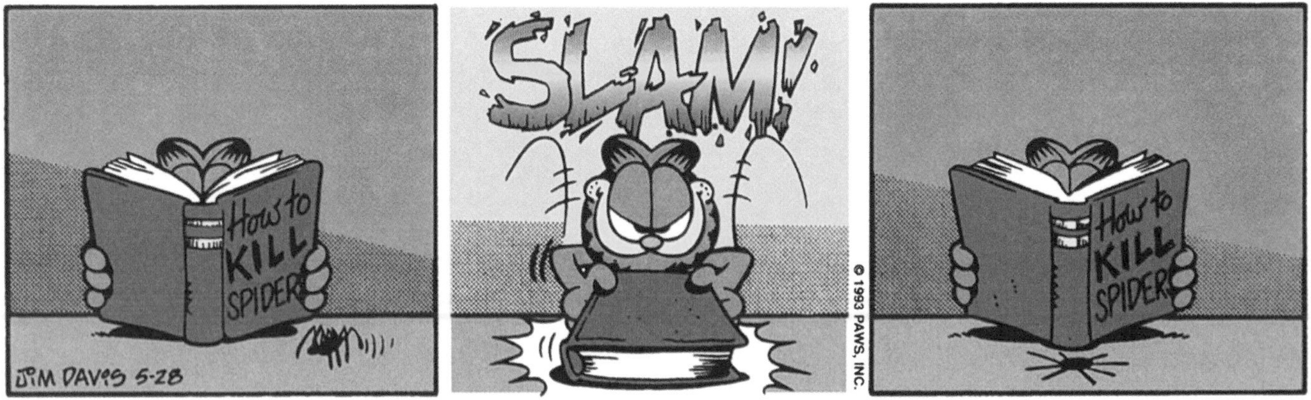
How to KILL SPIDERS
JIM DAVIS 5-28
SLAM!
© 1993 PAWS, INC.
How to KILL SPIDERS

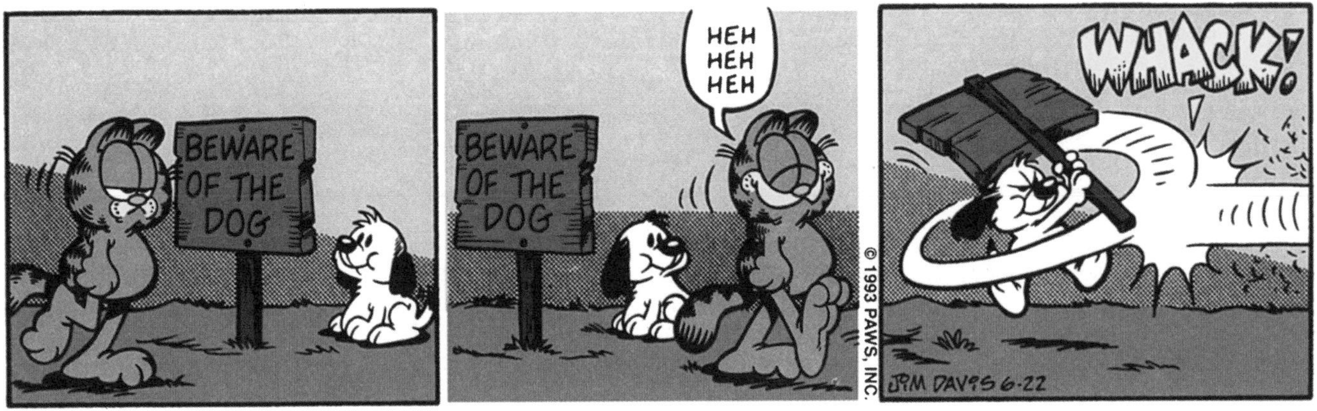

BEWARE OF THE DOG
BEWARE OF THE DOG
HEH HEH HEH
© 1993 PAWS, INC.
WHACK!
JIM DAVIS 6-22

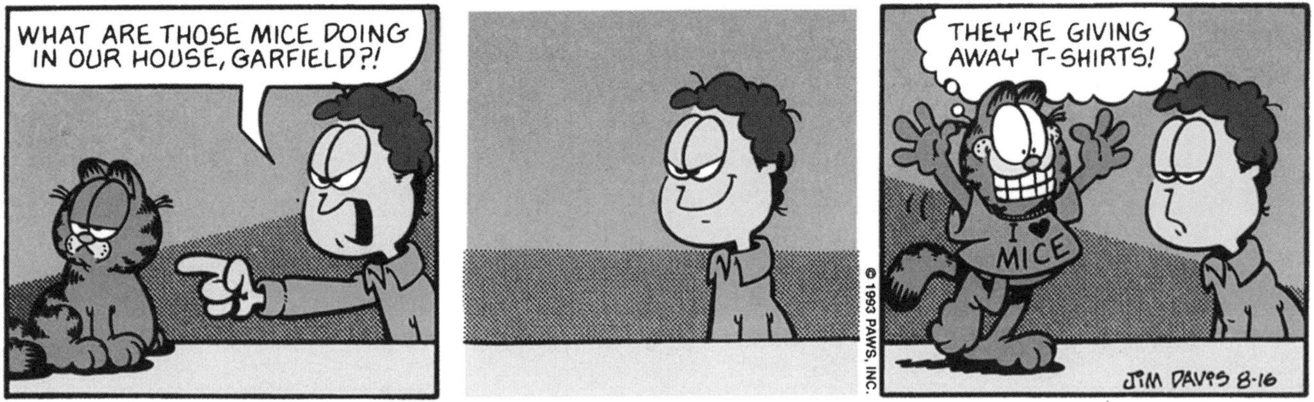

WHAT ARE THOSE MICE DOING IN OUR HOUSE, GARFIELD?!
© 1993 PAWS, INC.
THEY'RE GIVING AWAY T-SHIRTS!
I ♥ MICE
JIM DAVIS 8-16

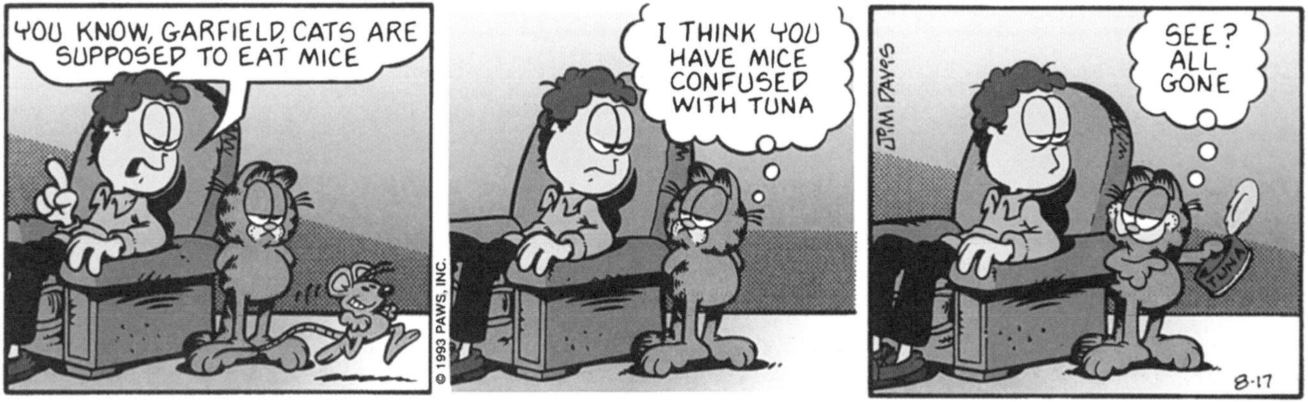
YOU KNOW, GARFIELD, CATS ARE SUPPOSED TO EAT MICE
I THINK YOU HAVE MICE CONFUSED WITH TUNA
SEE? ALL GONE
TUNA
JIM DAVIS
8-17
© 1993 PAWS, INC.

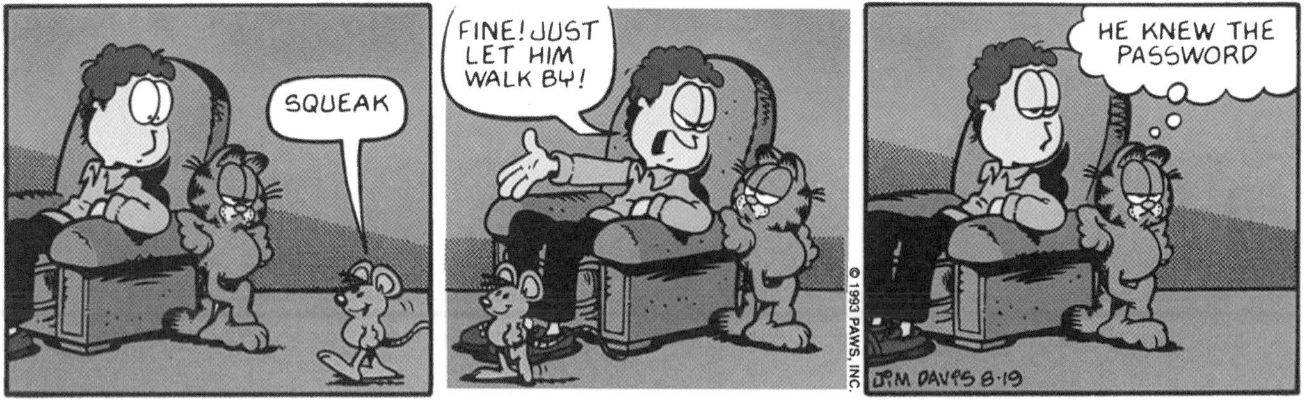
SQUEAK
FINE! JUST LET HIM WALK BY!
HE KNEW THE PASSWORD
JIM DAVIS 8-19
© 1993 PAWS, INC.

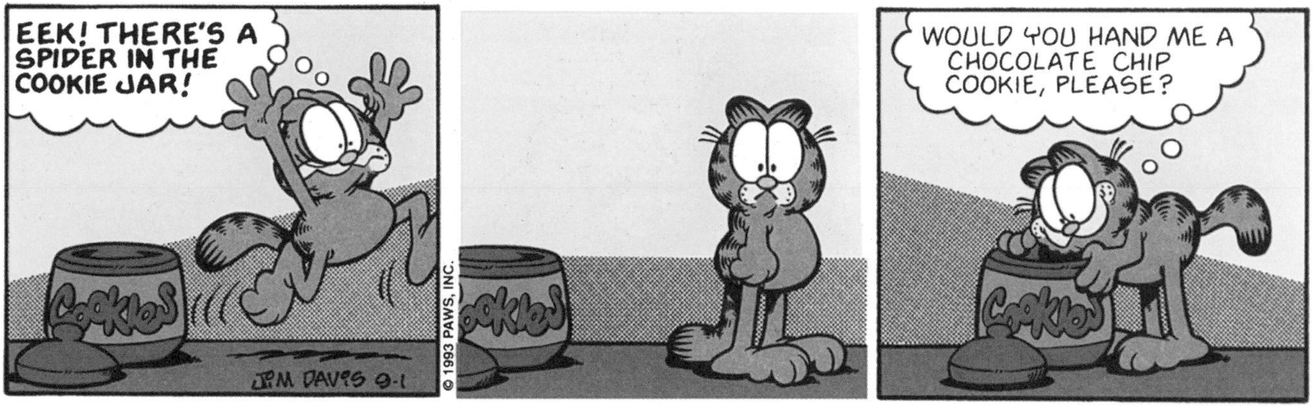
EEK! THERE'S A SPIDER IN THE COOKIE JAR!
COOKIES
JIM DAVIS 9-1
© 1993 PAWS, INC.
WOULD YOU HAND ME A CHOCOLATE CHIP COOKIE, PLEASE?

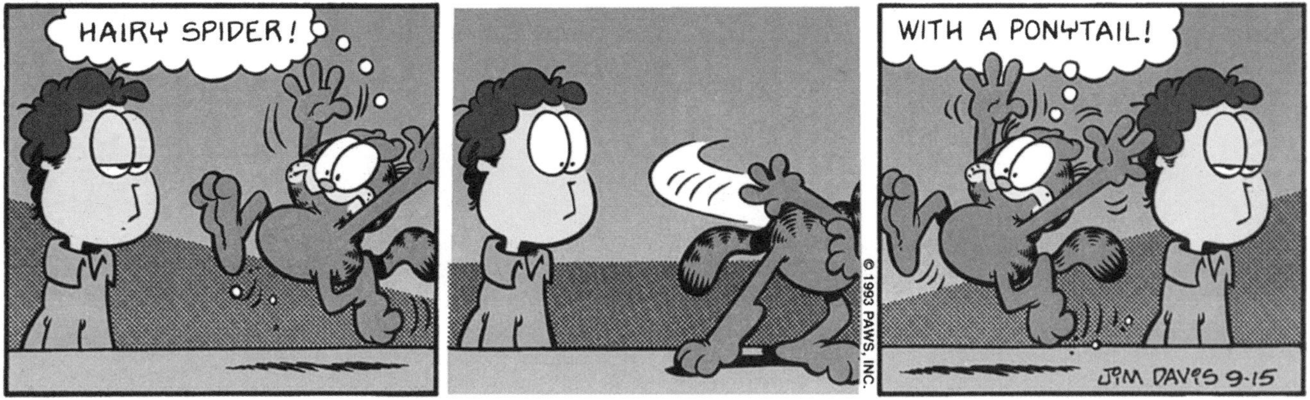
HAIRY SPIDER!
© 1993 PAWS, INC.
WITH A PONYTAIL!
JIM DAVIS 9-15

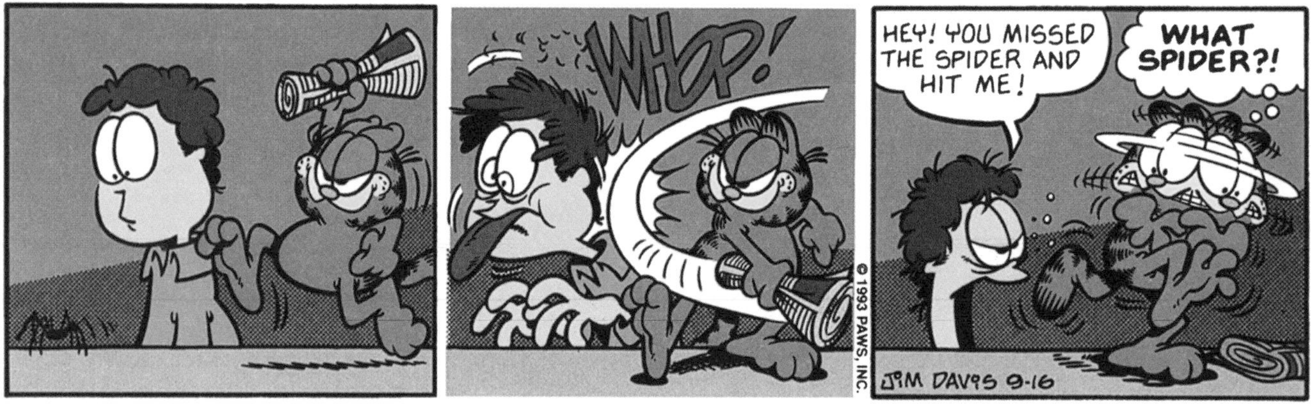
WHOP!
HEY! YOU MISSED THE SPIDER AND HIT ME!
WHAT SPIDER?!
© 1993 PAWS, INC.
JIM DAVIS 9-16

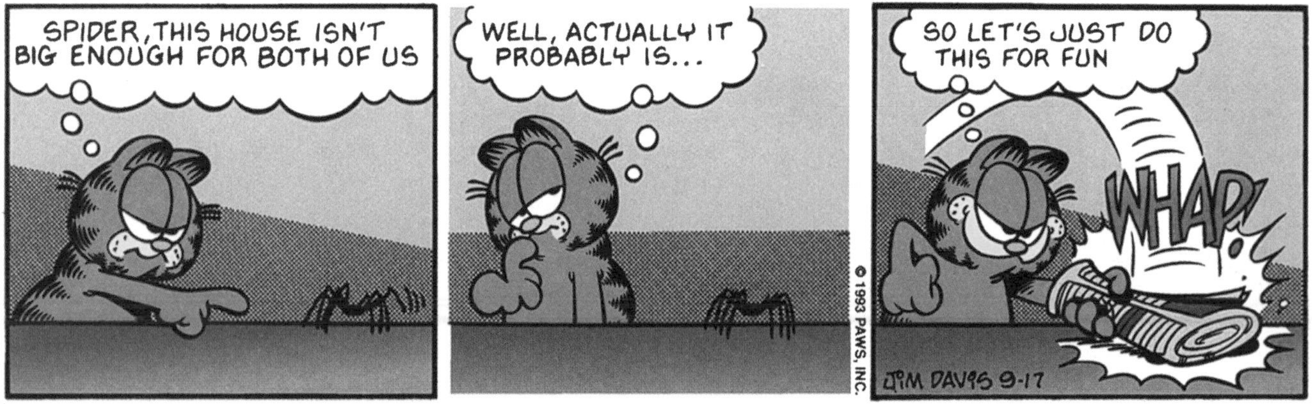
SPIDER, THIS HOUSE ISN'T BIG ENOUGH FOR BOTH OF US
WELL, ACTUALLY IT PROBABLY IS...
SO LET'S JUST DO THIS FOR FUN
WHAP!
© 1993 PAWS, INC.
JIM DAVIS 9-17

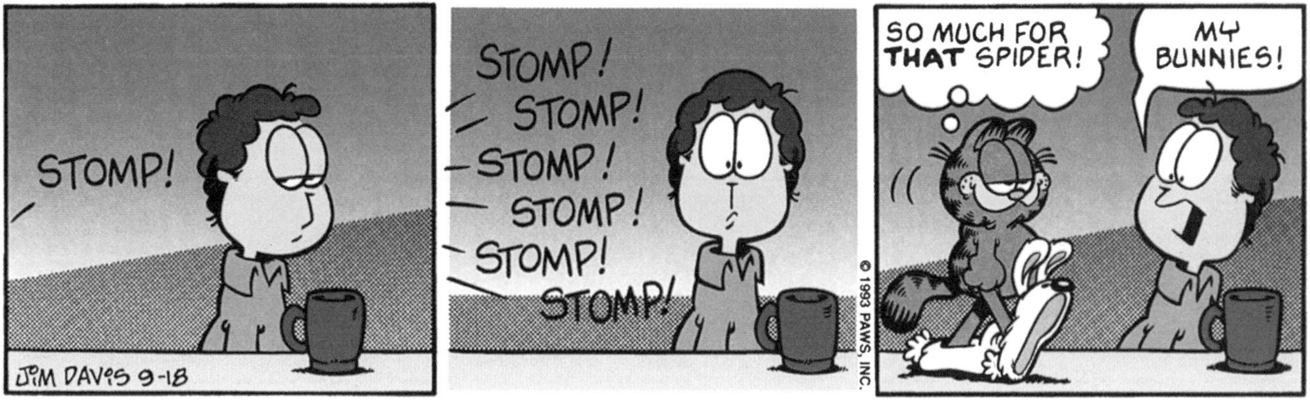
STOMP!
JIM DAVIS 9-18
STOMP!
STOMP!
STOMP!
STOMP!
STOMP!
STOMP!
© 1993 PAWS, INC.
SO MUCH FOR **THAT** SPIDER!
MY BUNNIES!

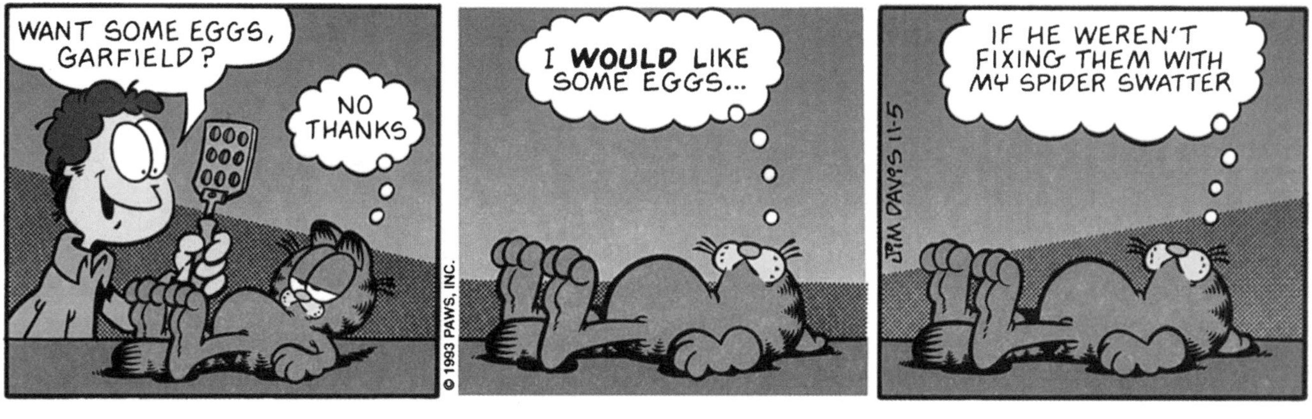
WANT SOME EGGS, GARFIELD?
NO THANKS
© 1993 PAWS, INC.
I **WOULD** LIKE SOME EGGS...
JIM DAVIS 11-5
IF HE WEREN'T FIXING THEM WITH MY SPIDER SWATTER

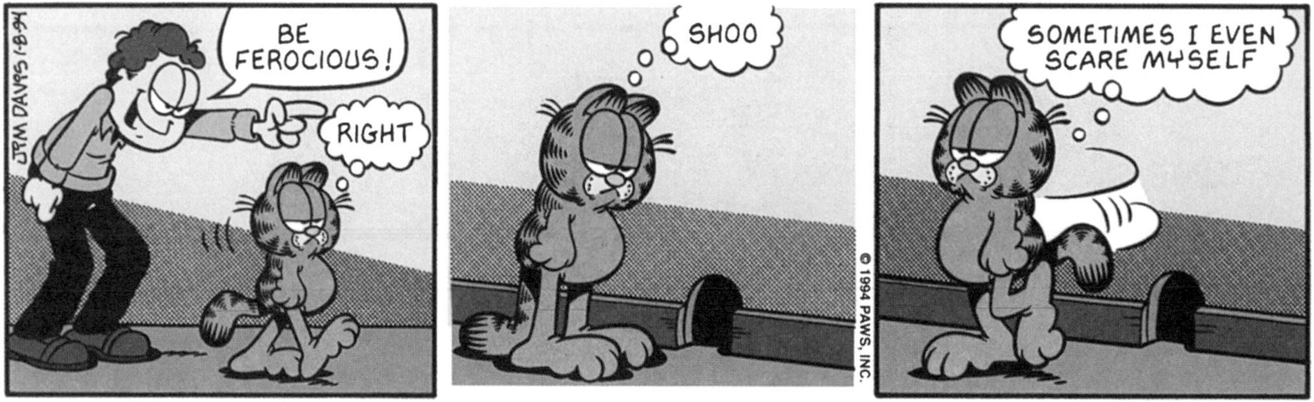
JPM DAVPS 1-8-94
BE FEROCIOUS!
RIGHT
SHOO
SOMETIMES I EVEN SCARE MYSELF
© 1994 PAWS, INC.

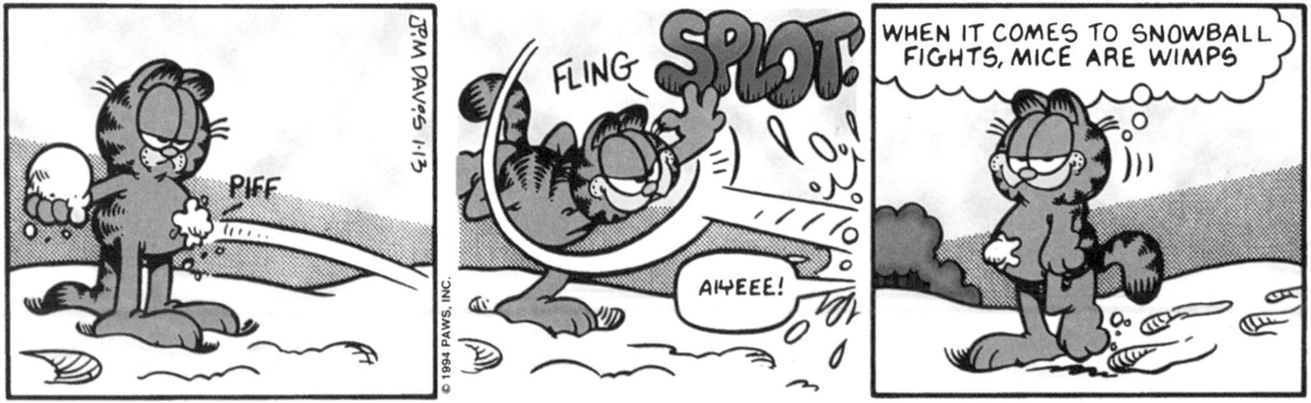
JPM DAVPS 1-13
PIFF
© 1994 PAWS, INC.
FLING
SPLOT!
AIYEEE!
WHEN IT COMES TO SNOWBALL FIGHTS, MICE ARE WIMPS

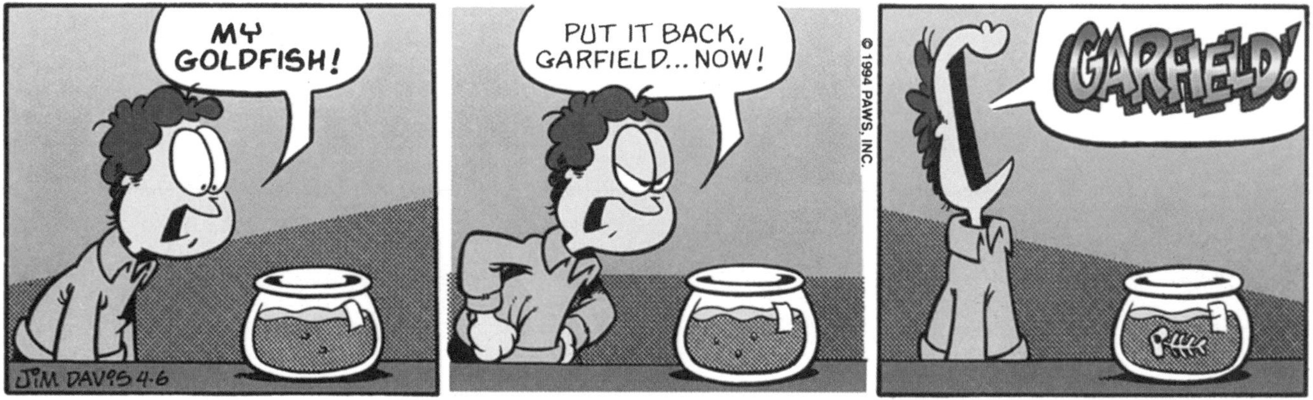

MY GOLDFISH!
JIM DAVIS 4-6
PUT IT BACK, GARFIELD... NOW!
© 1994 PAWS, INC.
GARFIELD!

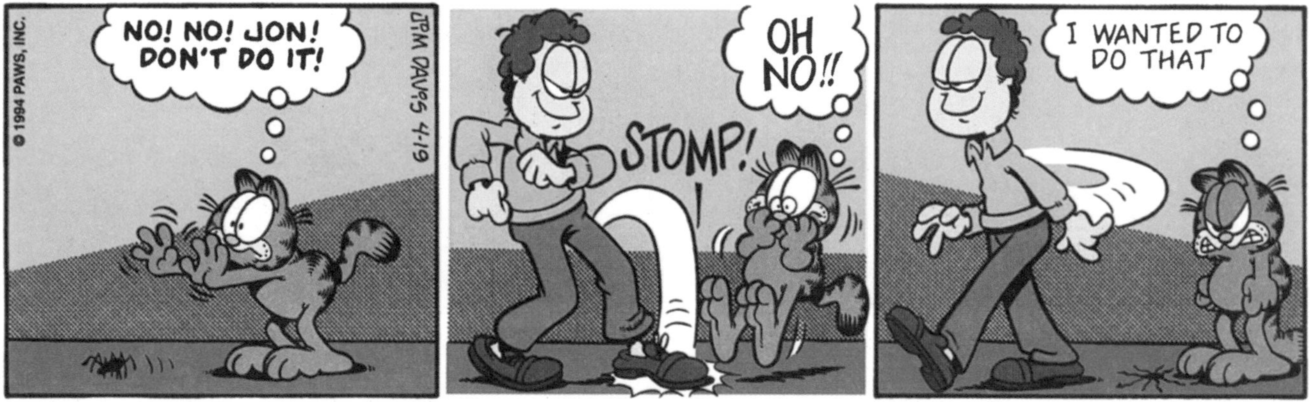

© 1994 PAWS, INC.
NO! NO! JON! DON'T DO IT!
JIM DAVIS 4-19
STOMP!
OH NO!!
I WANTED TO DO THAT

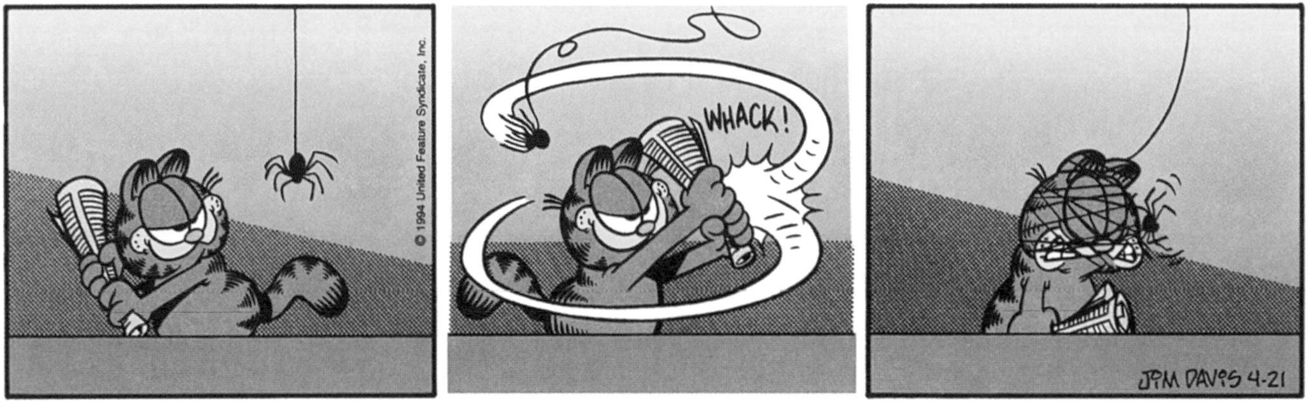
© 1994 United Feature Syndicate, Inc.
WHACK!
JIM DAVIS 4-21

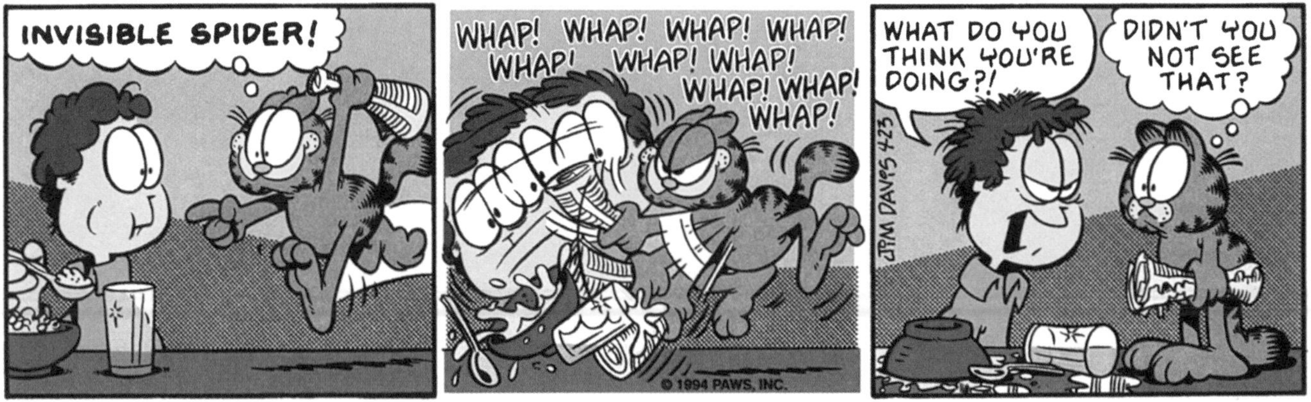
INVISIBLE SPIDER!
WHAP! WHAP! WHAP! WHAP! WHAP! WHAP! WHAP! WHAP! WHAP! WHAP!
© 1994 PAWS, INC.
JIM DAVIS 4-23
WHAT DO YOU THINK YOU'RE DOING?!
DIDN'T YOU NOT SEE THAT?

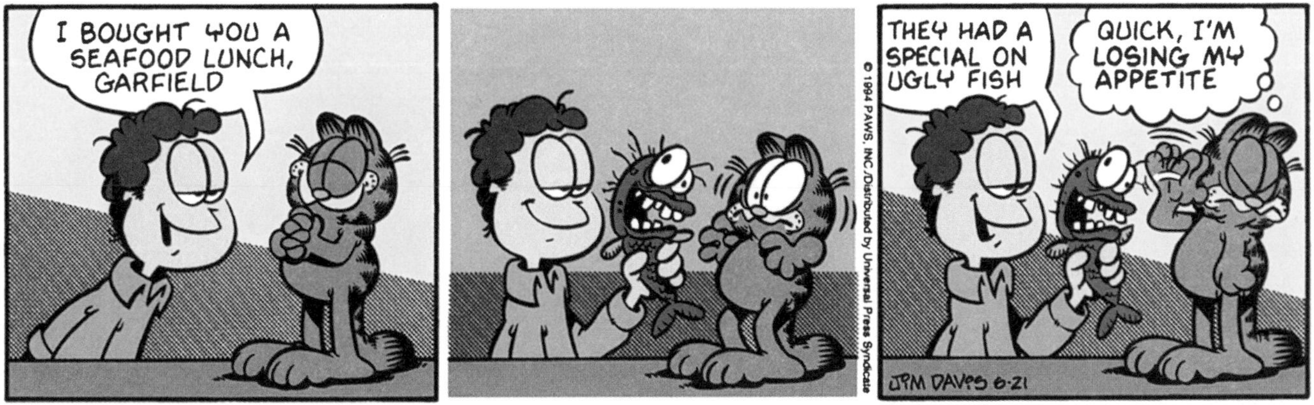
I BOUGHT YOU A SEAFOOD LUNCH, GARFIELD
THEY HAD A SPECIAL ON UGLY FISH
QUICK, I'M LOSING MY APPETITE
© 1994 PAWS, INC./Distributed by Universal Press Syndicate
JIM DAVIS 6-21

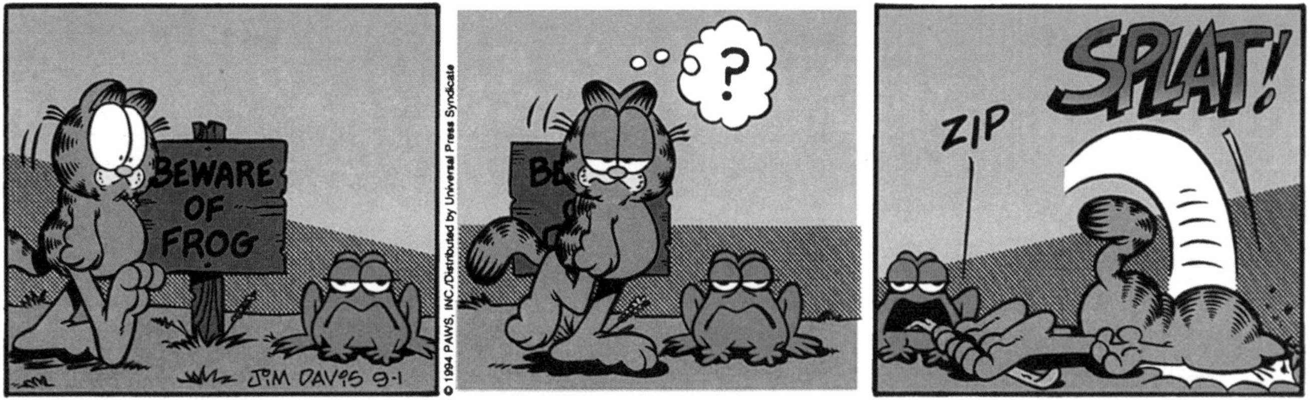
BEWARE OF FROG
JIM DAVIS 9-1
© 1994 PAWS, INC./Distributed by Universal Press Syndicate
?
ZIP
SPLAT!

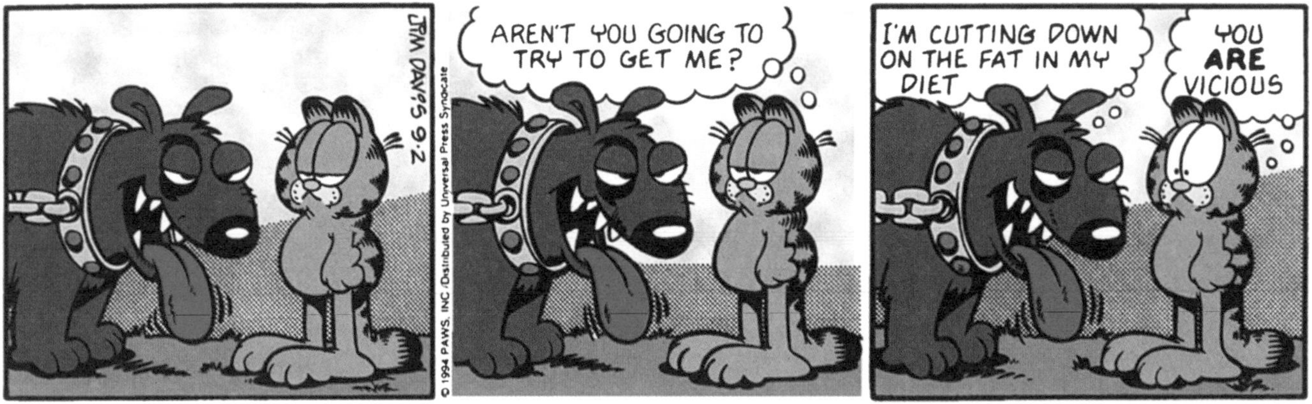
JPM DAVIS 9-2
© 1994 PAWS, INC./Distributed by Universal Press Syndicate
AREN'T YOU GOING TO TRY TO GET ME?
I'M CUTTING DOWN ON THE FAT IN MY DIET
YOU **ARE** VICIOUS

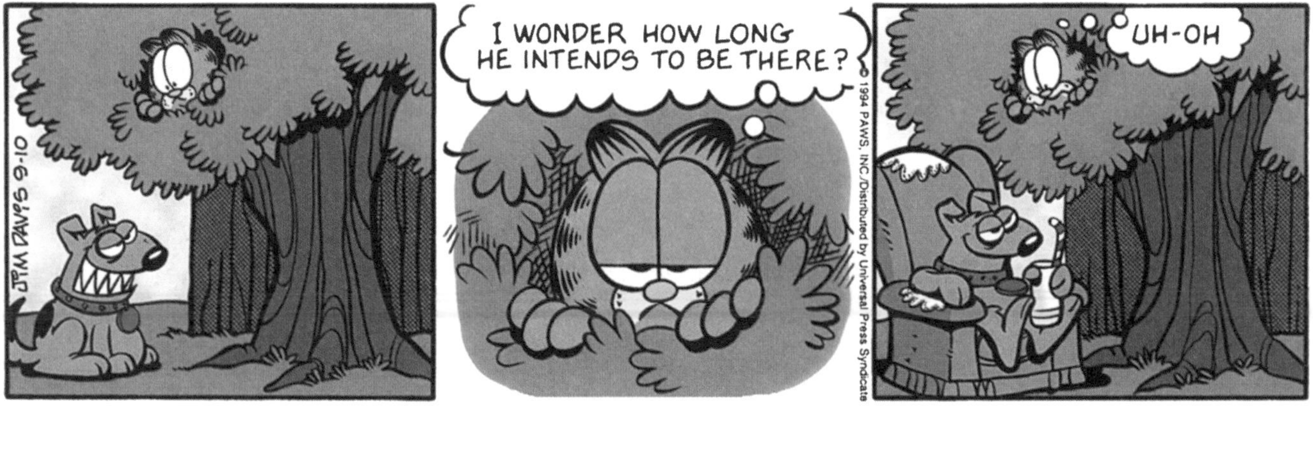
JPM DAVIS 9-10
I WONDER HOW LONG HE INTENDS TO BE THERE?
© 1994 PAWS, INC./Distributed by Universal Press Syndicate
UH-OH

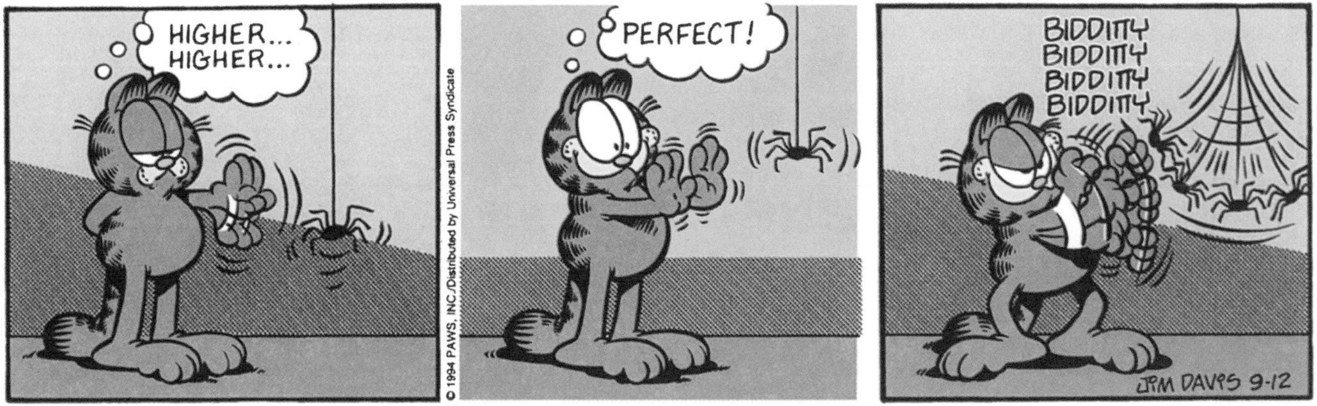
HIGHER... HIGHER...
PERFECT!
BIDDITTY
BIDDITTY
BIDDITTY
BIDDITTY
JIM DAVIS 9-12
© 1994 PAWS, INC./Distributed by Universal Press Syndicate

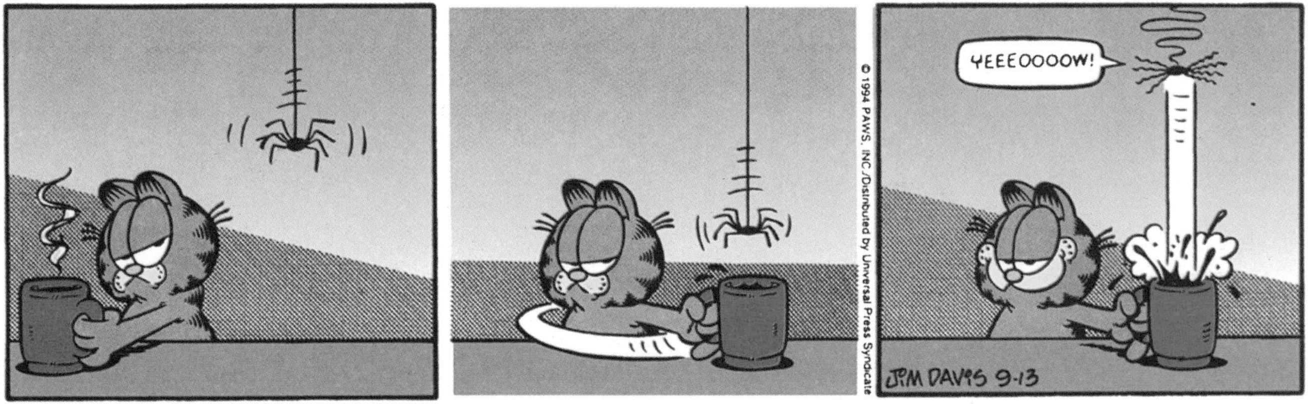
YEEEOOOOW!
JIM DAVIS 9-13
© 1994 PAWS, INC./Distributed by Universal Press Syndicate

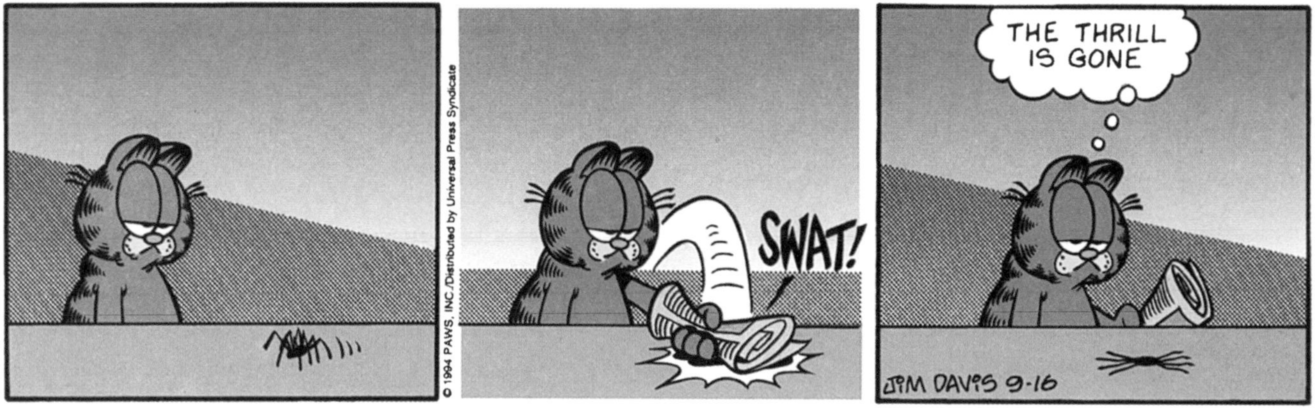
© 1994 PAWS, INC./Distributed by Universal Press Syndicate
SWAT!
THE THRILL IS GONE
JIM DAVIS 9-16

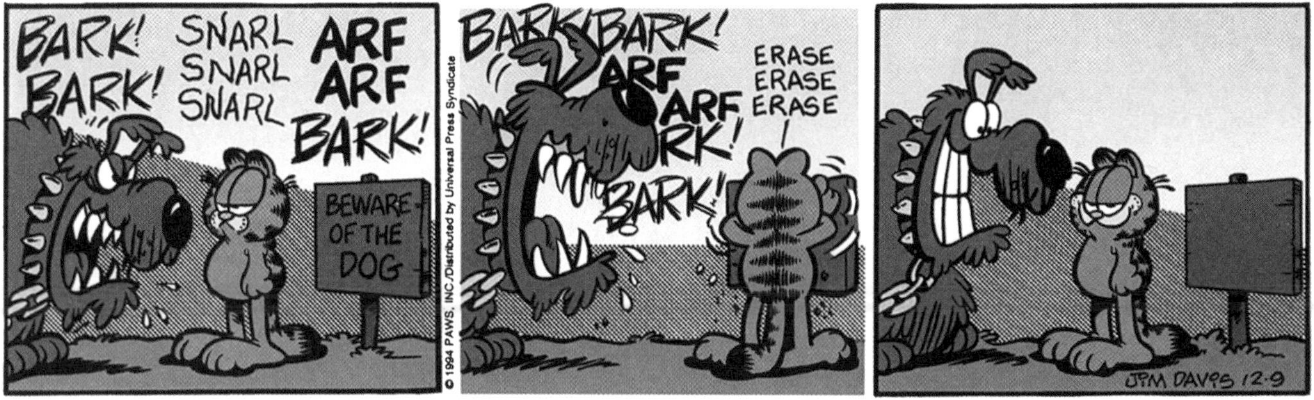
BARK! BARK!
SNARL SNARL SNARL
ARF ARF BARK!
BEWARE OF THE DOG
© 1994 PAWS, INC./Distributed by Universal Press Syndicate
BARK! BARK!
ERASE ERASE ERASE
BARK!
JIM DAVIS 12-9

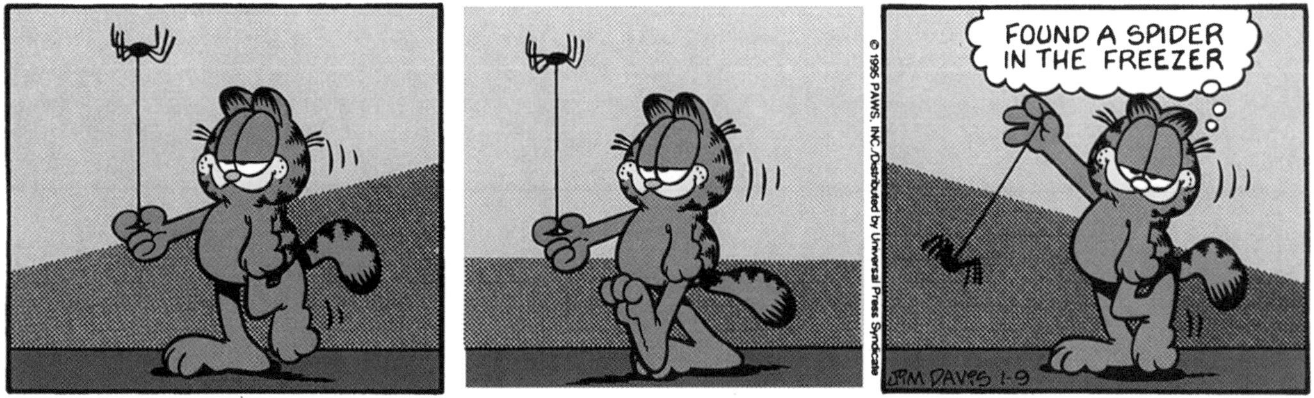
© 1995 PAWS, INC./Distributed by Universal Press Syndicate
FOUND A SPIDER IN THE FREEZER
JIM DAVIS 1-9

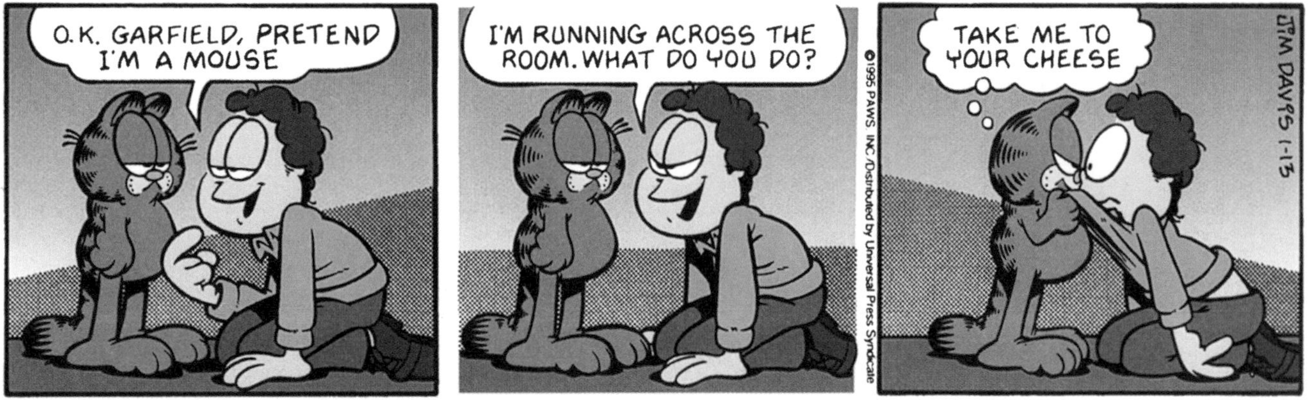
O.K. GARFIELD, PRETEND I'M A MOUSE
I'M RUNNING ACROSS THE ROOM. WHAT DO YOU DO?
© 1995 PAWS, INC./Distributed by Universal Press Syndicate
TAKE ME TO YOUR CHEESE
JIM DAVIS 1-13

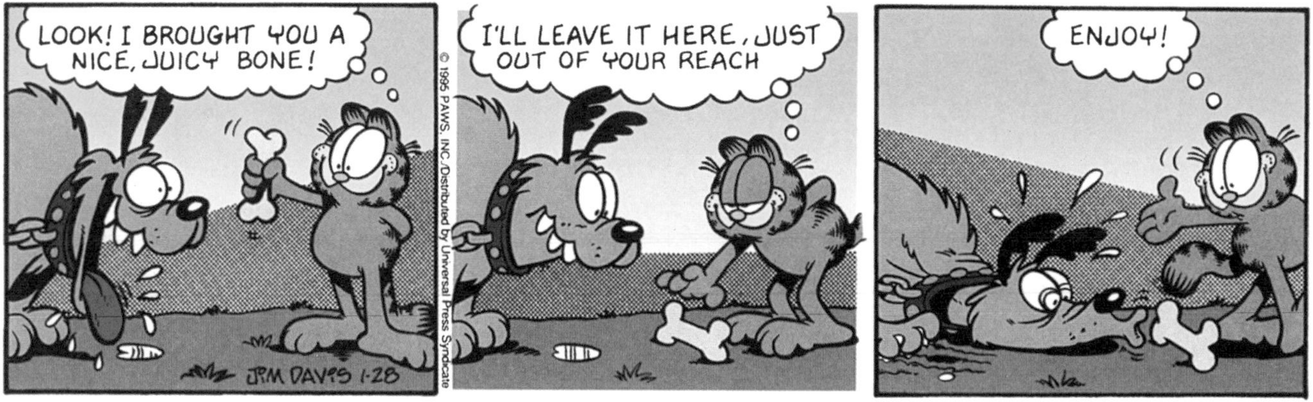
LOOK! I BROUGHT YOU A NICE, JUICY BONE!
JIM DAVIS 1-28
© 1995 PAWS, INC./Distributed by Universal Press Syndicate
I'LL LEAVE IT HERE, JUST OUT OF YOUR REACH
ENJOY!

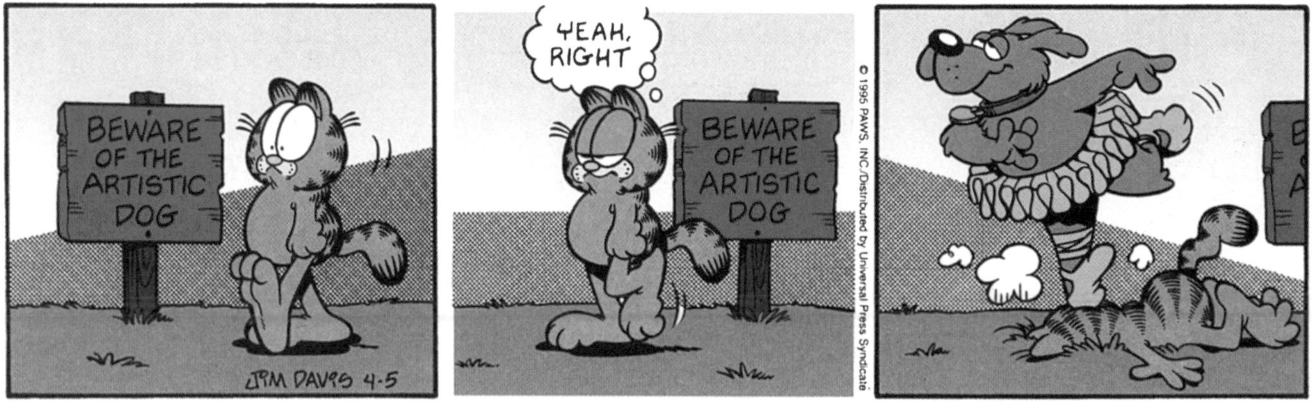
BEWARE OF THE ARTISTIC DOG
JIM DAVIS 4-5
YEAH, RIGHT
BEWARE OF THE ARTISTIC DOG
© 1995 PAWS, INC./Distributed by Universal Press Syndicate

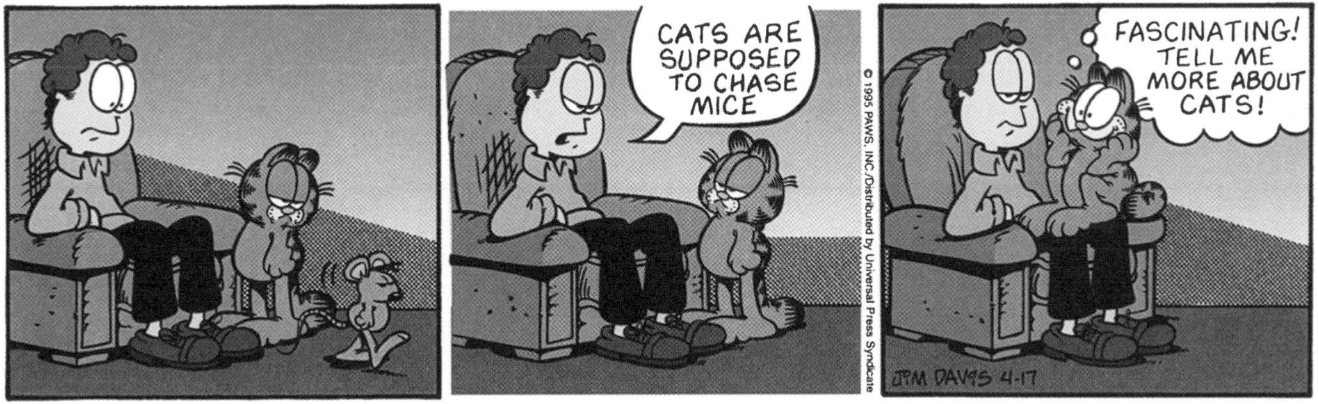
CATS ARE SUPPOSED TO CHASE MICE
© 1995 PAWS, INC./Distributed by Universal Press Syndicate
FASCINATING! TELL ME MORE ABOUT CATS!
JIM DAVIS 4-17

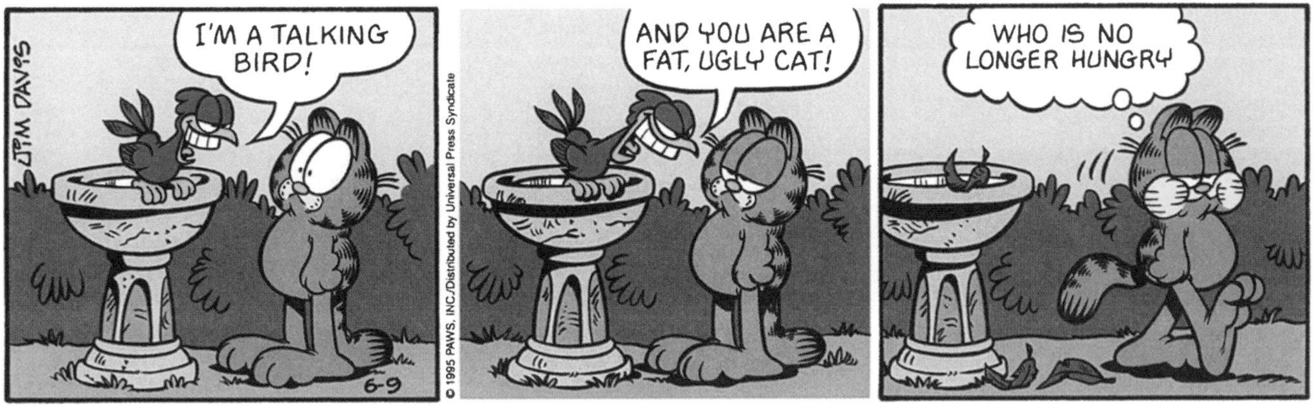
JIM DAVIS
I'M A TALKING BIRD!
6-9
© 1995 PAWS, INC./Distributed by Universal Press Syndicate
AND YOU ARE A FAT, UGLY CAT!
WHO IS NO LONGER HUNGRY

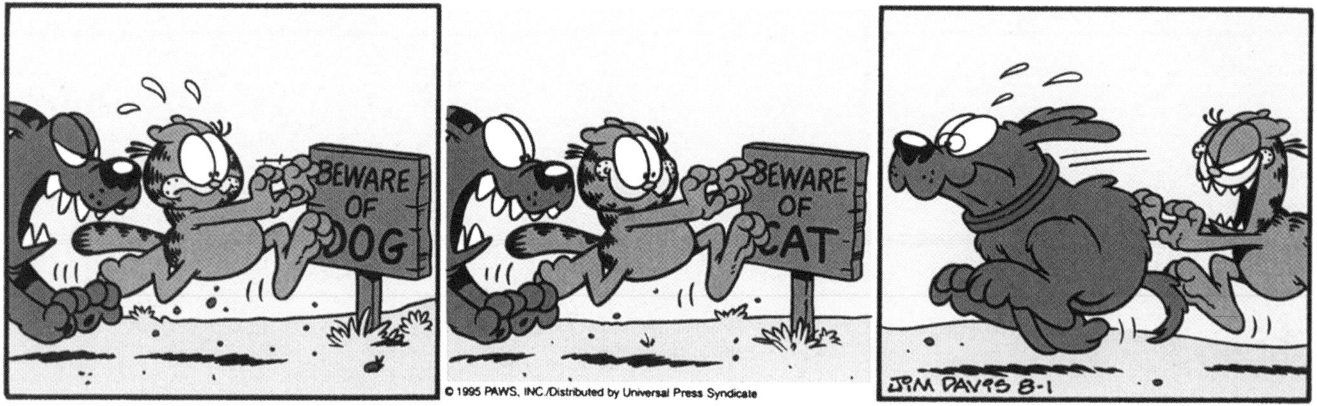
BEWARE OF DOG
BEWARE OF CAT
© 1995 PAWS, INC./Distributed by Universal Press Syndicate
JIM DAVIS 8-1

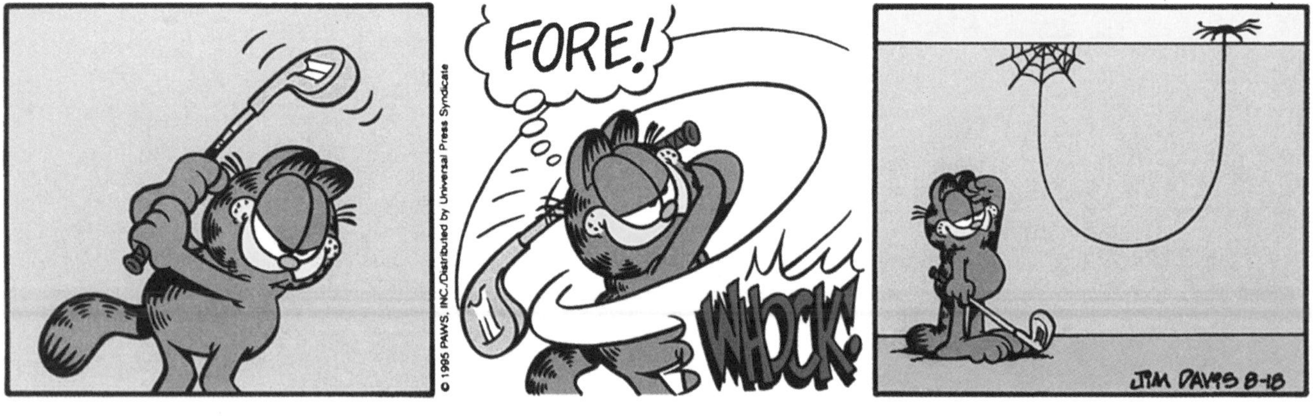
© 1995 PAWS, INC./Distributed by Universal Press Syndicate
FORE!
WHOCK!
JIM DAVIS 8-18

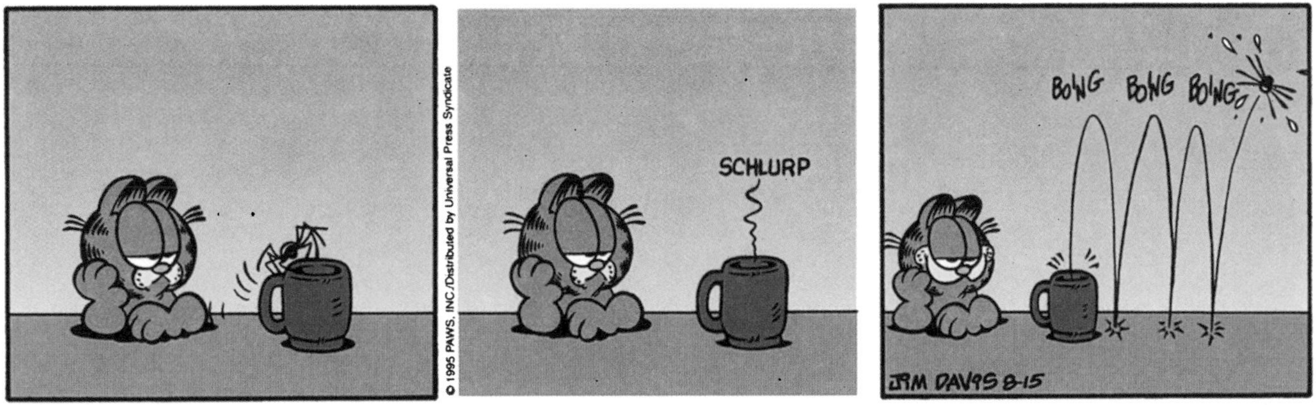
© 1995 PAWS, INC./Distributed by Universal Press Syndicate
SCHLURP
BOING BOING BOING
JIM DAVIS 8-15

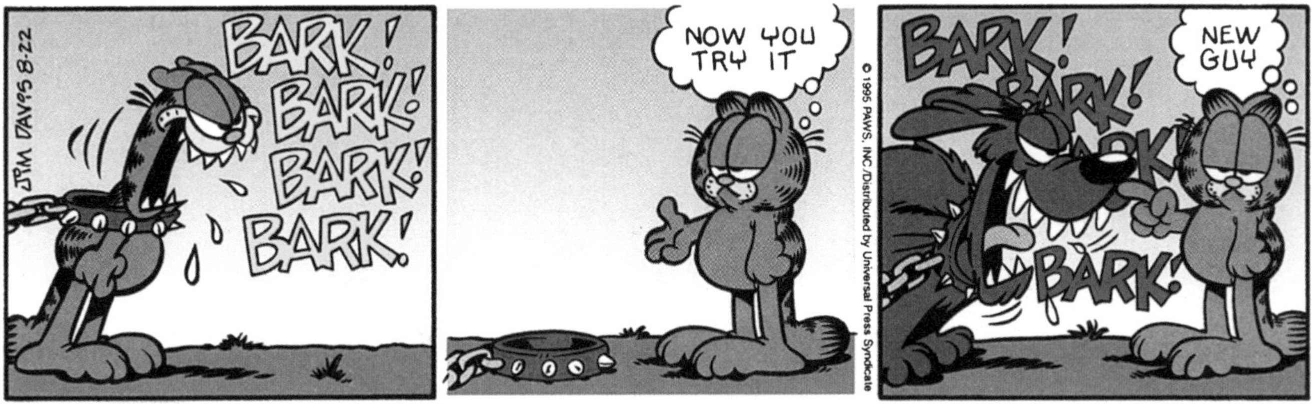
JIM DAVIS 8-22
BARK! BARK! BARK! BARK!
NOW YOU TRY IT
© 1995 PAWS, INC./Distributed by Universal Press Syndicate
BARK! BARK! ARK! BARK!
NEW GUY

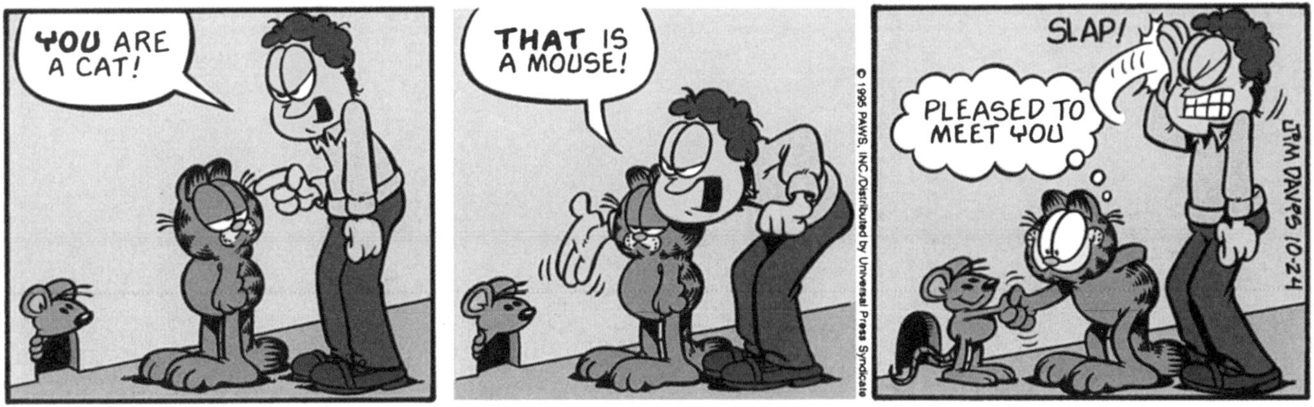
YOU ARE A CAT!
THAT IS A MOUSE!
© 1995 PAWS, INC./Distributed by Universal Press Syndicate
SLAP!
PLEASED TO MEET YOU
JIM DAVIS 10-24

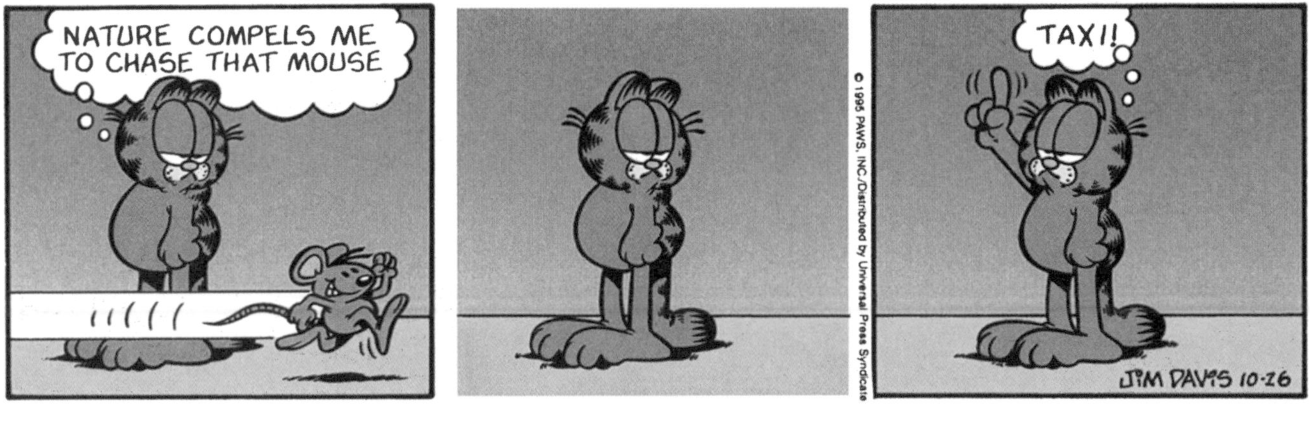
NATURE COMPELS ME TO CHASE THAT MOUSE
© 1995 PAWS, INC./Distributed by Universal Press Syndicate
TAXI!
JIM DAVIS 10-26

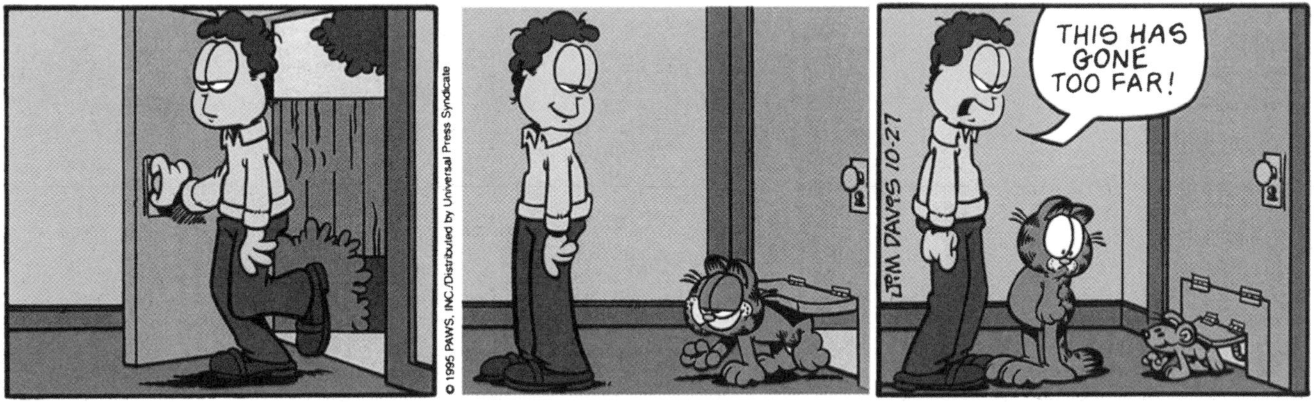
© 1995 PAWS, INC./Distributed by Universal Press Syndicate
JIM DAVIS 10-27
THIS HAS GONE TOO FAR!

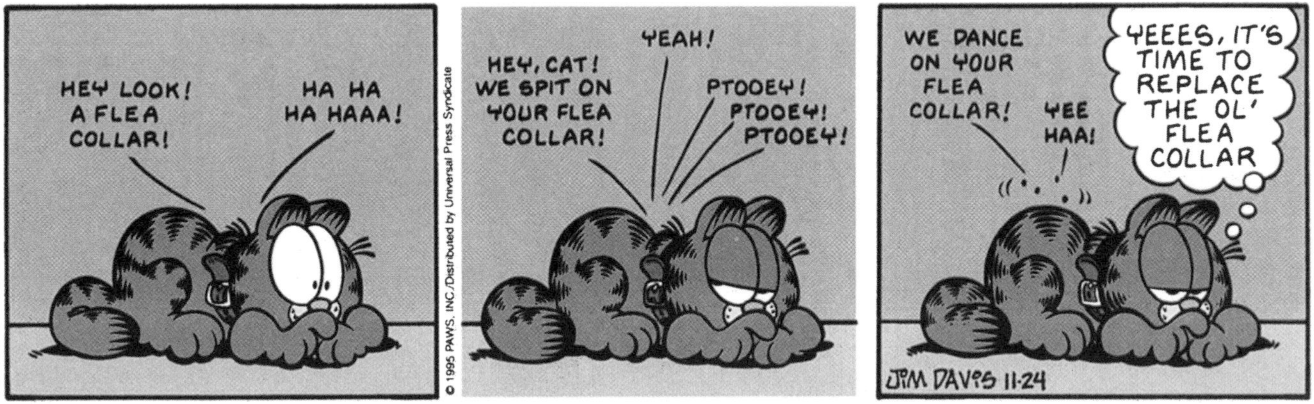
HEY LOOK! A FLEA COLLAR!
HA HA HA HAAA!
© 1995 PAWS, INC./Distributed by Universal Press Syndicate
HEY, CAT! WE SPIT ON YOUR FLEA COLLAR!
YEAH!
PTOOEY! PTOOEY! PTOOEY!
WE DANCE ON YOUR FLEA COLLAR!
YEE HAA!
YEEES, IT'S TIME TO REPLACE THE OL' FLEA COLLAR
JIM DAVIS 11-24

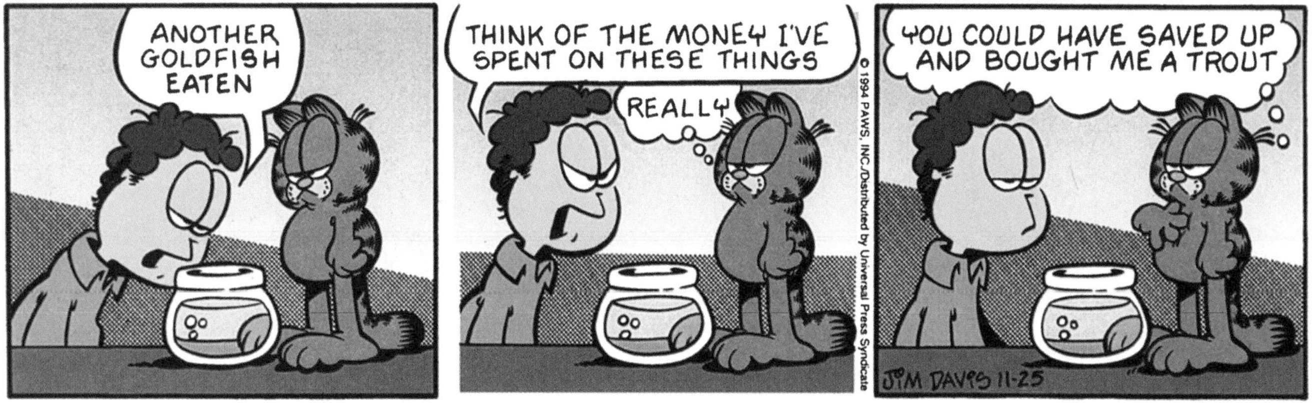
ANOTHER GOLDFISH EATEN
THINK OF THE MONEY I'VE SPENT ON THESE THINGS
REALLY
YOU COULD HAVE SAVED UP AND BOUGHT ME A TROUT
© 1994 PAWS, INC./Distributed by Universal Press Syndicate
JIM DAVIS 11-25

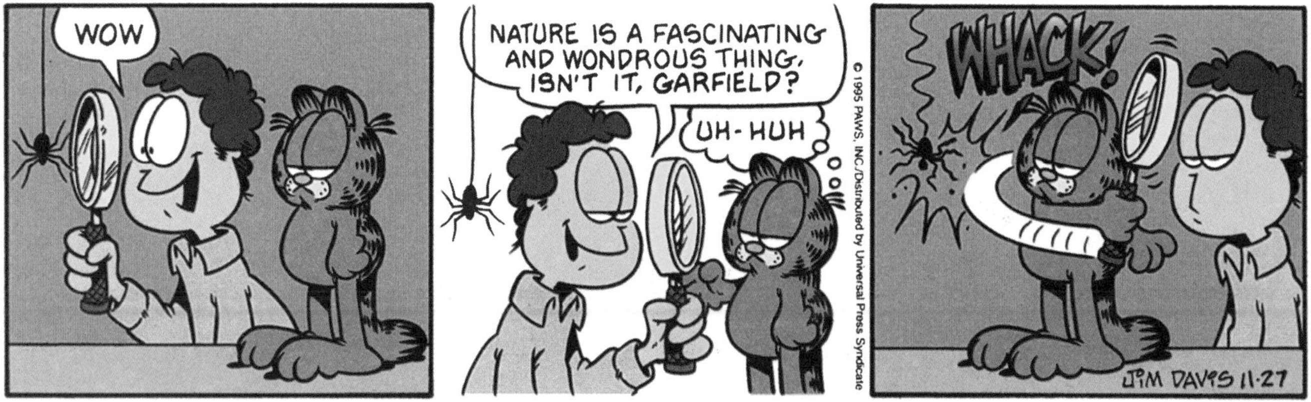
WOW
NATURE IS A FASCINATING AND WONDROUS THING, ISN'T IT, GARFIELD?
UH-HUH
WHACK!
© 1995 PAWS, INC./Distributed by Universal Press Syndicate
JIM DAVIS 11-27

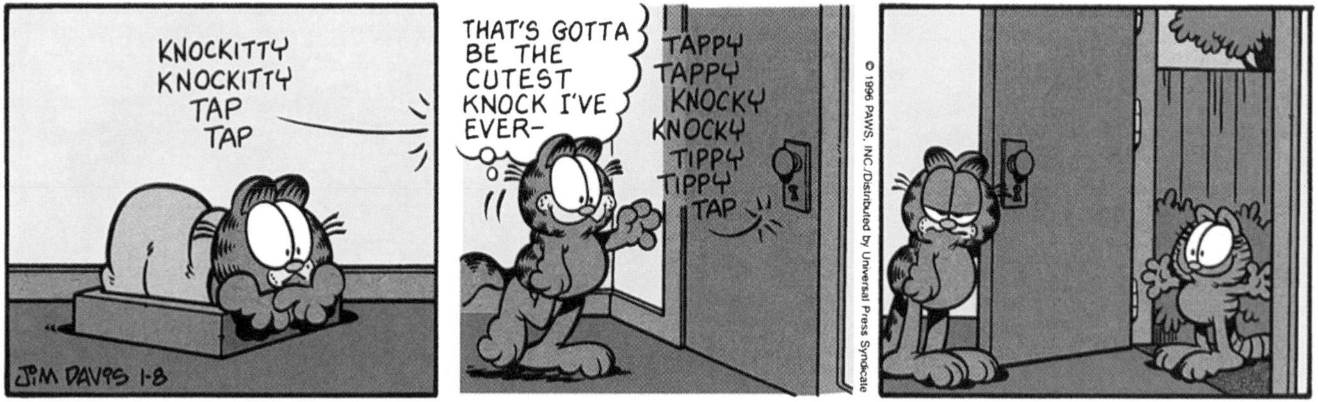
KNOCKITTY KNOCKITTY TAP TAP
JIM DAVIS 1-8
THAT'S GOTTA BE THE CUTEST KNOCK I'VE EVER-
TAPPY TAPPY KNOCKY KNOCKY TIPPY TIPPY TAP
© 1996 PAWS, INC./Distributed by Universal Press Syndicate

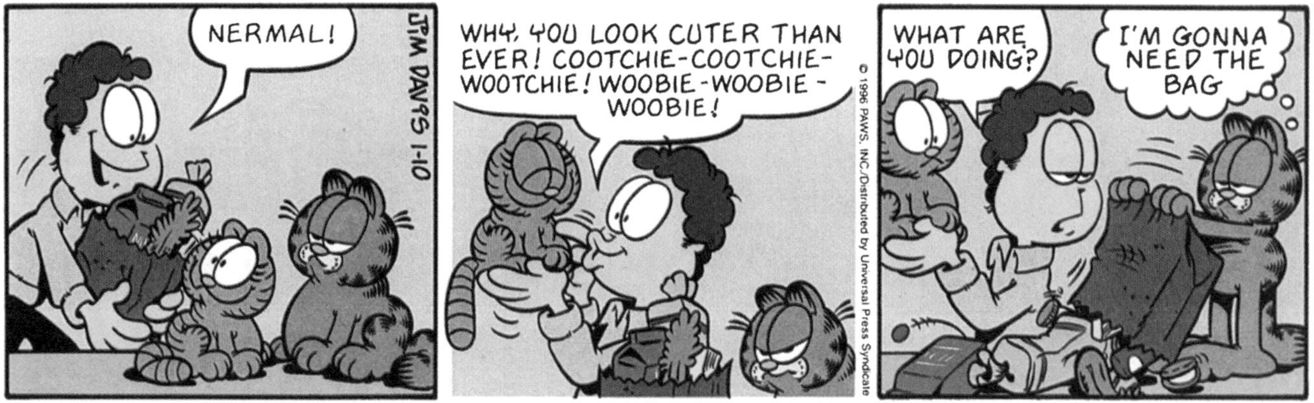
NERMAL!
JIM DAVIS 1-10
WHY, YOU LOOK CUTER THAN EVER! COOTCHIE-COOTCHIE-WOOTCHIE! WOOBIE-WOOBIE-WOOBIE!
© 1996 PAWS, INC./Distributed by Universal Press Syndicate
WHAT ARE YOU DOING?
I'M GONNA NEED THE BAG

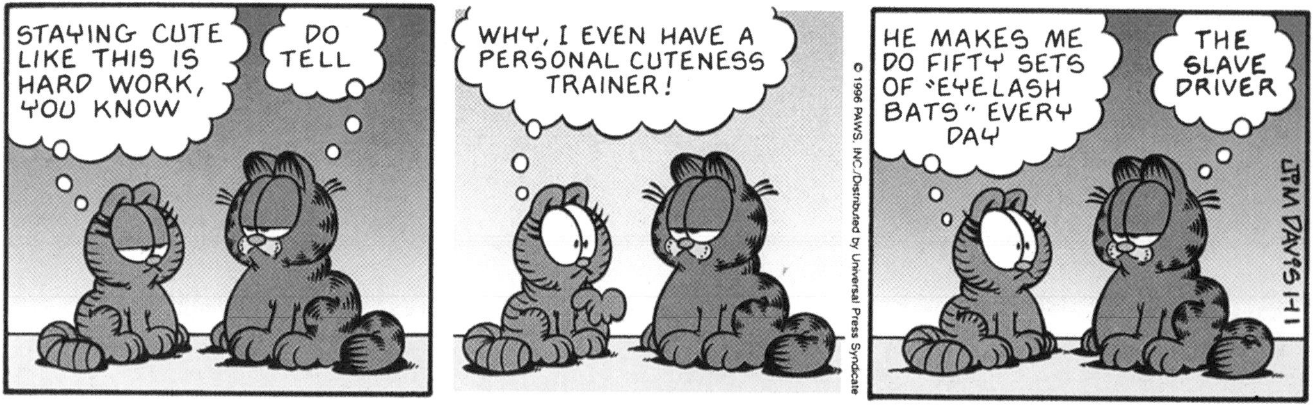
STAYING CUTE LIKE THIS IS HARD WORK, YOU KNOW
DO TELL
WHY, I EVEN HAVE A PERSONAL CUTENESS TRAINER!
© 1996 PAWS, INC./Distributed by Universal Press Syndicate
HE MAKES ME DO FIFTY SETS OF "EYELASH BATS" EVERY DAY
THE SLAVE DRIVER
JIM DAVIS 1-11

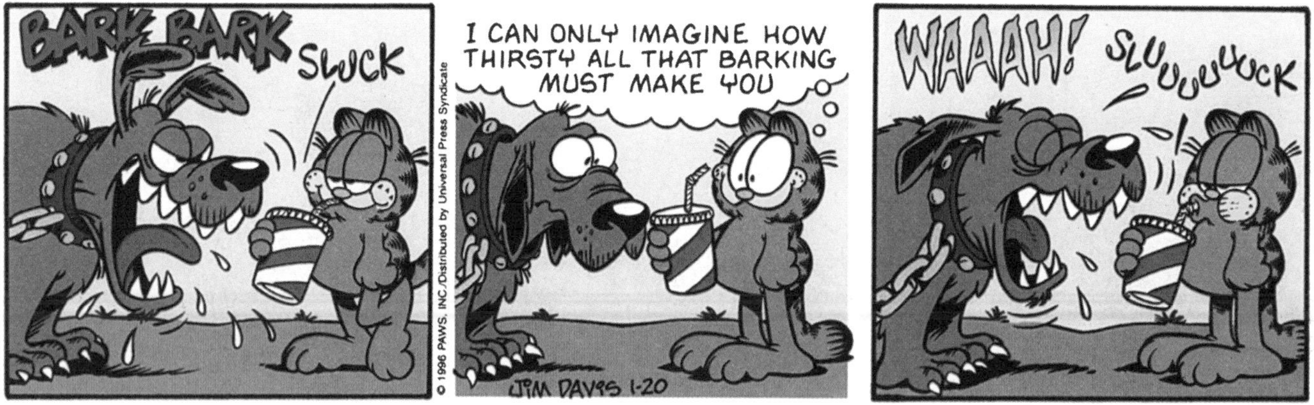
BARK BARK
SLUCK
© 1996 PAWS, INC./Distributed by Universal Press Syndicate
I CAN ONLY IMAGINE HOW THIRSTY ALL THAT BARKING MUST MAKE YOU
JIM DAVIS 1-20
WAAAH!
SLUUUUUUCK

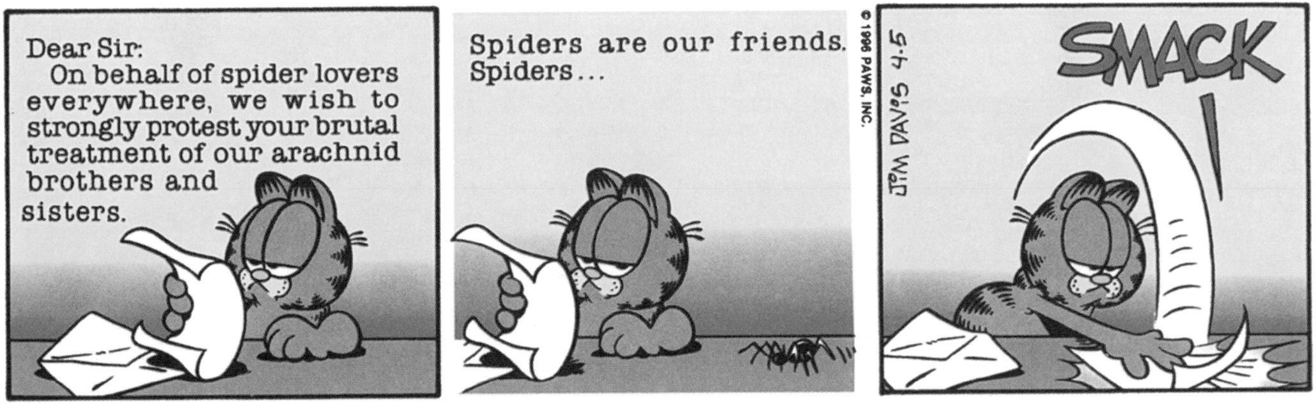
Dear Sir:
On behalf of spider lovers everywhere, we wish to strongly protest your brutal treatment of our arachnid brothers and sisters.
Spiders are our friends. Spiders...
© 1996 PAWS, INC.
JIM DAVIS 4-5
SMACK
!

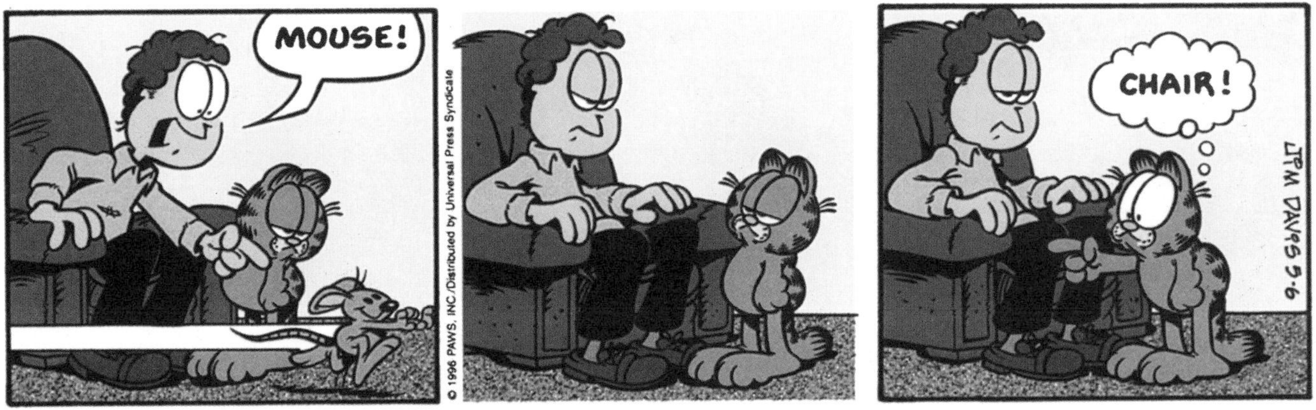
MOUSE!
© 1996 PAWS, INC./Distributed by Universal Press Syndicate
CHAIR!
JIM DAVIS 5-6

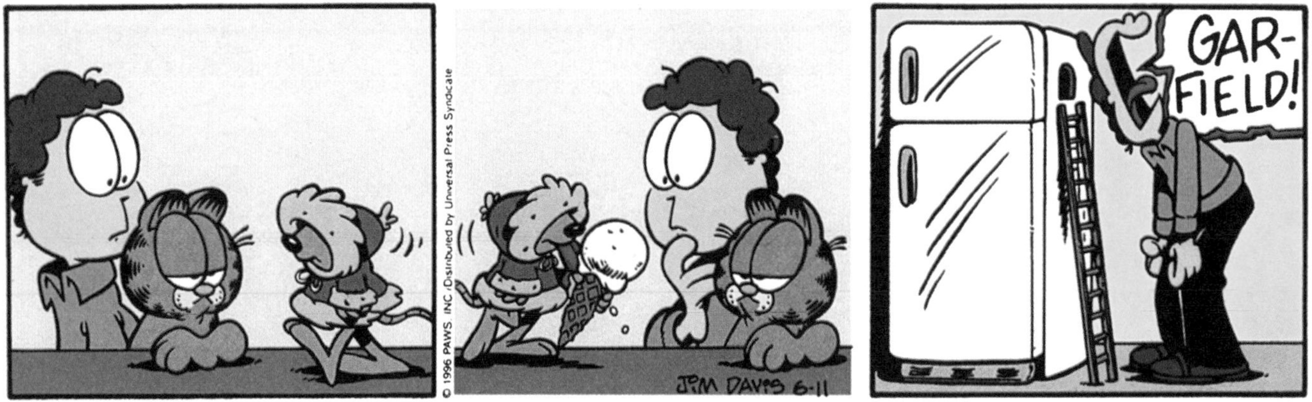
© 1996 PAWS, INC./Distributed by Universal Press Syndicate
JIM DAVIS 6-11
GAR-FIELD!

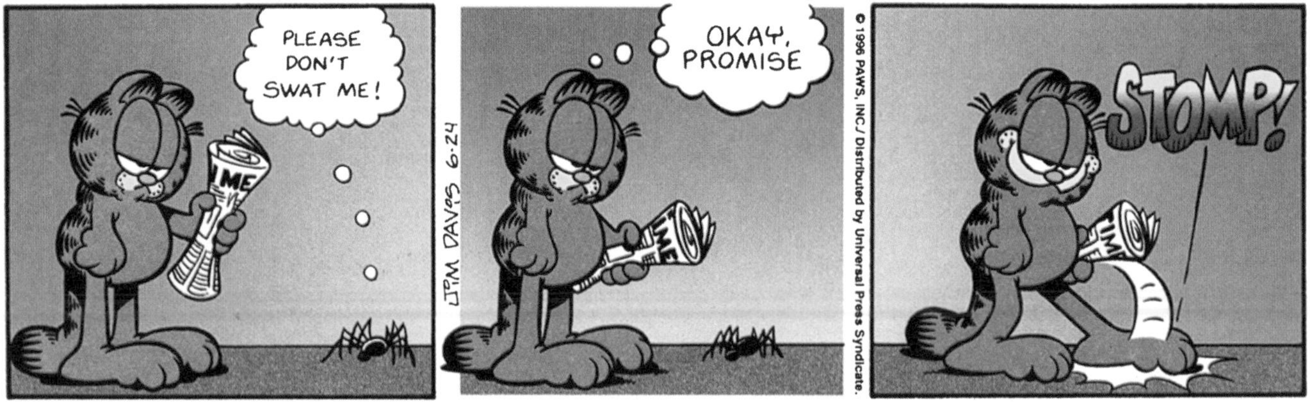
PLEASE DON'T SWAT ME!
JIM DAVIS 6-24
OKAY, PROMISE
© 1996 PAWS, INC./ Distributed by Universal Press Syndicate.
STOMP!

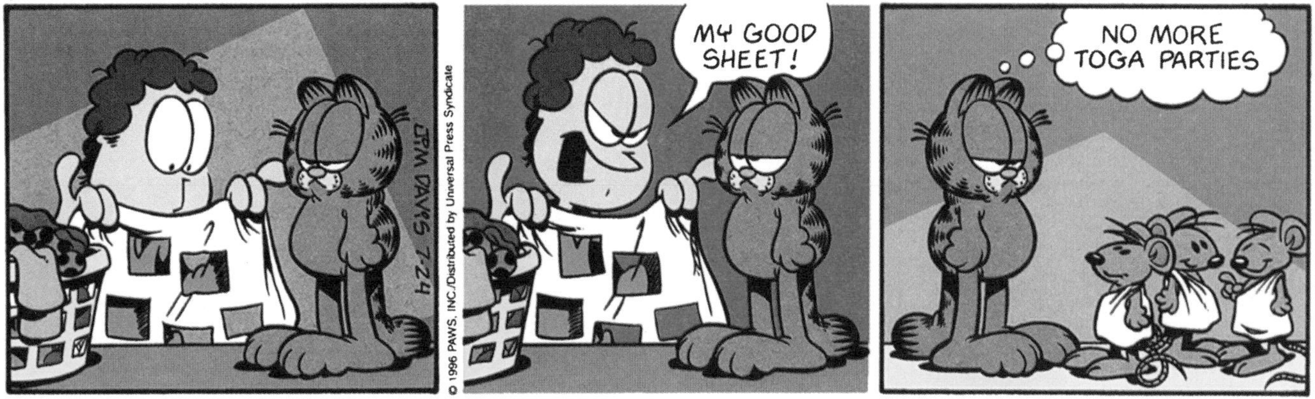
JIM DAVIS 7-24
© 1996 PAWS, INC./Distributed by Universal Press Syndicate
MY GOOD SHEET!
NO MORE TOGA PARTIES

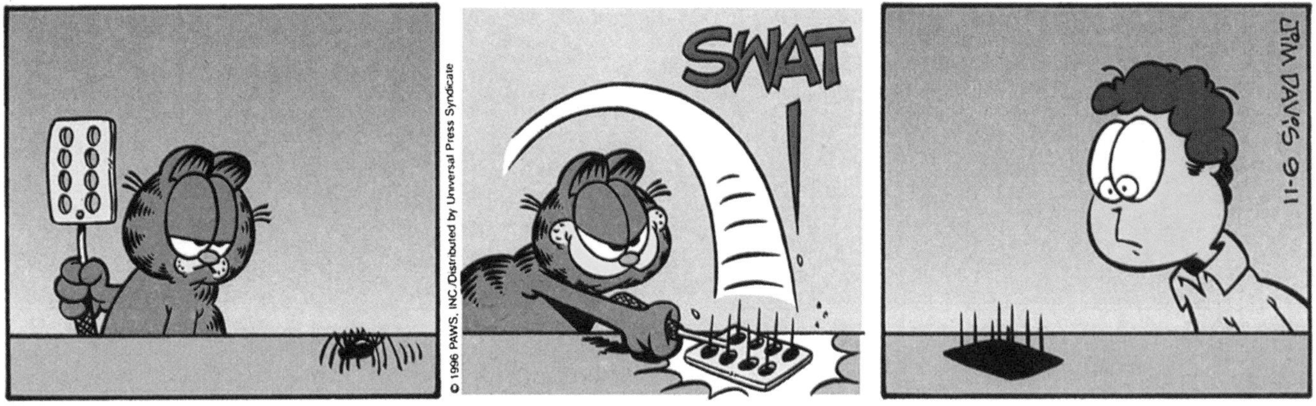
© 1996 PAWS, INC./Distributed by Universal Press Syndicate
SWAT
JIM DAVIS 9-11

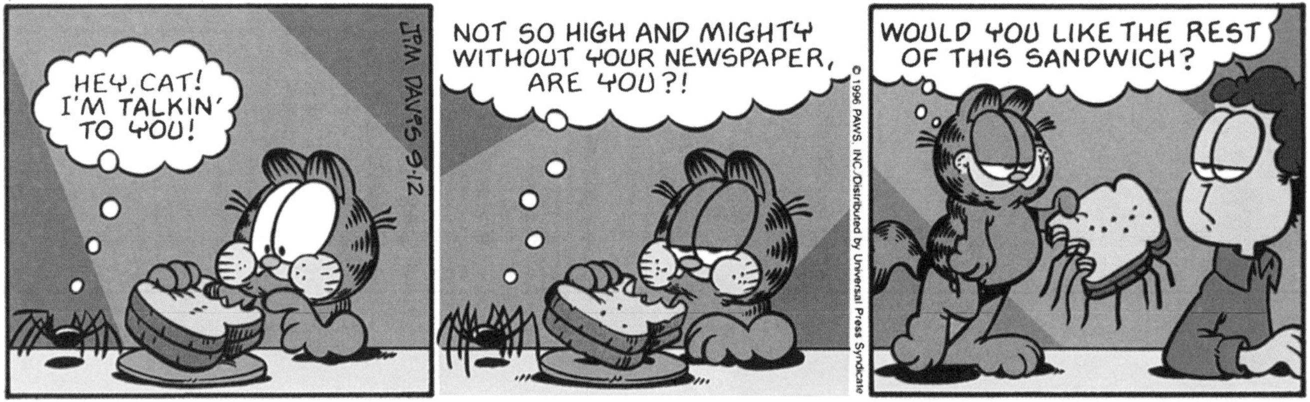
HEY, CAT! I'M TALKIN' TO YOU!
JIM DAVIS 9-12
NOT SO HIGH AND MIGHTY WITHOUT YOUR NEWSPAPER, ARE YOU?!
© 1996 PAWS, INC./Distributed by Universal Press Syndicate
WOULD YOU LIKE THE REST OF THIS SANDWICH?

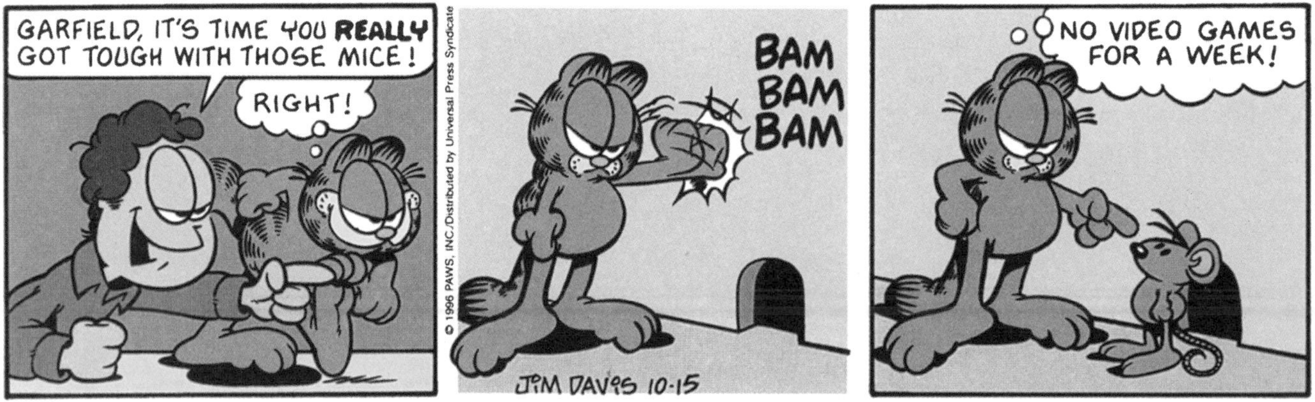
GARFIELD, IT'S TIME YOU **REALLY** GOT TOUGH WITH THOSE MICE!
RIGHT!
© 1996 PAWS, INC./Distributed by Universal Press Syndicate
BAM BAM BAM
JIM DAVIS 10-15
NO VIDEO GAMES FOR A WEEK!

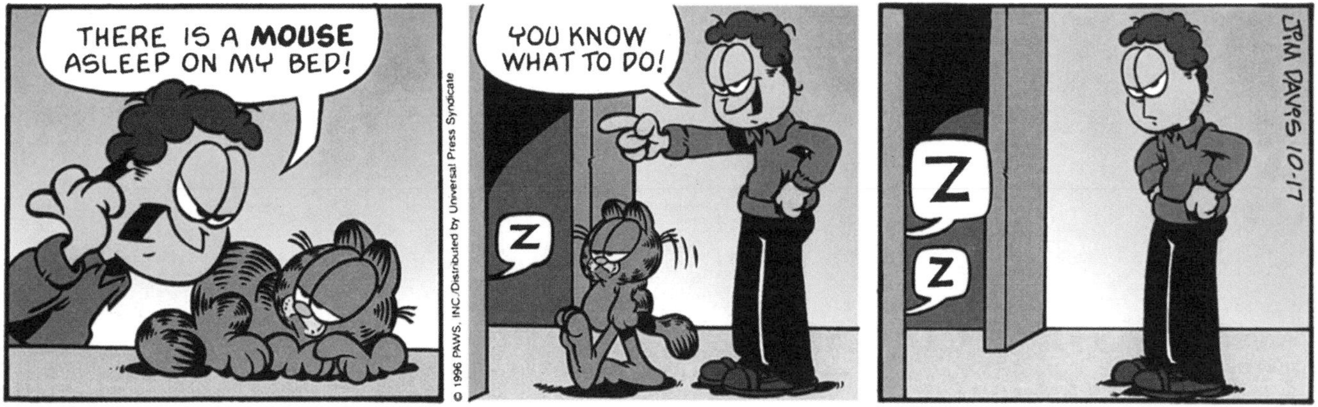
THERE IS A **MOUSE** ASLEEP ON MY BED!
Z
YOU KNOW WHAT TO DO!
Z
Z
JIM DAVIS 10-17

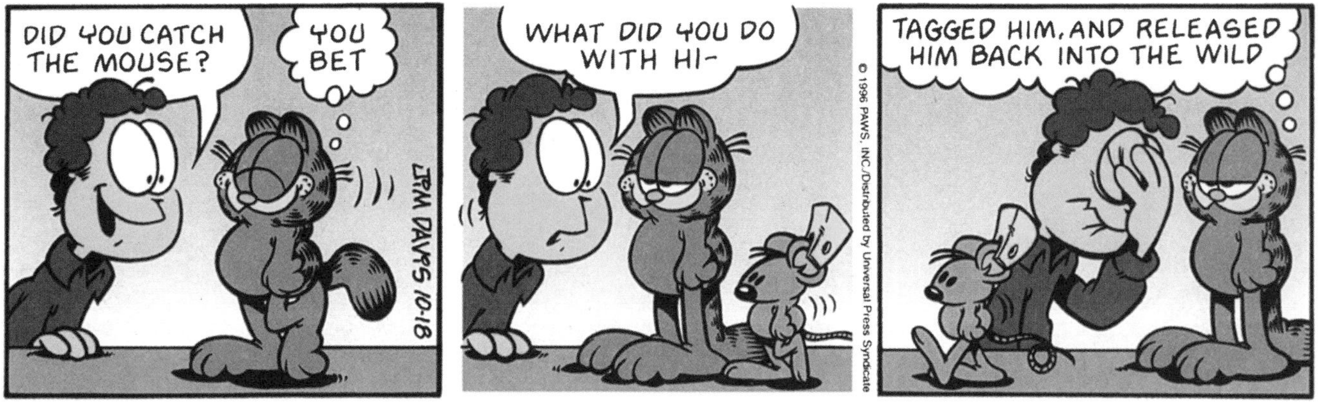
DID YOU CATCH THE MOUSE?
YOU BET
JIM DAVIS 10-18
WHAT DID YOU DO WITH HI-
TAGGED HIM, AND RELEASED HIM BACK INTO THE WILD

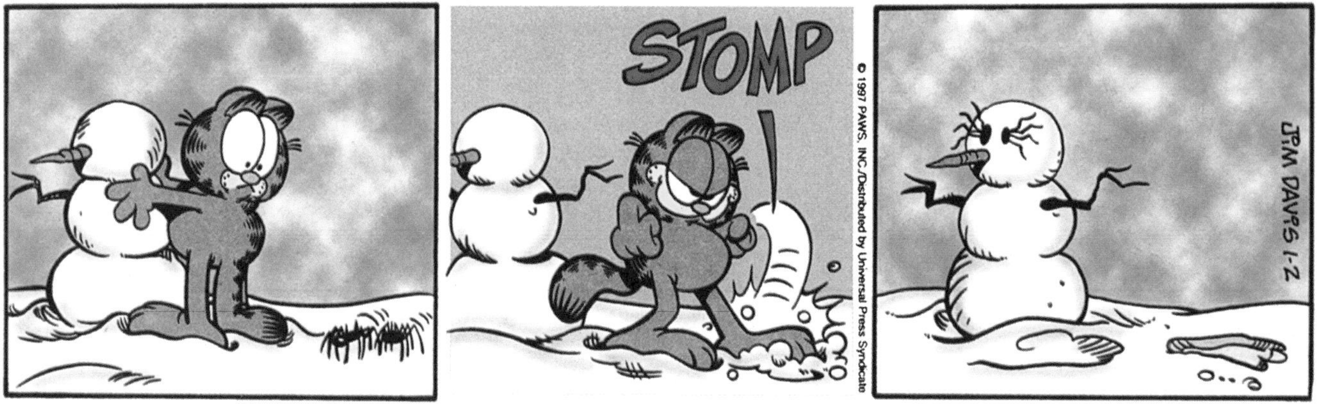
STOMP
© 1997 PAWS, INC./Distributed by Universal Press Syndicate
JIM DAVIS 1-2

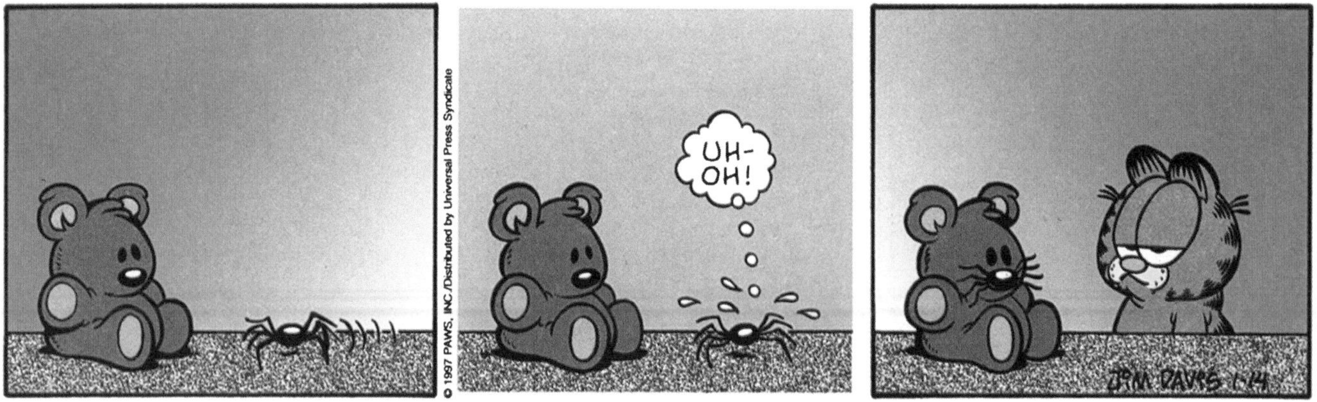
© 1997 PAWS, INC./Distributed by Universal Press Syndicate
UH-OH!
JIM DAVIS 1-14

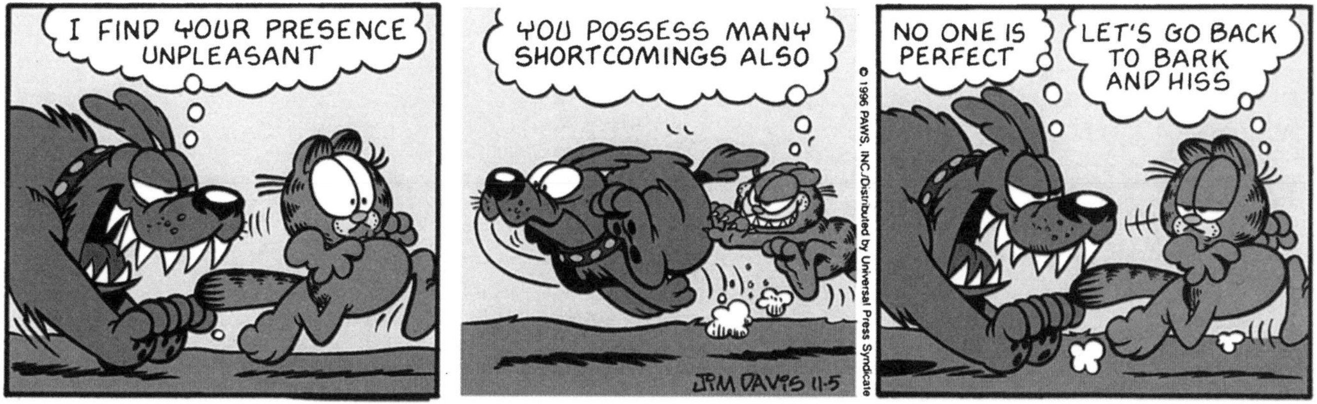
I FIND YOUR PRESENCE UNPLEASANT
YOU POSSESS MANY SHORTCOMINGS ALSO
JIM DAVIS 11-5
© 1996 PAWS, INC./Distributed by Universal Press Syndicate
NO ONE IS PERFECT
LET'S GO BACK TO BARK AND HISS

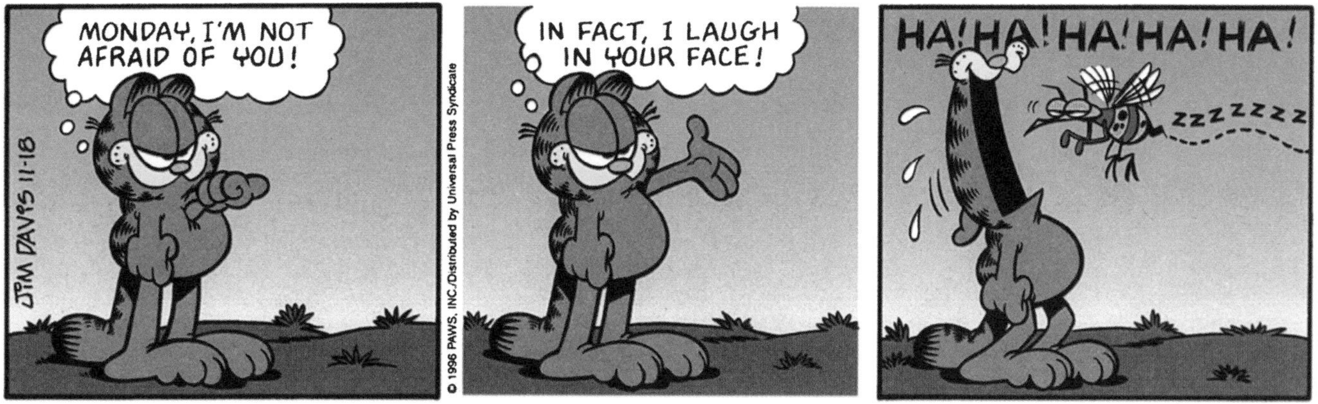
MONDAY, I'M NOT AFRAID OF YOU!
JIM DAVIS 11-18
© 1996 PAWS, INC./Distributed by Universal Press Syndicate
IN FACT, I LAUGH IN YOUR FACE!
HA! HA! HA! HA! HA!
ZZZZZZZ

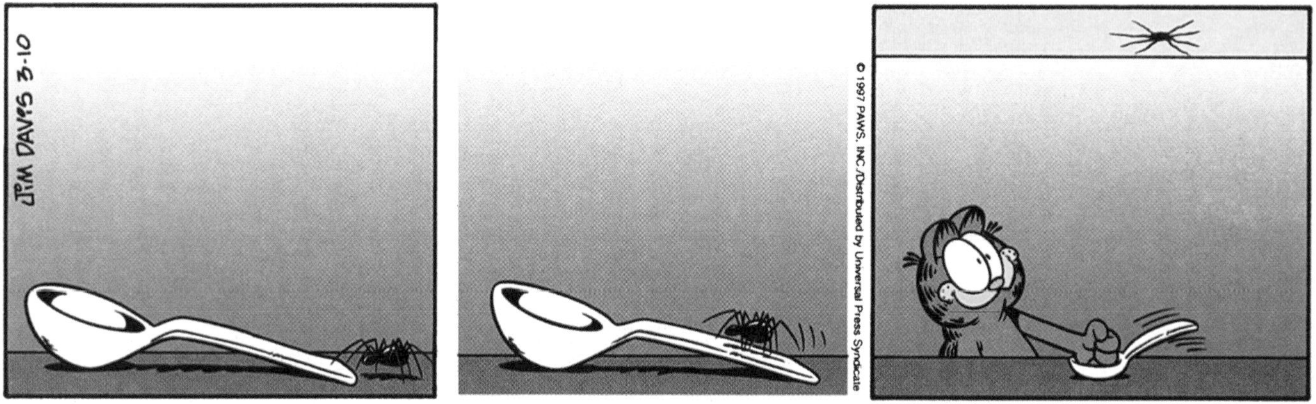
JIM DAVIS 3-10
© 1997 PAWS, INC./Distributed by Universal Press Syndicate

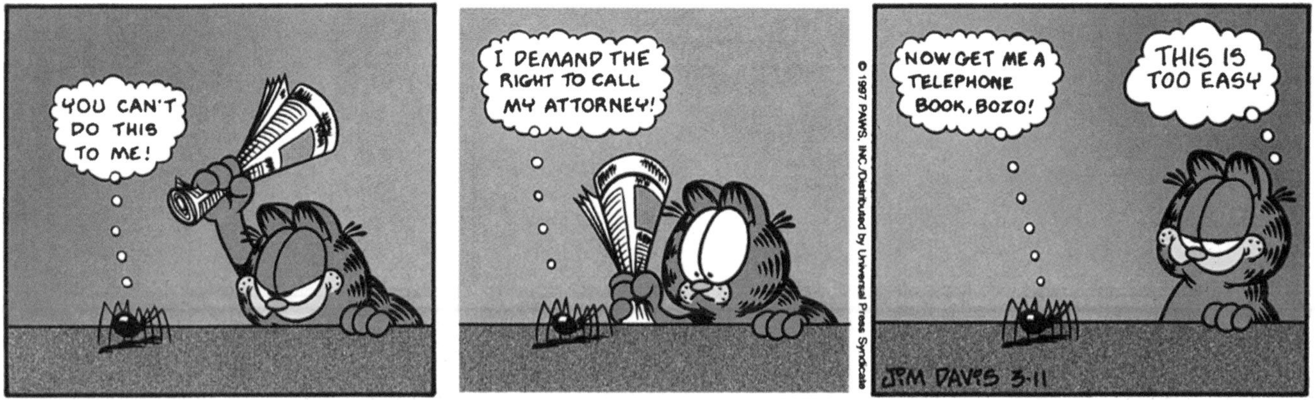
YOU CAN'T DO THIS TO ME!
I DEMAND THE RIGHT TO CALL MY ATTORNEY!
NOW GET ME A TELEPHONE BOOK, BOZO!
THIS IS TOO EASY
JIM DAVIS 3-11
© 1997 PAWS, INC./Distributed by Universal Press Syndicate

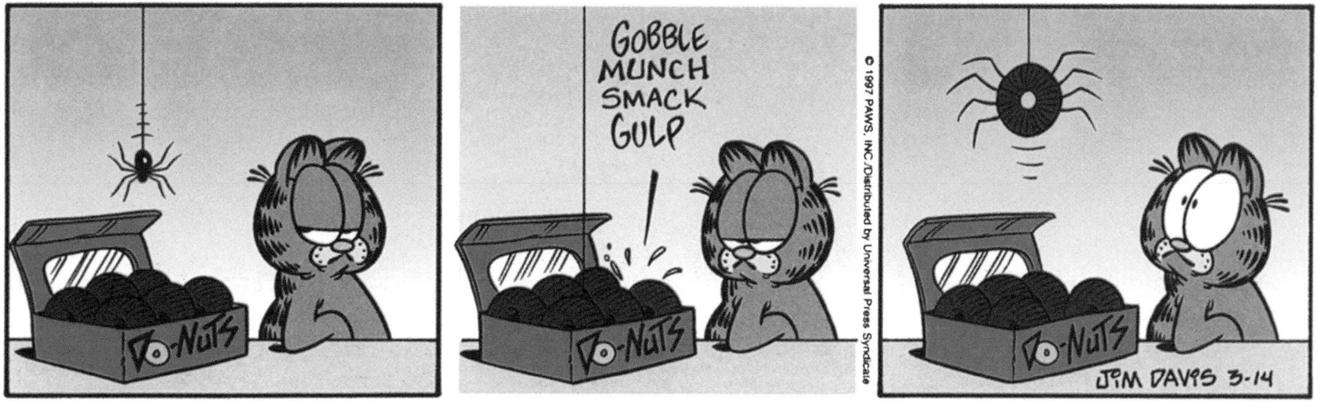

DO-NUTS
GOBBLE
MUNCH
SMACK
GULP
DO-NUTS
© 1997 PAWS, INC./Distributed by Universal Press Syndicate
DO-NUTS
JIM DAVIS 3-14

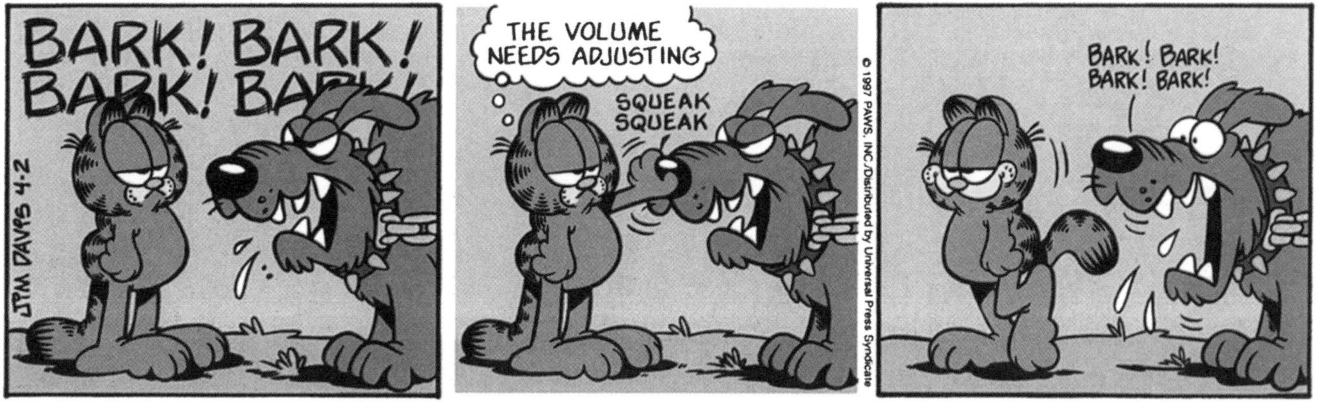

BARK! BARK!
BARK! BA
JIM DAVIS 4-2
THE VOLUME NEEDS ADJUSTING
SQUEAK SQUEAK
© 1997 PAWS, INC./Distributed by Universal Press Syndicate
BARK! BARK!
BARK! BARK!

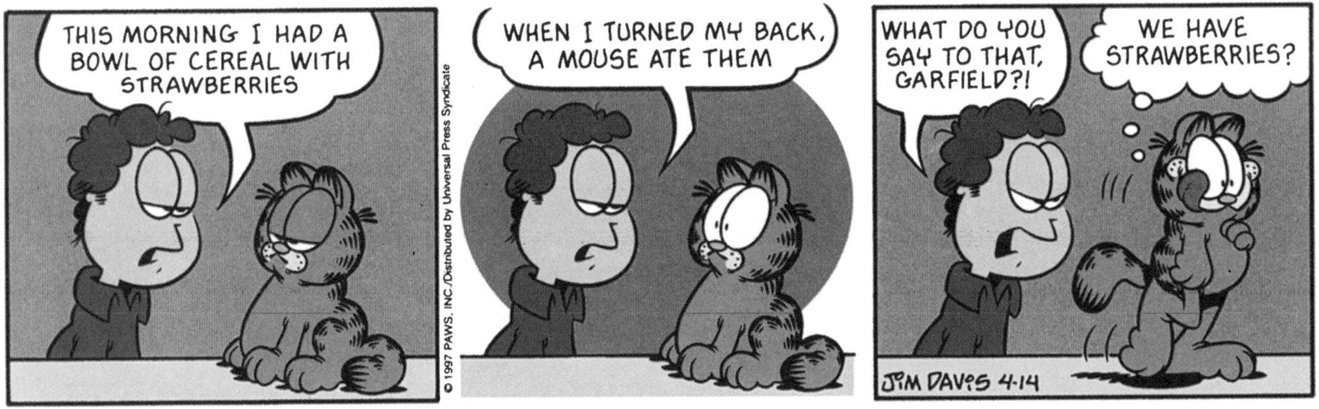
THIS MORNING I HAD A BOWL OF CEREAL WITH STRAWBERRIES
© 1997 PAWS, INC./Distributed by Universal Press Syndicate
WHEN I TURNED MY BACK, A MOUSE ATE THEM
WHAT DO YOU SAY TO THAT, GARFIELD?!
WE HAVE STRAWBERRIES?
JIM DAVIS 4-14

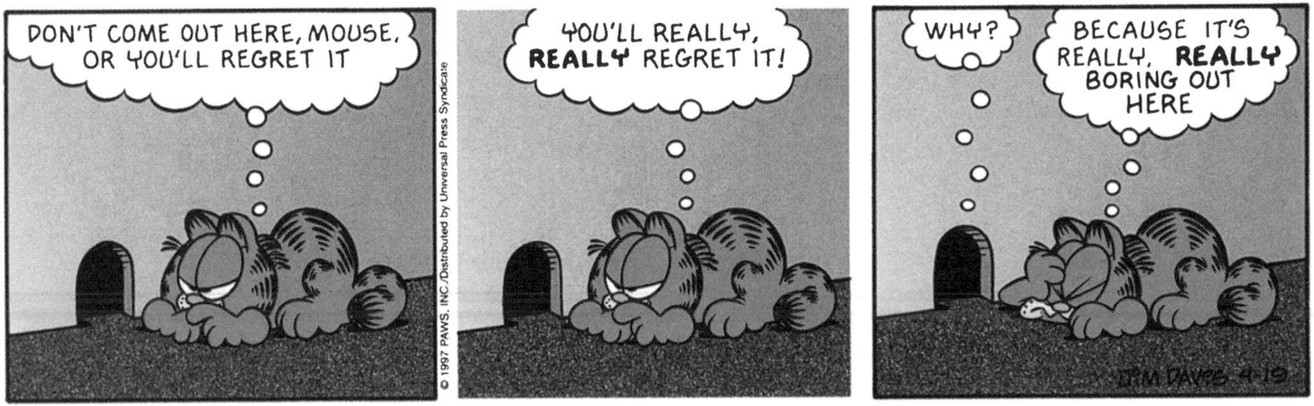
DON'T COME OUT HERE, MOUSE, OR YOU'LL REGRET IT
© 1997 PAWS, INC./Distributed by Universal Press Syndicate
YOU'LL REALLY, **REALLY** REGRET IT!
WHY?
BECAUSE IT'S REALLY, **REALLY** BORING OUT HERE
JIM DAVIS 4-19

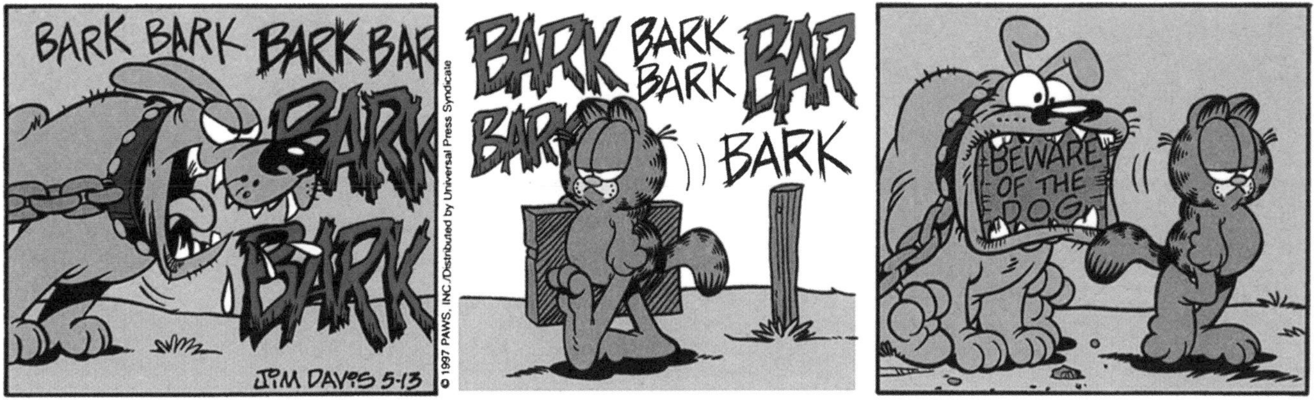

BARK BARK BARK BAR
BARK
BARK
JIM DAVIS 5-13
© 1997 PAWS, INC./Distributed by Universal Press Syndicate
BARK BARK BARK BAR
BARK
BAR
BARK
BEWARE OF THE DOG

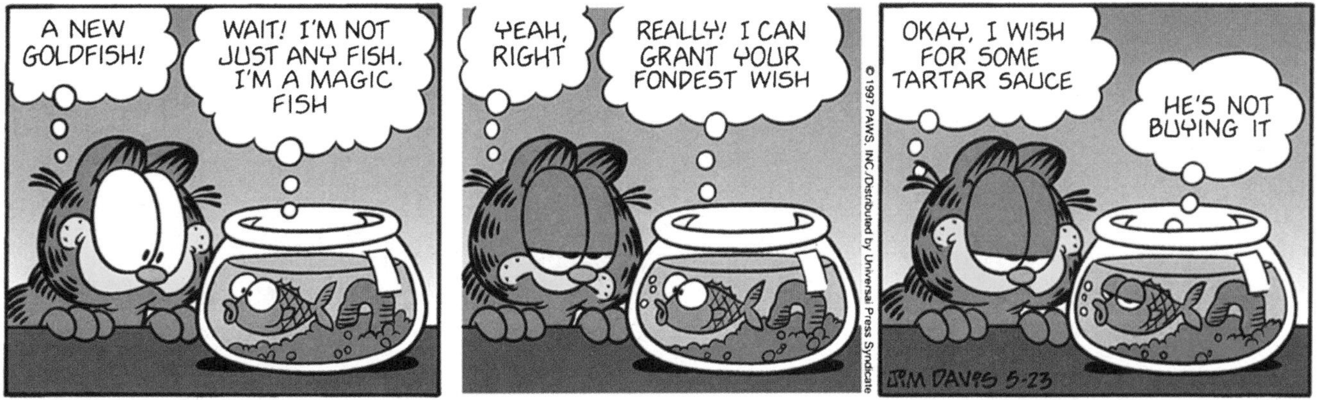

A NEW GOLDFISH!
WAIT! I'M NOT JUST ANY FISH. I'M A MAGIC FISH
YEAH, RIGHT
REALLY! I CAN GRANT YOUR FONDEST WISH
© 1997 PAWS, INC./Distributed by Universal Press Syndicate
OKAY, I WISH FOR SOME TARTAR SAUCE
HE'S NOT BUYING IT
JIM DAVIS 5-23

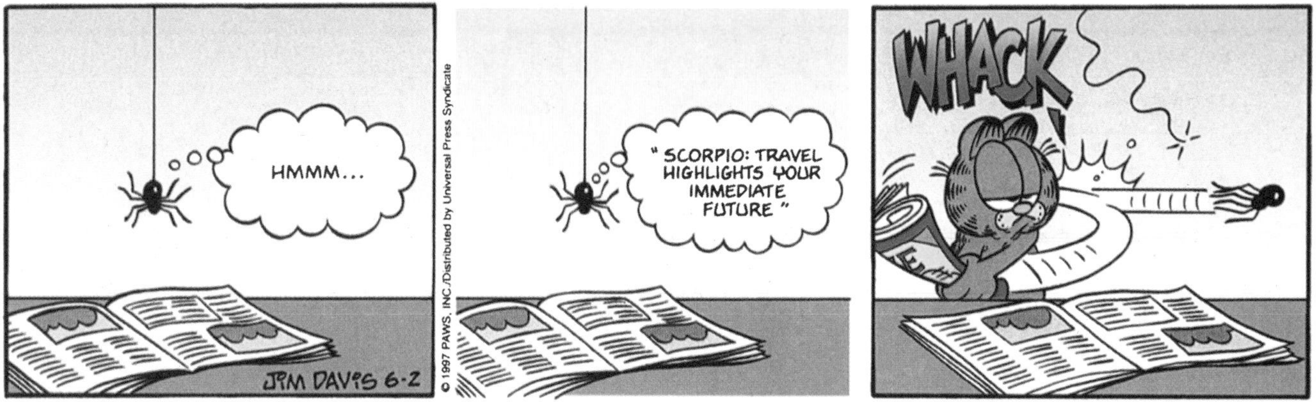
HMMM...
"SCORPIO: TRAVEL HIGHLIGHTS YOUR IMMEDIATE FUTURE"
WHACK
JIM DAVIS 6-2
© 1997 PAWS, INC./Distributed by Universal Press Syndicate

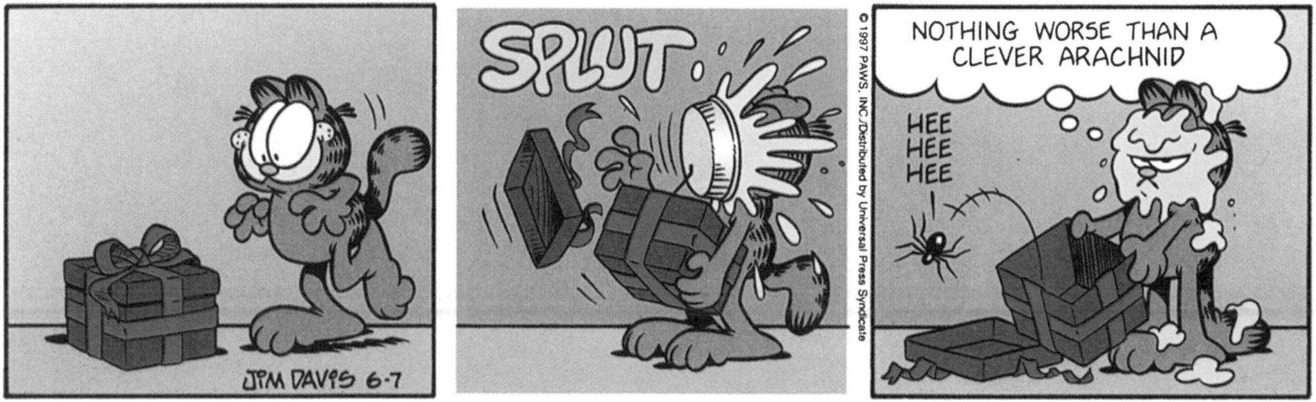
JIM DAVIS 6-7
SPLUT
NOTHING WORSE THAN A CLEVER ARACHNID
HEE HEE HEE
© 1997 PAWS, INC./Distributed by Universal Press Syndicate

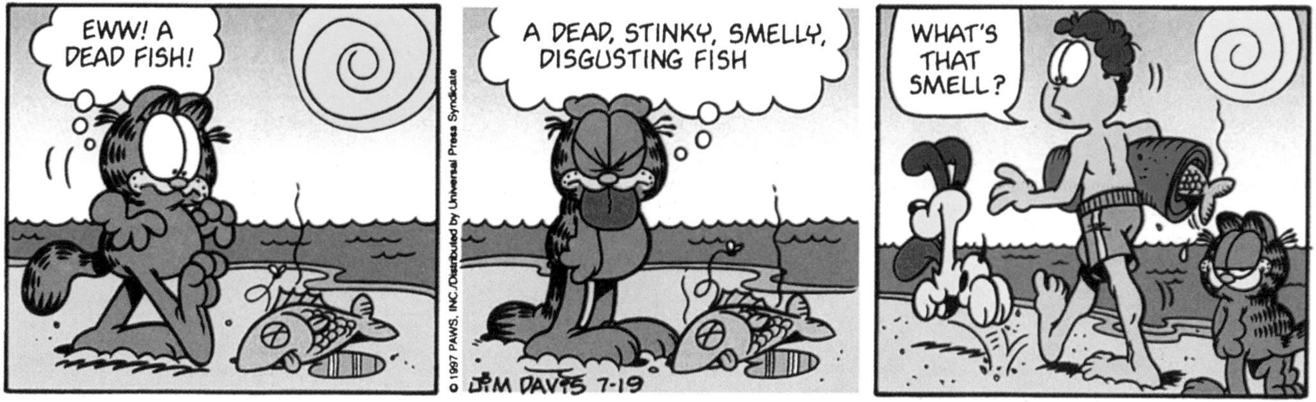
EWW! A DEAD FISH!
A DEAD, STINKY, SMELLY, DISGUSTING FISH
WHAT'S THAT SMELL?
JIM DAVIS 7-19
© 1997 PAWS, INC./Distributed by Universal Press Syndicate

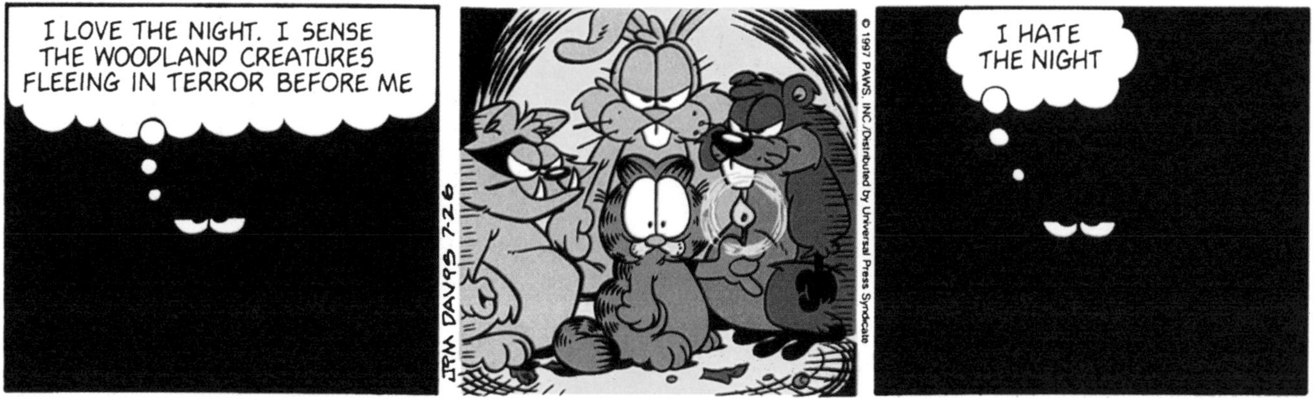
I LOVE THE NIGHT. I SENSE THE WOODLAND CREATURES FLEEING IN TERROR BEFORE ME
I HATE THE NIGHT
JIM DAVIS 7-26
© 1997 PAWS, INC./Distributed by Universal Press Syndicate

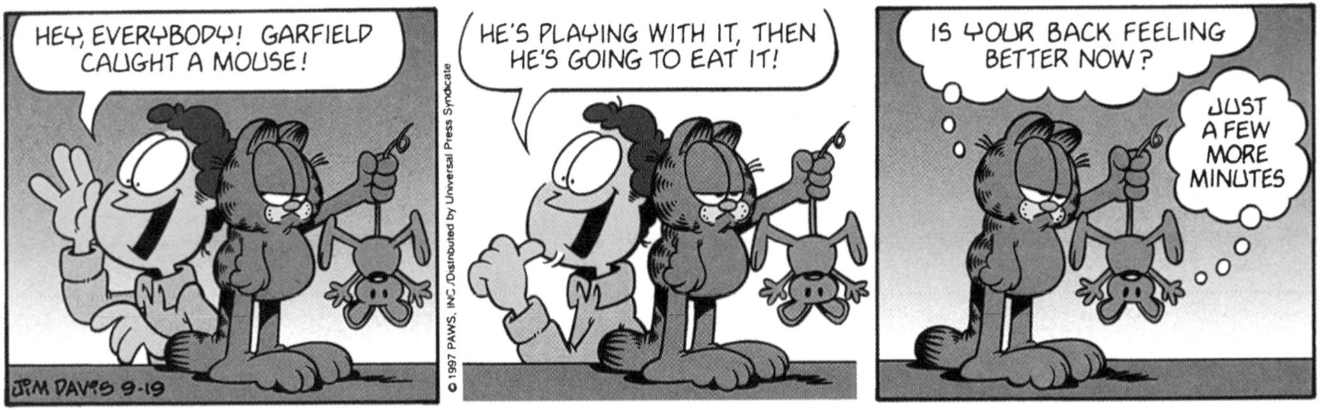
HEY, EVERYBODY! GARFIELD CAUGHT A MOUSE!
JIM DAVIS 9-19
© 1997 PAWS, INC./Distributed by Universal Press Syndicate
HE'S PLAYING WITH IT, THEN HE'S GOING TO EAT IT!
IS YOUR BACK FEELING BETTER NOW?
JUST A FEW MORE MINUTES

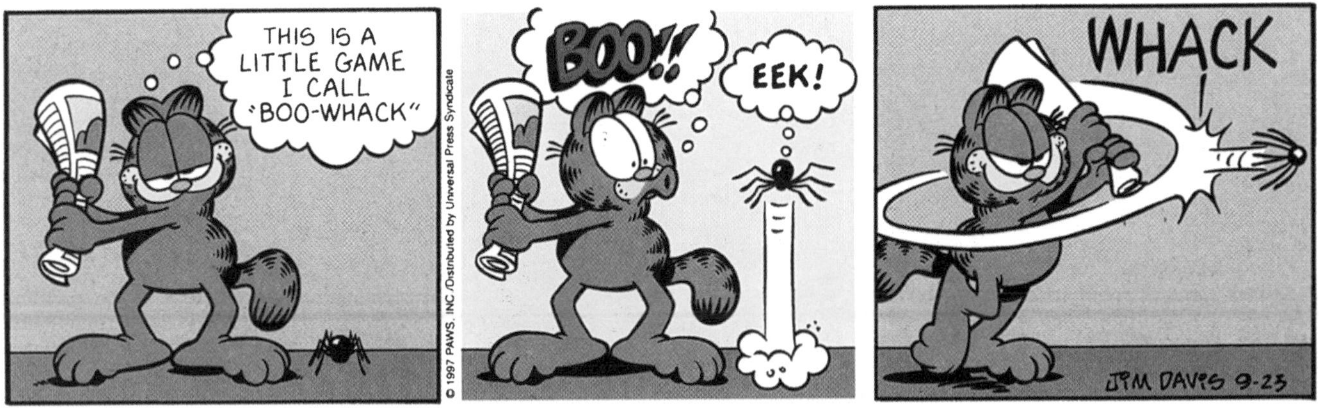
THIS IS A LITTLE GAME I CALL "BOO-WHACK"
© 1997 PAWS, INC./Distributed by Universal Press Syndicate
BOO!!
EEK!
WHACK
JIM DAVIS 9-23

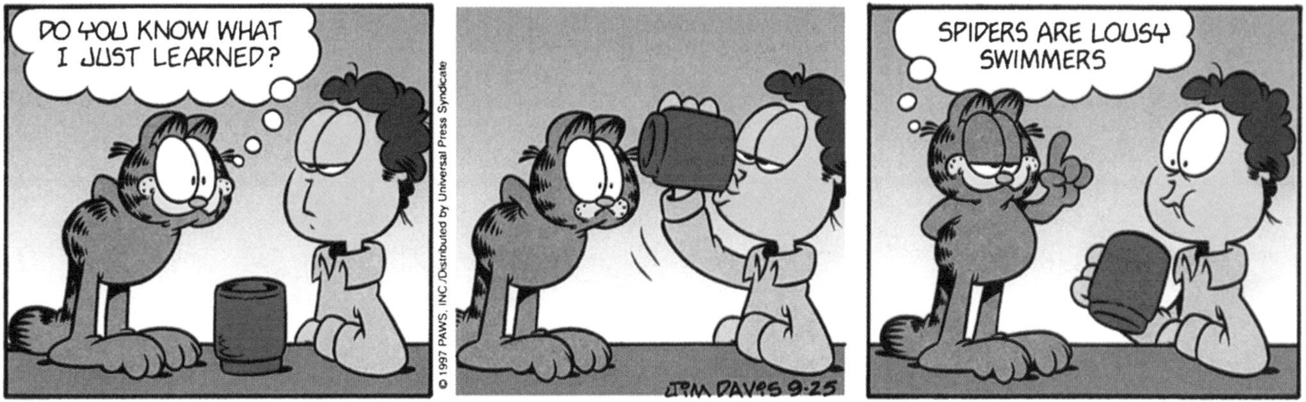
DO YOU KNOW WHAT I JUST LEARNED?
© 1997 PAWS, INC./Distributed by Universal Press Syndicate
JIM DAVIS 9-25
SPIDERS ARE LOUSY SWIMMERS

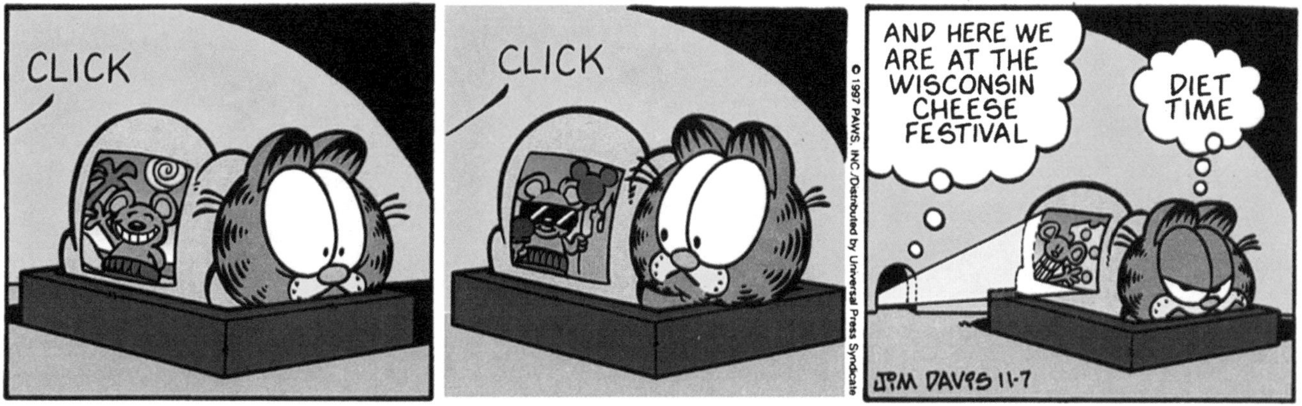
CLICK
CLICK
© 1997 PAWS, INC./Distributed by Universal Press Syndicate
AND HERE WE ARE AT THE WISCONSIN CHEESE FESTIVAL
DIET TIME
JIM DAVIS 11-7

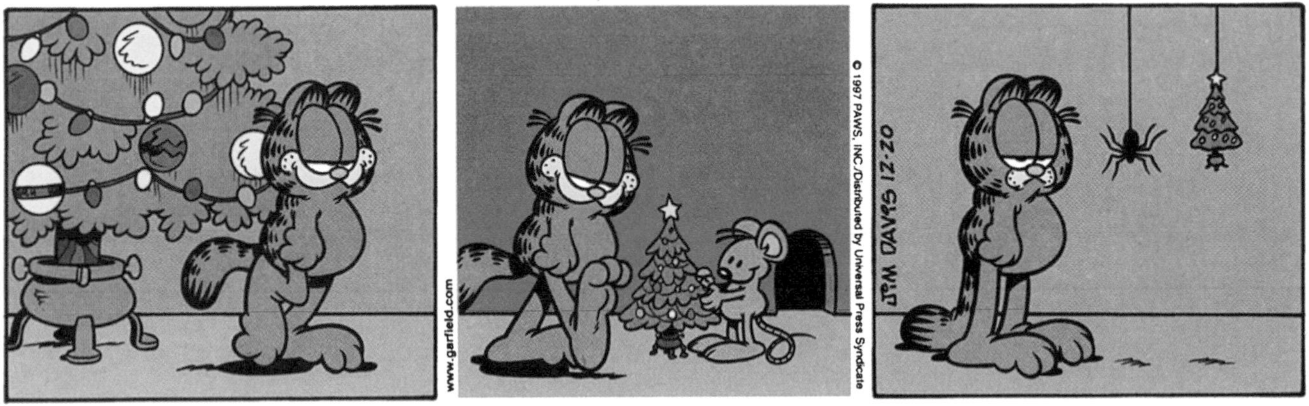
www.garfield.com
© 1997 PAWS, INC./Distributed by Universal Press Syndicate
JIM DAVIS 12-20

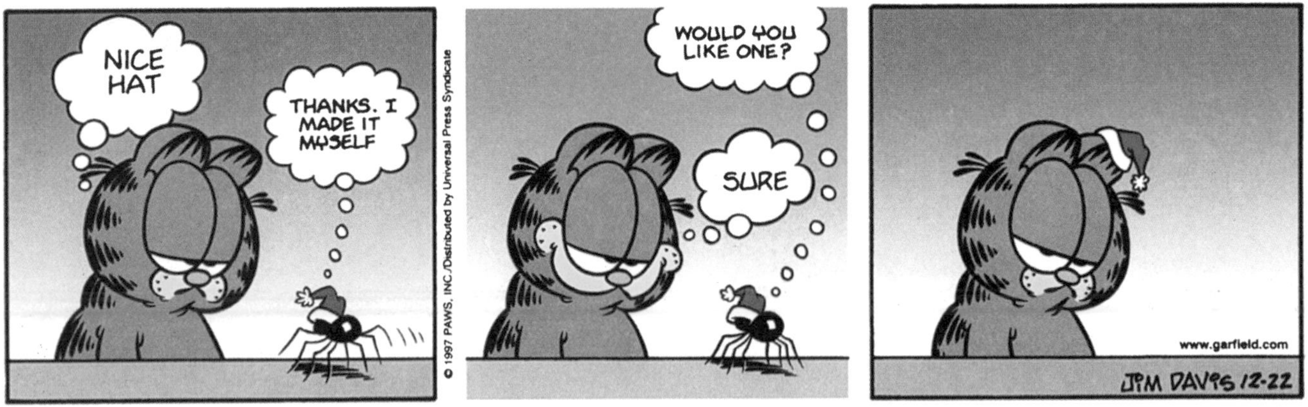
NICE HAT
THANKS. I MADE IT MYSELF
© 1997 PAWS, INC./Distributed by Universal Press Syndicate
WOULD YOU LIKE ONE?
SURE
www.garfield.com
JIM DAVIS 12-22

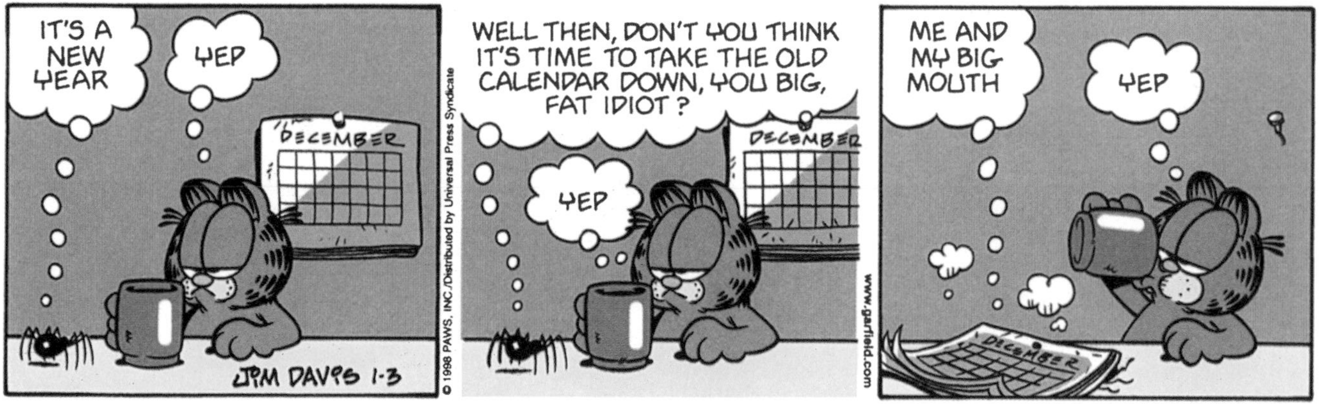
IT'S A NEW YEAR
YEP
WELL THEN, DON'T YOU THINK IT'S TIME TO TAKE THE OLD CALENDAR DOWN, YOU BIG, FAT IDIOT ?
YEP
ME AND MY BIG MOUTH
YEP
DECEMBER
JIM DAVIS 1-3
© 1998 PAWS, INC./Distributed by Universal Press Syndicate
www.garfield.com

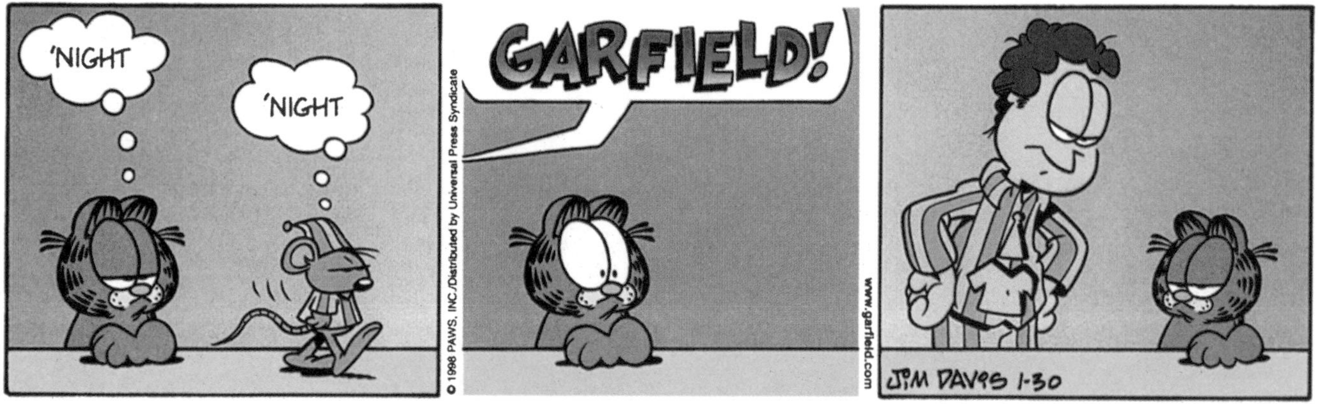
'NIGHT
'NIGHT
GARFIELD!
JIM DAVIS 1-30
© 1998 PAWS, INC./Distributed by Universal Press Syndicate
www.garfield.com

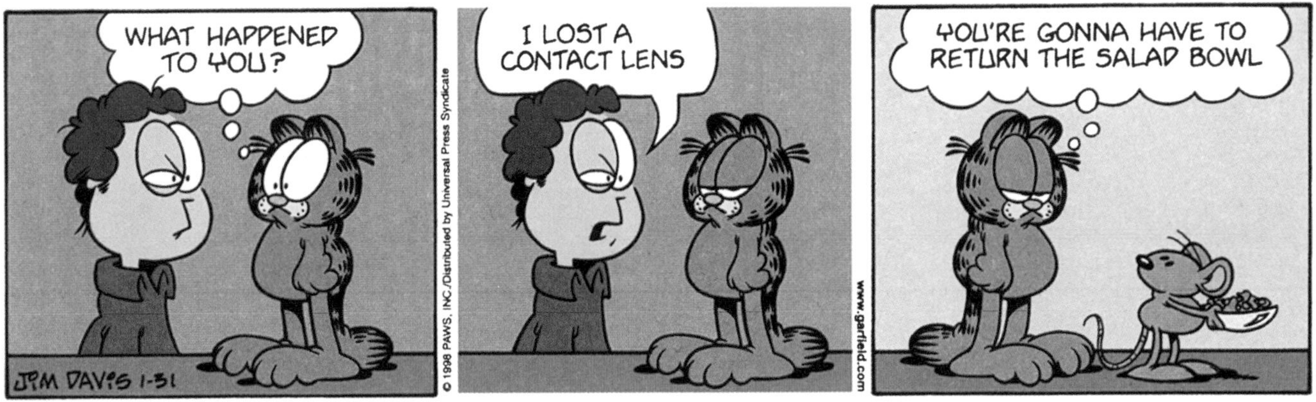
WHAT HAPPENED TO YOU?
JIM DAVIS 1-31
© 1998 PAWS, INC./Distributed by Universal Press Syndicate
I LOST A CONTACT LENS
www.garfield.com
YOU'RE GONNA HAVE TO RETURN THE SALAD BOWL

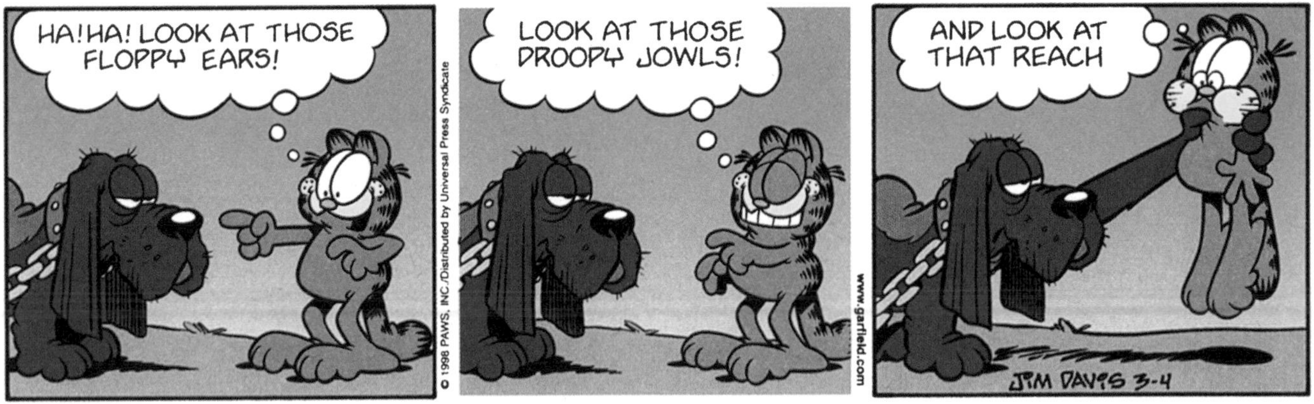
HA! HA! LOOK AT THOSE FLOPPY EARS!
© 1998 PAWS, INC./Distributed by Universal Press Syndicate
LOOK AT THOSE DROOPY JOWLS!
www.garfield.com
AND LOOK AT THAT REACH
JIM DAVIS 3-4

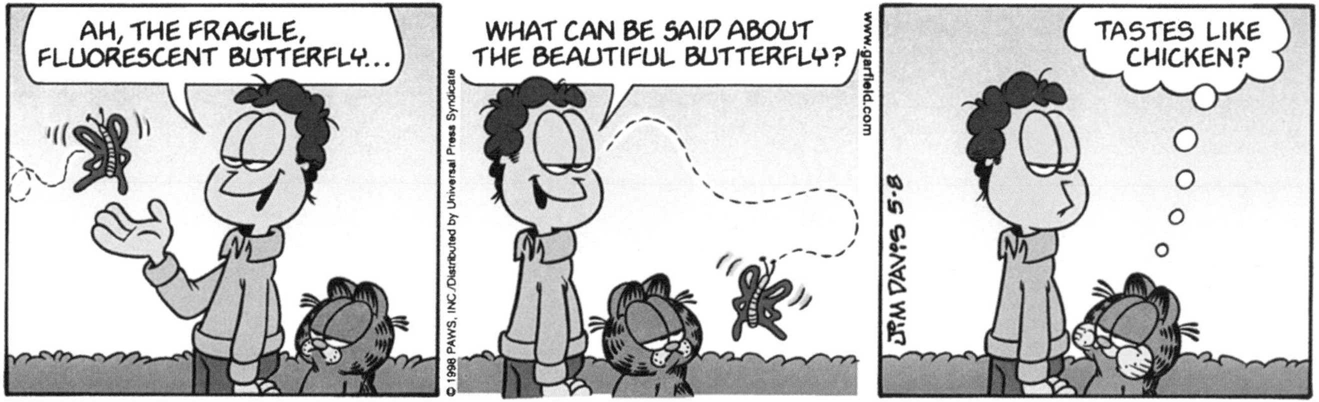
AH, THE FRAGILE, FLUORESCENT BUTTERFLY...
© 1998 PAWS, INC./Distributed by Universal Press Syndicate
WHAT CAN BE SAID ABOUT THE BEAUTIFUL BUTTERFLY?
www.garfield.com
JIM DAVIS 5-8
TASTES LIKE CHICKEN?

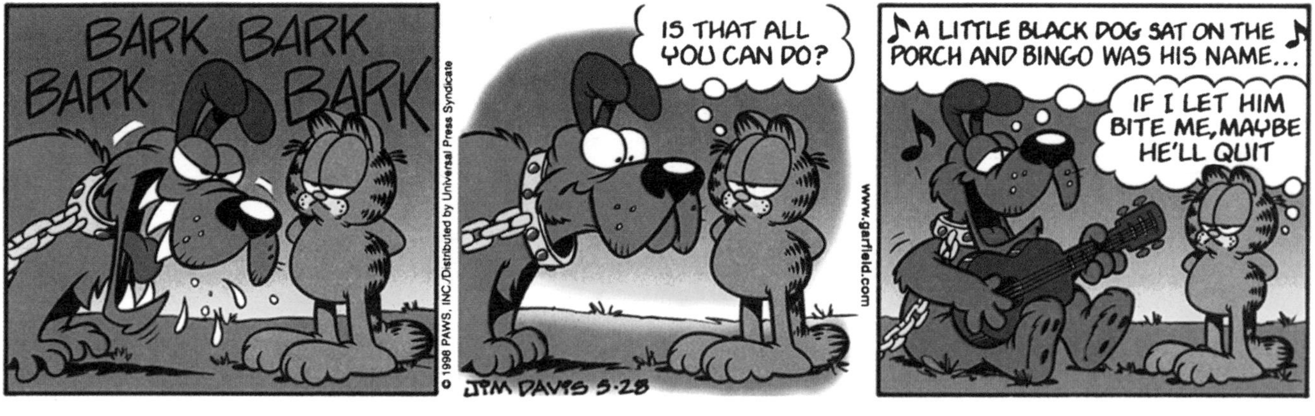
BARK BARK
BARK BARK
© 1998 PAWS, INC./Distributed by Universal Press Syndicate
IS THAT ALL YOU CAN DO?
JIM DAVIS 5-28
www.garfield.com
A LITTLE BLACK DOG SAT ON THE PORCH AND BINGO WAS HIS NAME...
IF I LET HIM BITE ME, MAYBE HE'LL QUIT

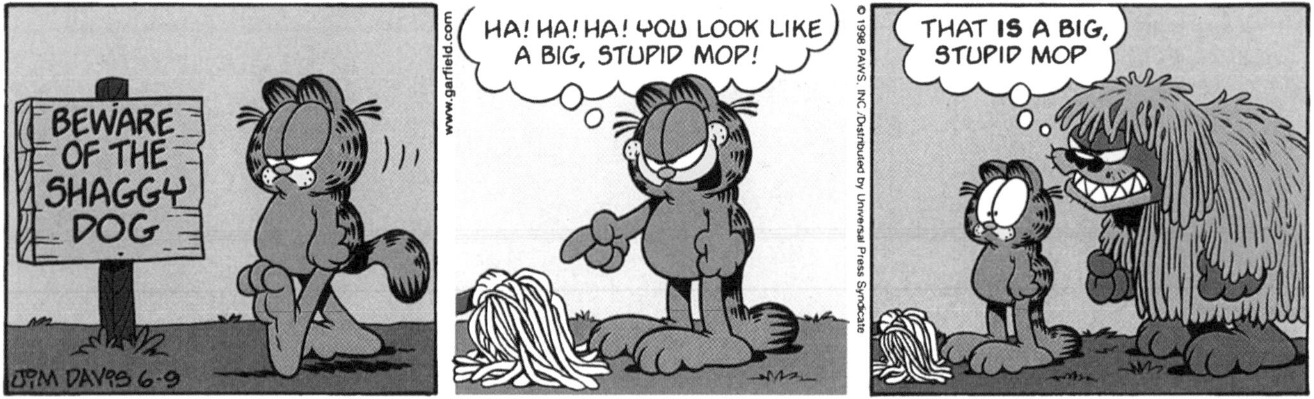
BEWARE OF THE SHAGGY DOG
JIM DAVIS 6-9
www.garfield.com
HA! HA! HA! YOU LOOK LIKE A BIG, STUPID MOP!
© 1998 PAWS, INC./Distributed by Universal Press Syndicate
THAT **IS** A BIG, STUPID MOP

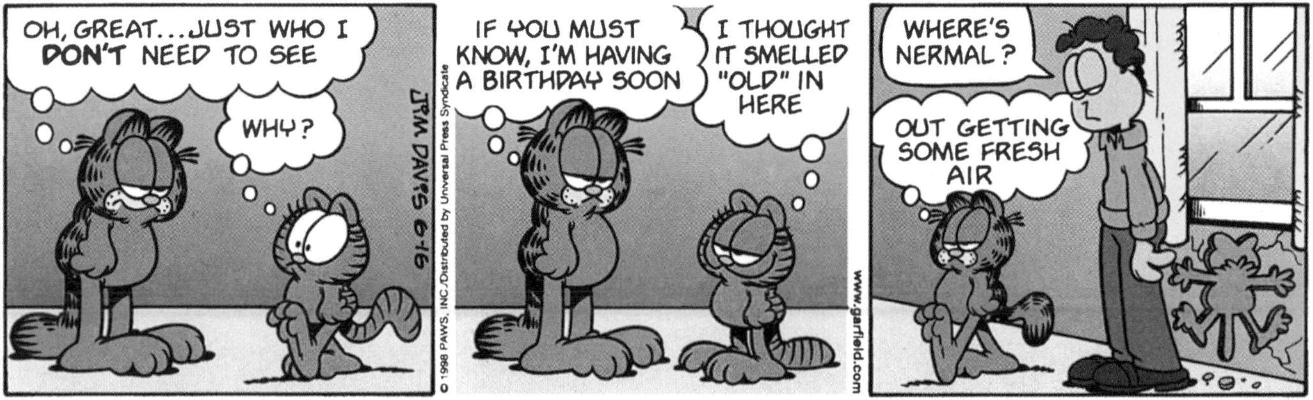
OH, GREAT...JUST WHO I **DON'T** NEED TO SEE
WHY?
JIM DAVIS 6-16
© 1998 PAWS, INC./Distributed by Universal Press Syndicate
IF YOU MUST KNOW, I'M HAVING A BIRTHDAY SOON
I THOUGHT IT SMELLED "OLD" IN HERE
www.garfield.com
WHERE'S NERMAL?
OUT GETTING SOME FRESH AIR

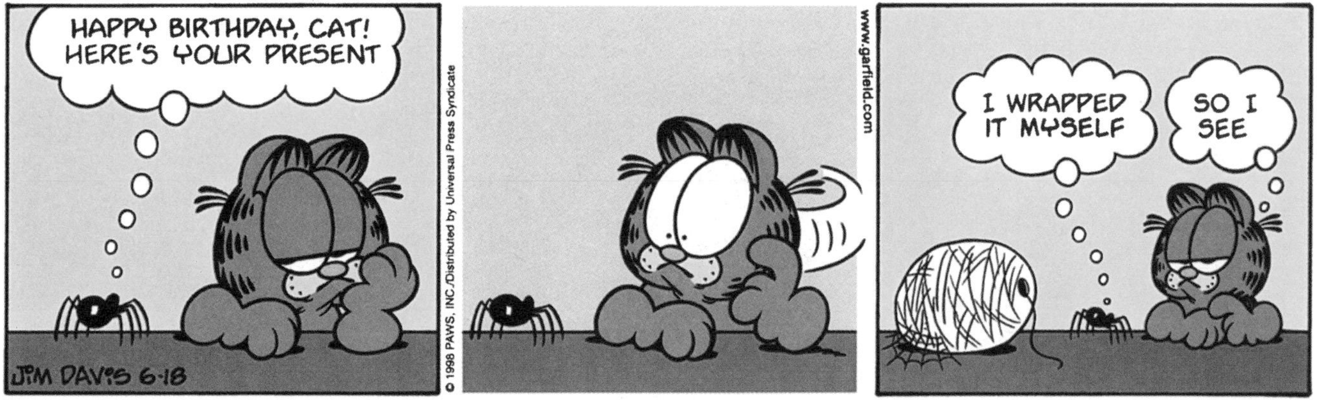
HAPPY BIRTHDAY, CAT! HERE'S YOUR PRESENT
I WRAPPED IT MYSELF
SO I SEE
JIM DAVIS 6-18
© 1998 PAWS, INC./Distributed by Universal Press Syndicate
www.garfield.com

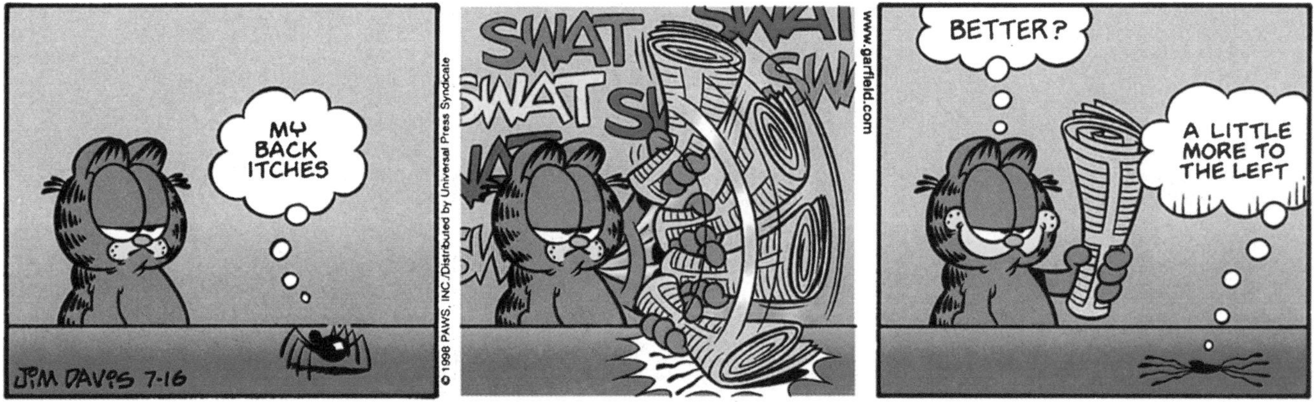
MY BACK ITCHES
SWAT
SWAT
BETTER?
A LITTLE MORE TO THE LEFT
JIM DAVIS 7-16
© 1998 PAWS, INC./Distributed by Universal Press Syndicate
www.garfield.com

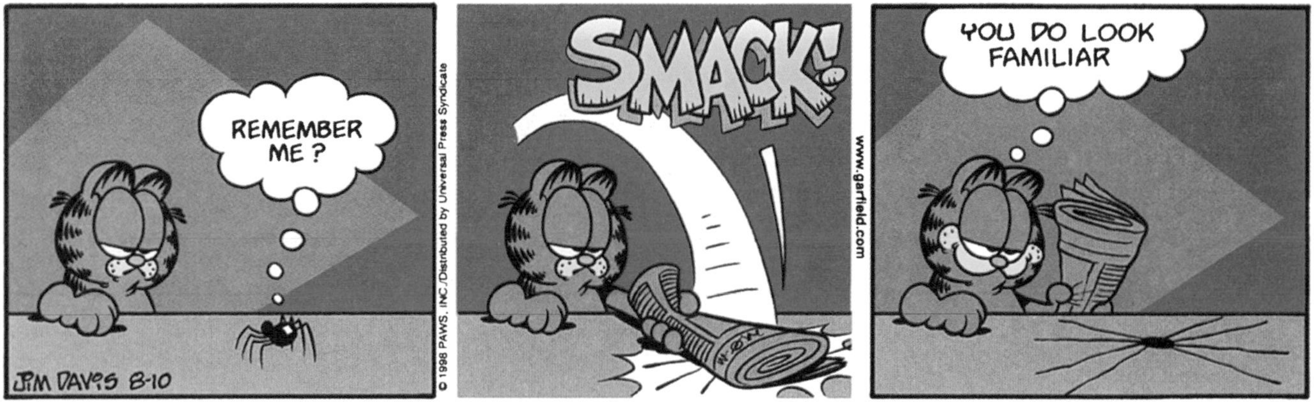
JIM DAVIS 8-10
REMEMBER ME?
© 1998 PAWS, INC./Distributed by Universal Press Syndicate
SMACK!
www.garfield.com
YOU DO LOOK FAMILIAR

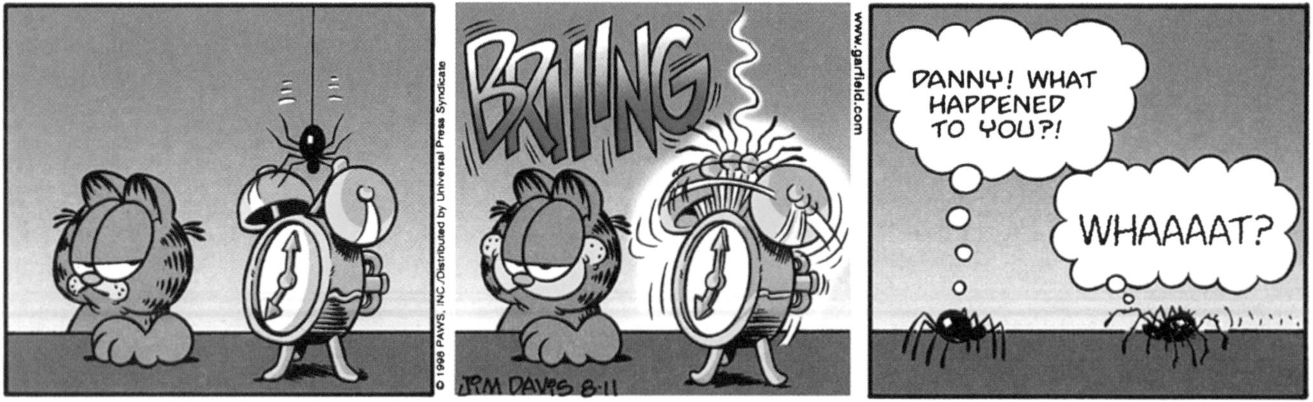
© 1998 PAWS, INC./Distributed by Universal Press Syndicate
BRIIING
JIM DAVIS 8-11
www.garfield.com
DANNY! WHAT HAPPENED TO YOU?!
WHAAAAT?

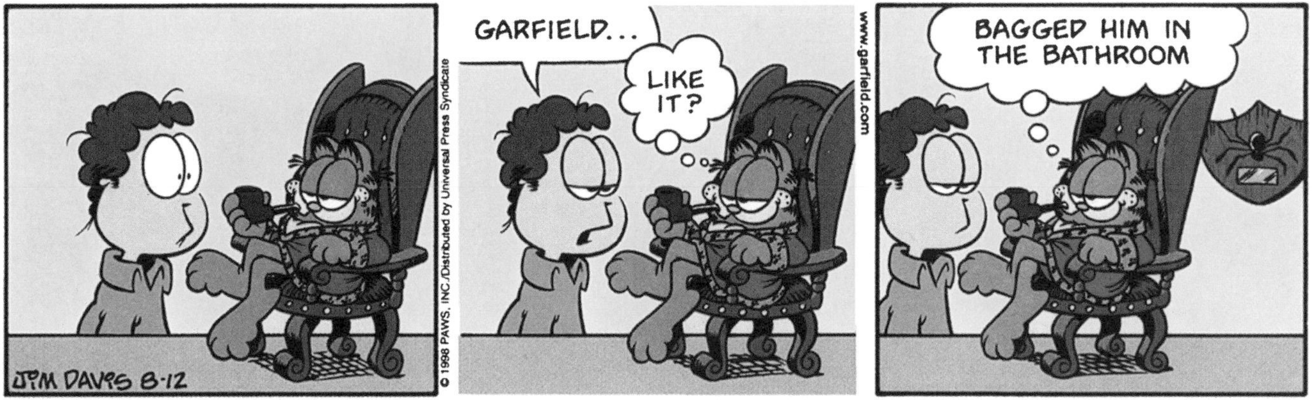
JIM DAVIS 8-12
© 1998 PAWS, INC./Distributed by Universal Press Syndicate
GARFIELD...
LIKE IT?
www.garfield.com
BAGGED HIM IN THE BATHROOM

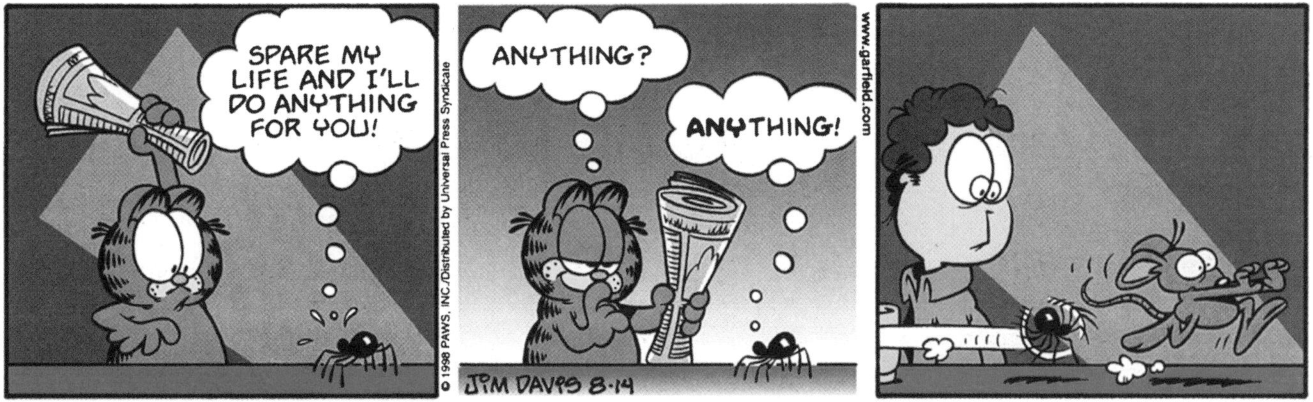
SPARE MY LIFE AND I'LL DO ANYTHING FOR YOU!
© 1998 PAWS, INC./Distributed by Universal Press Syndicate
ANYTHING?
ANYTHING!
JIM DAVIS 8-14
www.garfield.com

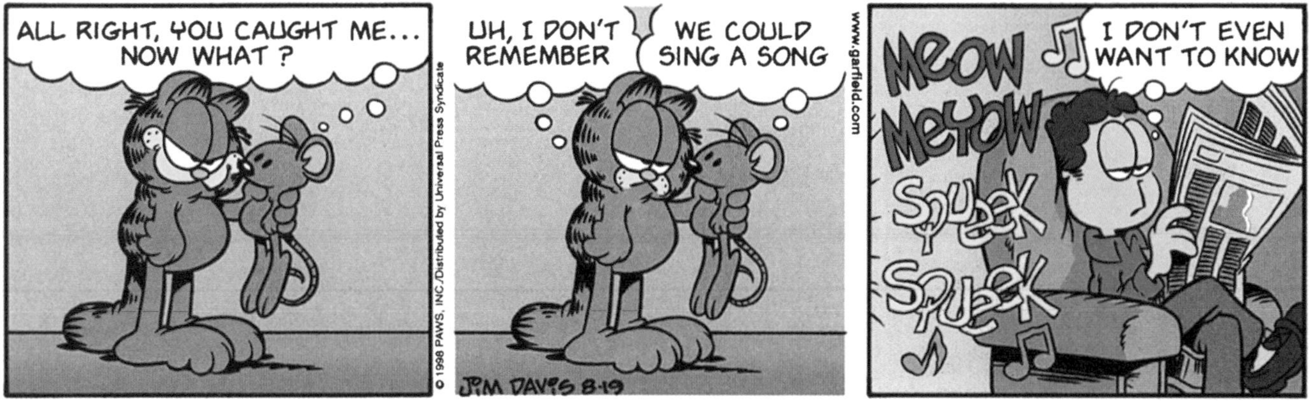
ALL RIGHT, YOU CAUGHT ME... NOW WHAT ?
UH, I DON'T REMEMBER
WE COULD SING A SONG
© 1998 PAWS, INC./Distributed by Universal Press Syndicate
JIM DAVIS 8-19
www.garfield.com
MEOW
MEYOW
SQUEEK
SQUEEK
I DON'T EVEN WANT TO KNOW

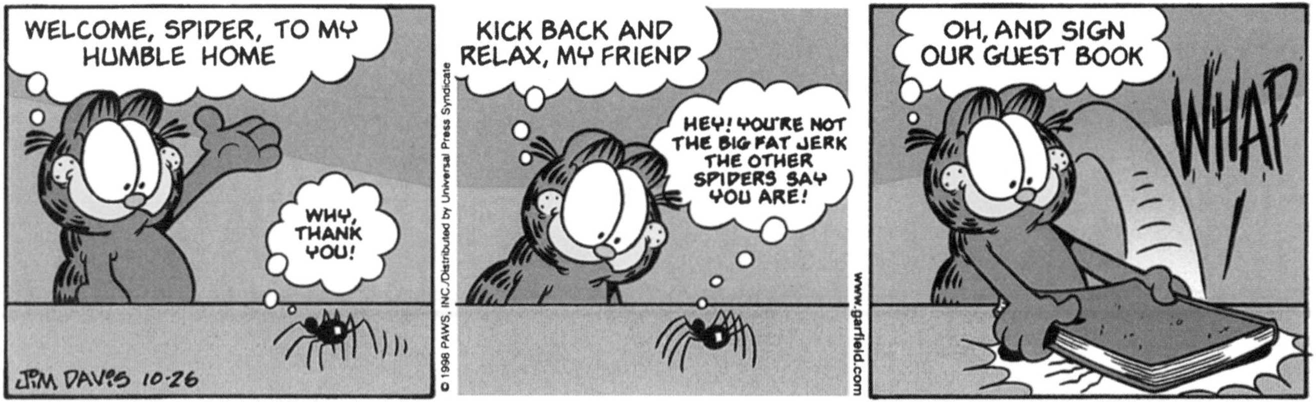
WELCOME, SPIDER, TO MY HUMBLE HOME
WHY, THANK YOU!
JIM DAVIS 10-26
© 1998 PAWS, INC./Distributed by Universal Press Syndicate
KICK BACK AND RELAX, MY FRIEND
HEY! YOU'RE NOT THE BIG FAT JERK THE OTHER SPIDERS SAY YOU ARE!
www.garfield.com
OH, AND SIGN OUR GUEST BOOK
WHAP

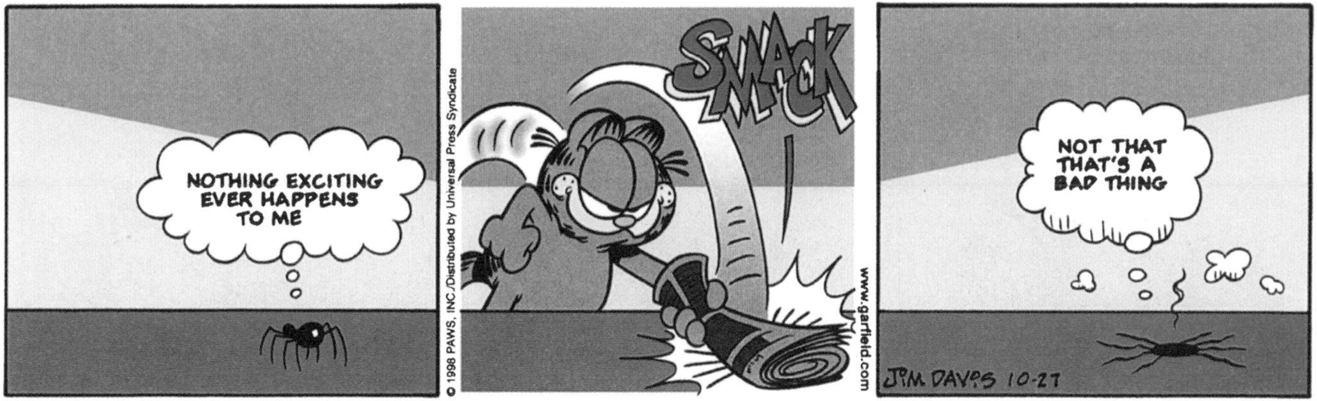
NOTHING EXCITING EVER HAPPENS TO ME
SMACK
NOT THAT THAT'S A BAD THING
JIM DAVIS 10-27
© 1998 PAWS, INC./Distributed by Universal Press Syndicate
www.garfield.com

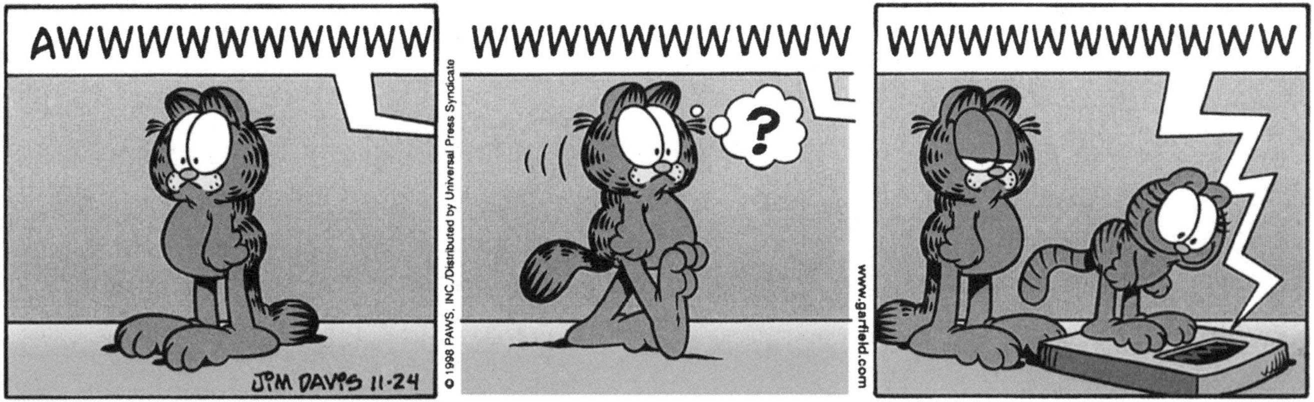
AWWWWWWWWWWW
WWWWWWWWWWWW
?
WWWWWWWWWWWWW
JIM DAVIS 11-24
© 1998 PAWS, INC./Distributed by Universal Press Syndicate
www.garfield.com

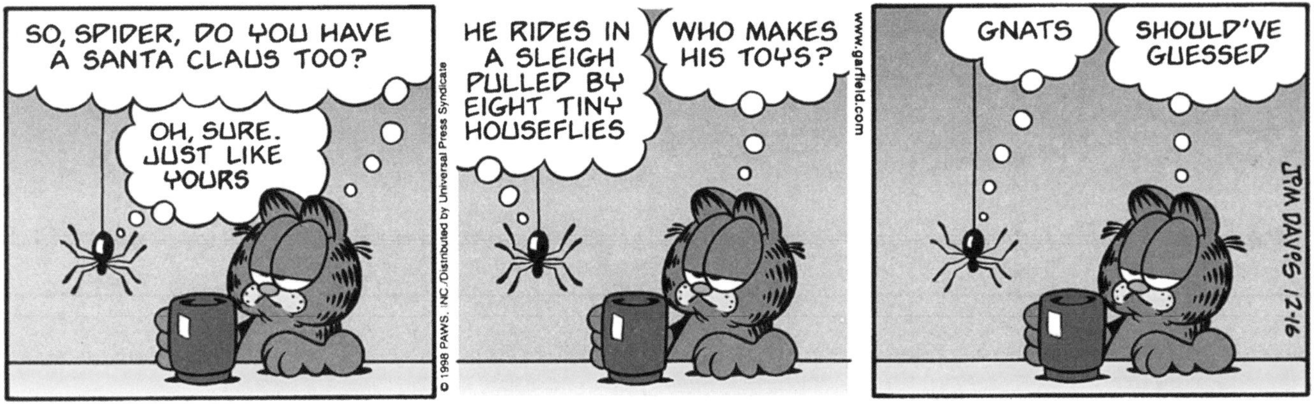
SO, SPIDER, DO YOU HAVE A SANTA CLAUS TOO?
OH, SURE. JUST LIKE YOURS
© 1998 PAWS, INC./Distributed by Universal Press Syndicate
HE RIDES IN A SLEIGH PULLED BY EIGHT TINY HOUSEFLIES
WHO MAKES HIS TOYS?
www.garfield.com
GNATS
SHOULD'VE GUESSED
JIM DAVIS 12-16

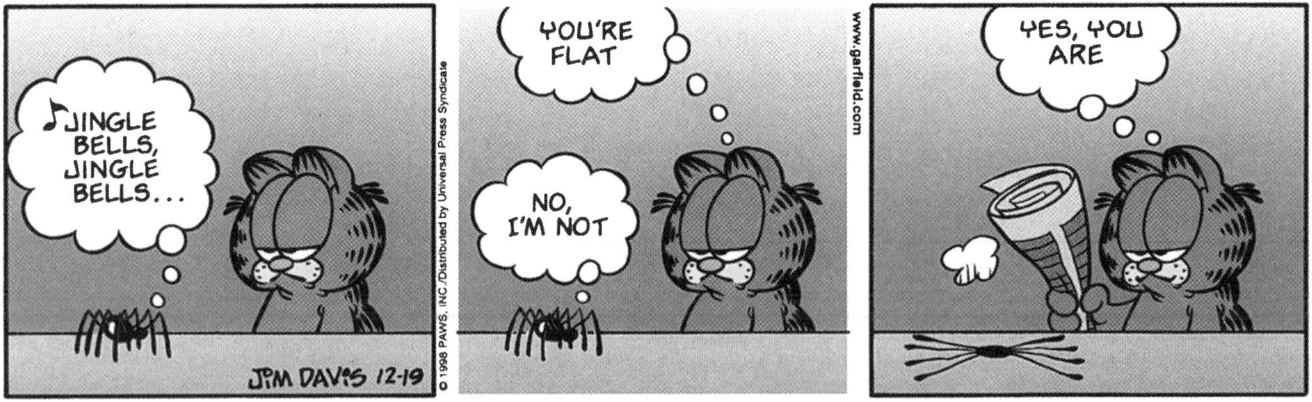
♪JINGLE BELLS, JINGLE BELLS...
JIM DAVIS 12-19
© 1998 PAWS, INC./Distributed by Universal Press Syndicate
YOU'RE FLAT
NO, I'M NOT
www.garfield.com
YES, YOU ARE

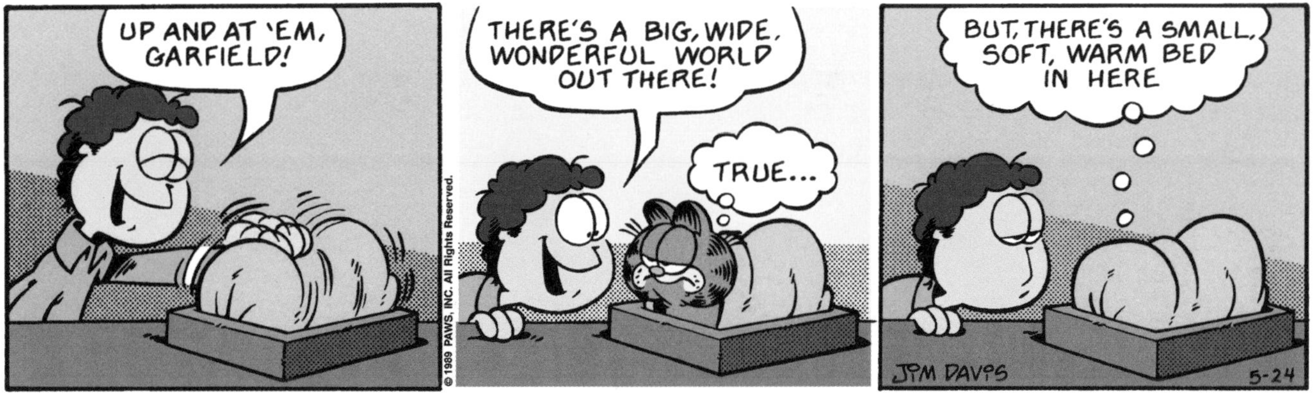
UP AND AT 'EM, GARFIELD!
© 1989 PAWS, INC. All Rights Reserved.
THERE'S A BIG, WIDE, WONDERFUL WORLD OUT THERE!
TRUE...
BUT, THERE'S A SMALL, SOFT, WARM BED IN HERE
JIM DAVIS
5-24

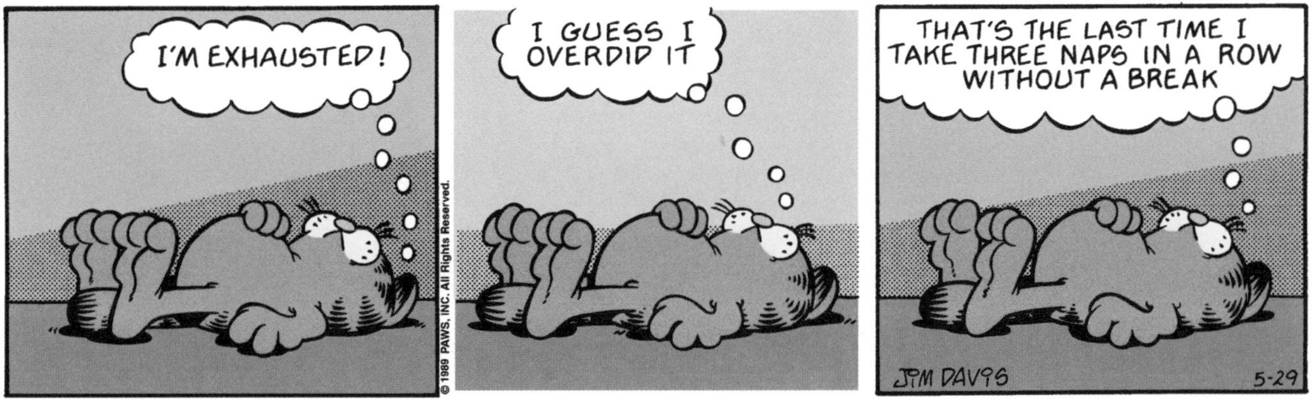
I'M EXHAUSTED!
© 1989 PAWS, INC. All Rights Reserved.
I GUESS I OVERDID IT
THAT'S THE LAST TIME I TAKE THREE NAPS IN A ROW WITHOUT A BREAK
JIM DAVIS
5-29

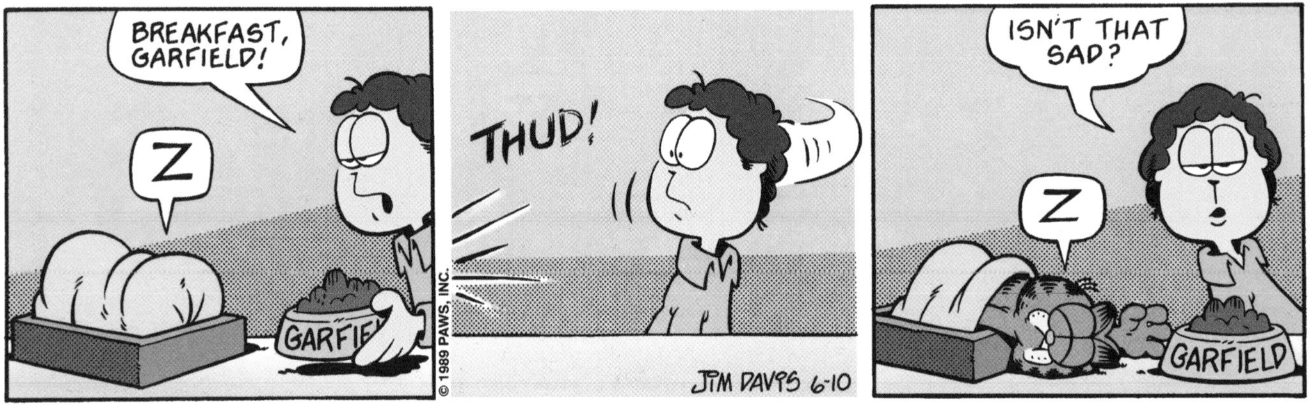
BREAKFAST, GARFIELD!
Z
GARFIE
© 1989 PAWS, INC.
THUD!
JIM DAVIS 6-10
ISN'T THAT SAD?
Z
GARFIELD

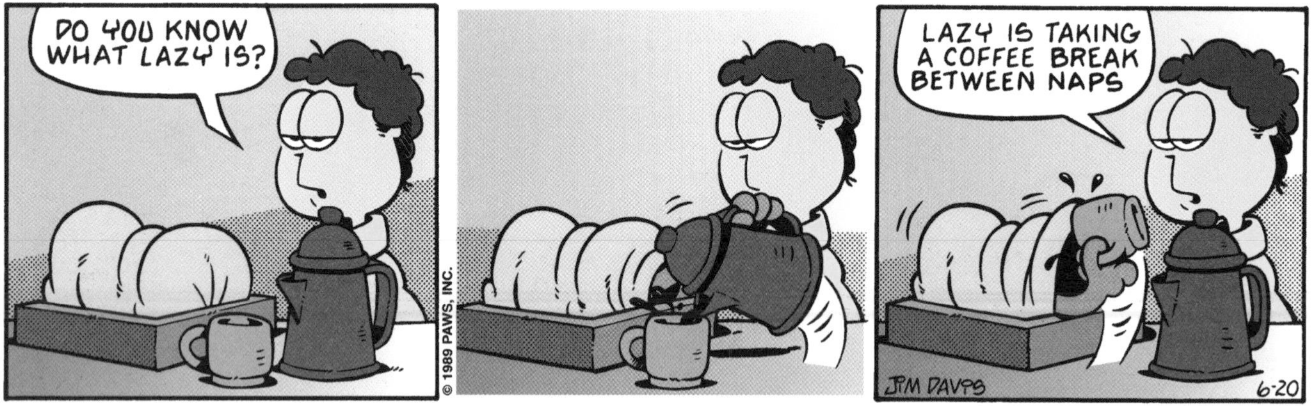
DO YOU KNOW WHAT LAZY IS?
© 1989 PAWS, INC.
LAZY IS TAKING A COFFEE BREAK BETWEEN NAPS
JIM DAVIS
6-20

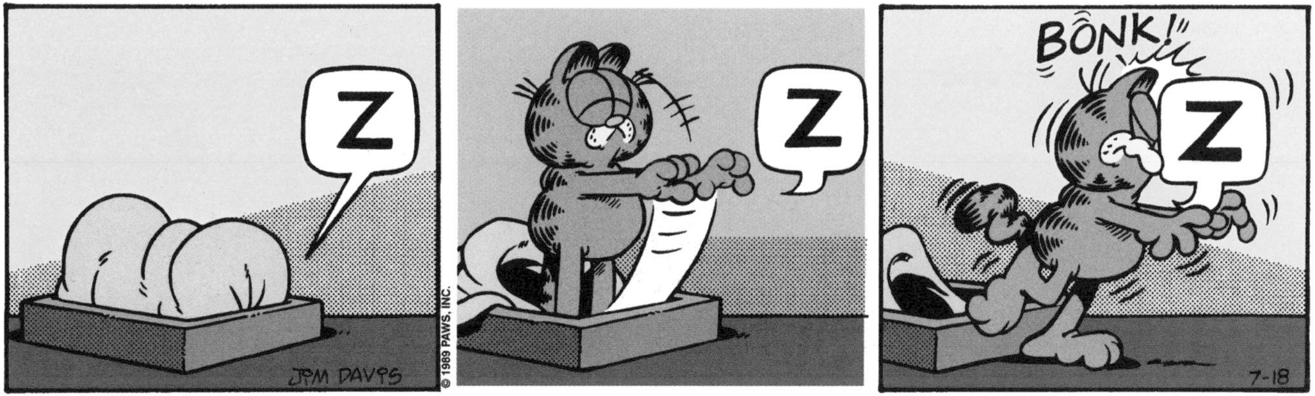
Z
JIM DAVIS
© 1989 PAWS, INC.
Z
BONK!
Z
7-18

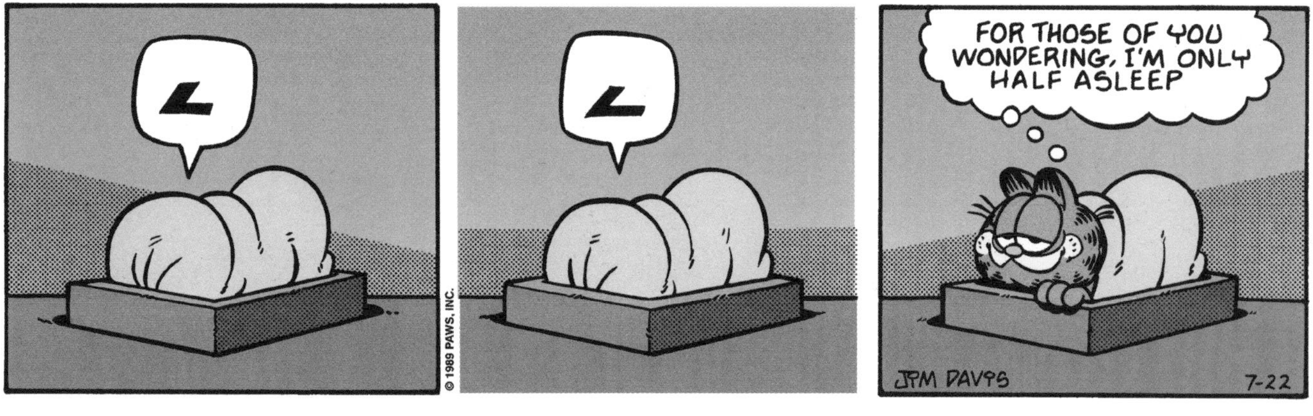
© 1989 PAWS, INC.
FOR THOSE OF YOU WONDERING, I'M ONLY HALF ASLEEP
JIM DAVIS
7-22

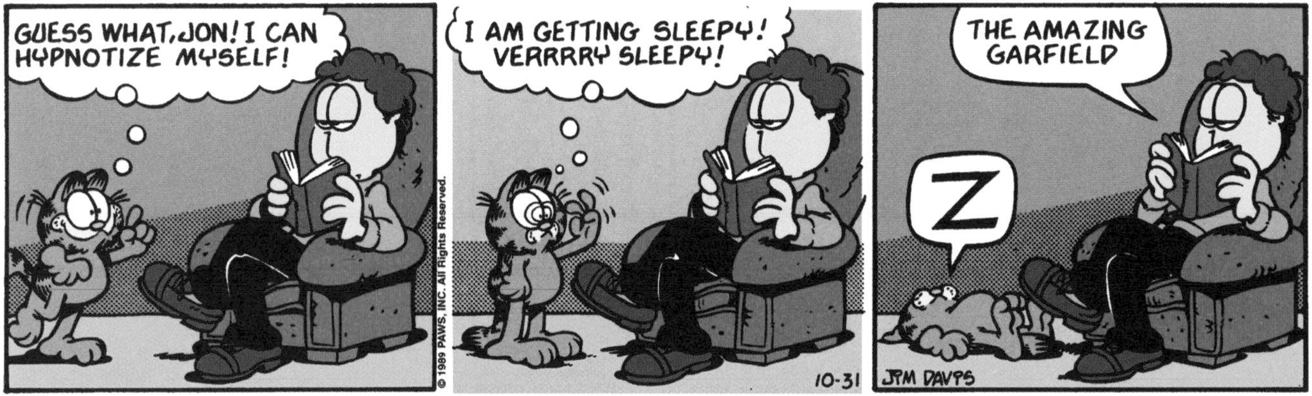
GUESS WHAT, JON! I CAN HYPNOTIZE MYSELF!
© 1989 PAWS, INC. All Rights Reserved.
I AM GETTING SLEEPY! VERRRRY SLEEPY!
10-31
THE AMAZING GARFIELD
Z
JIM DAVIS

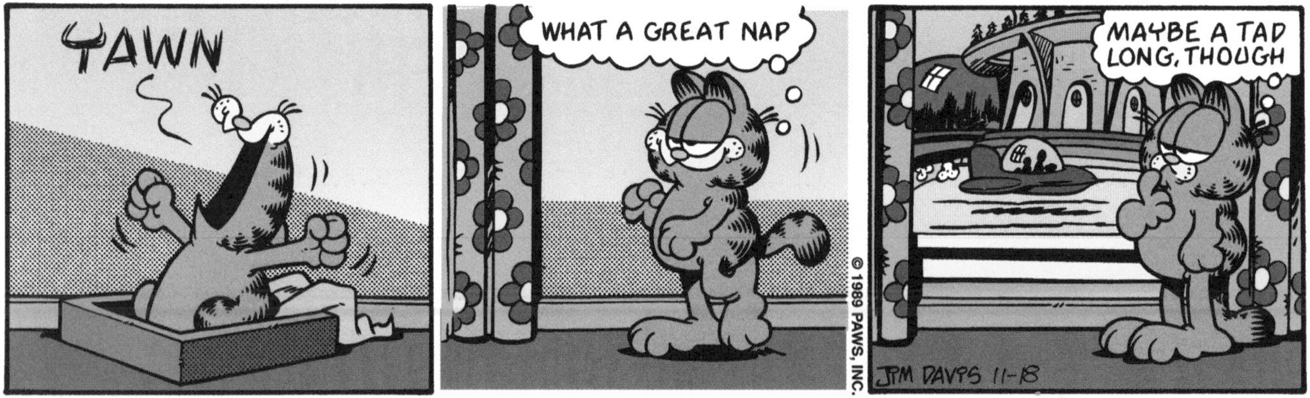
YAWN
WHAT A GREAT NAP
© 1989 PAWS, INC.
MAYBE A TAD LONG, THOUGH
JIM DAVIS 11-18

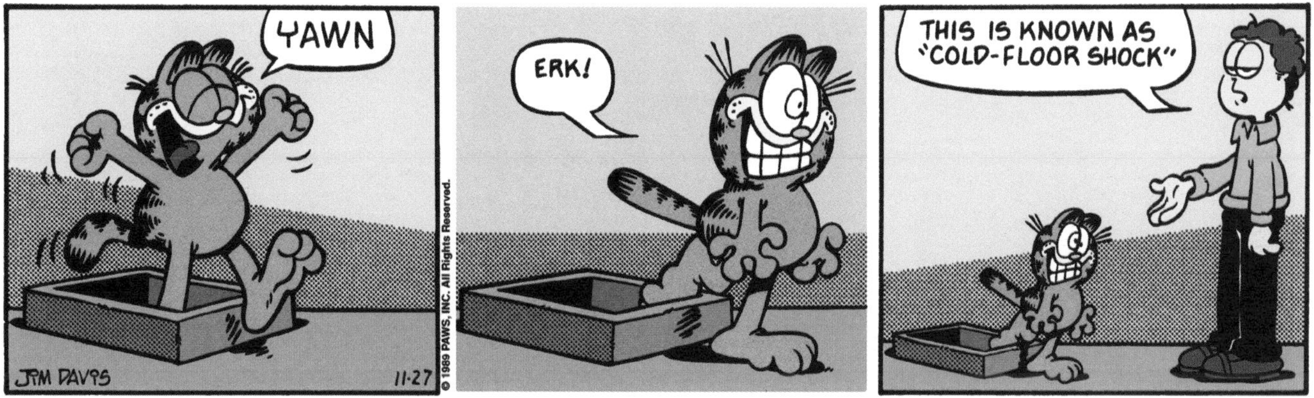
YAWN
ERK!
THIS IS KNOWN AS "COLD-FLOOR SHOCK"
JIM DAVIS
11-27
© 1989 PAWS, INC. All Rights Reserved.

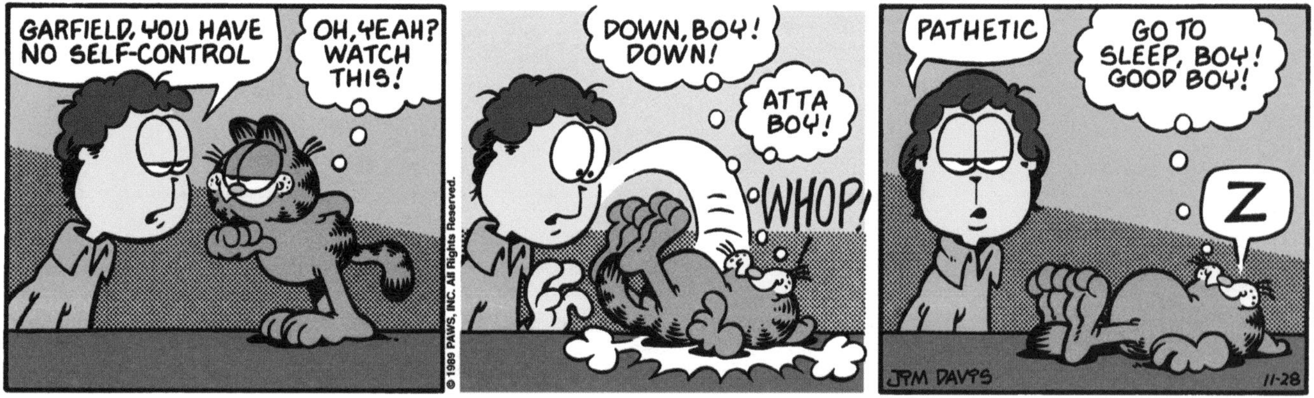
GARFIELD, YOU HAVE NO SELF-CONTROL
OH, YEAH? WATCH THIS!
DOWN, BOY! DOWN!
ATTA BOY!
WHOP!
PATHETIC
GO TO SLEEP, BOY! GOOD BOY!
Z
JIM DAVIS
11-28
© 1989 PAWS, INC. All Rights Reserved.

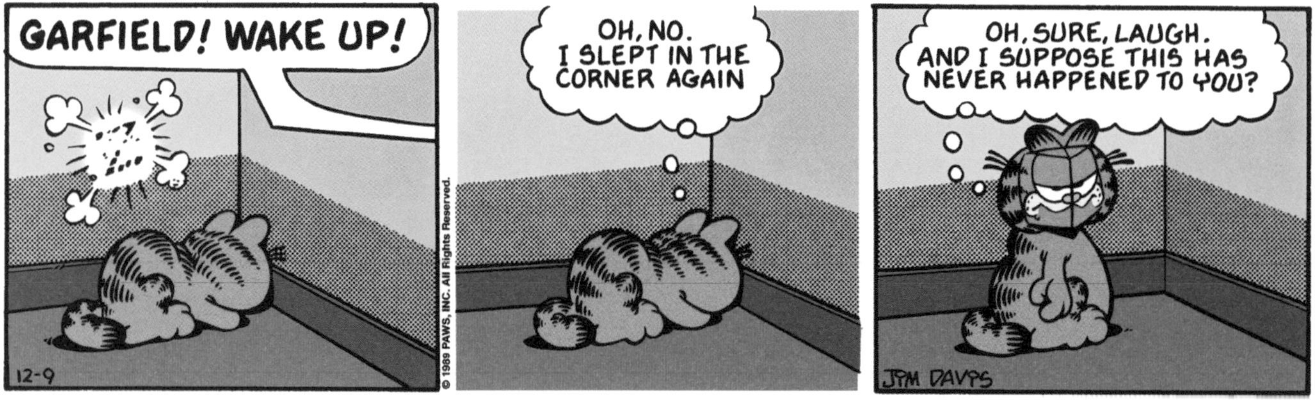
GARFIELD! WAKE UP!
12-9
© 1989 PAWS, INC. All Rights Reserved.
OH, NO. I SLEPT IN THE CORNER AGAIN
OH, SURE, LAUGH. AND I SUPPOSE THIS HAS NEVER HAPPENED TO YOU?
JIM DAVIS

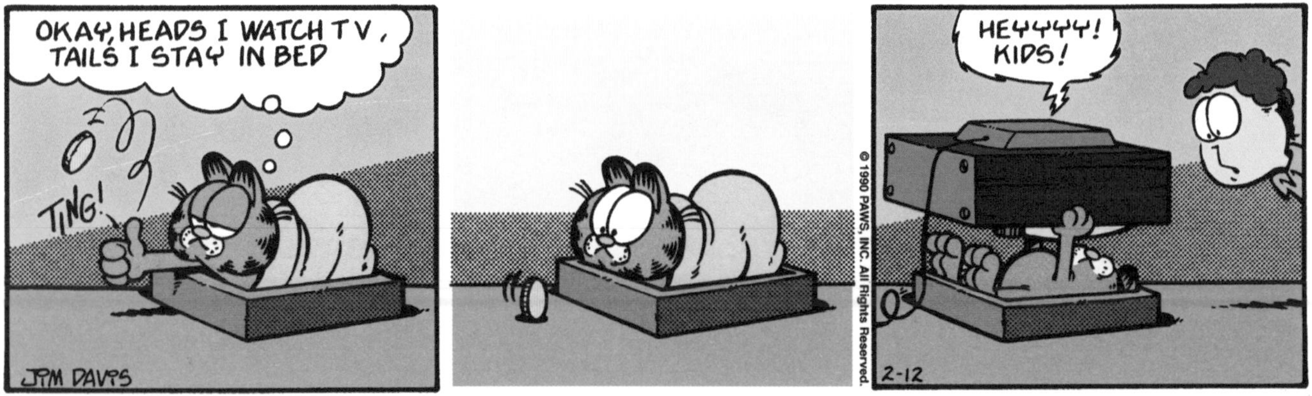
OKAY, HEADS I WATCH TV, TAILS I STAY IN BED
TING!
JIM DAVIS
© 1990 PAWS, INC. All Rights Reserved.
HEYYYY! KIDS!
2-12

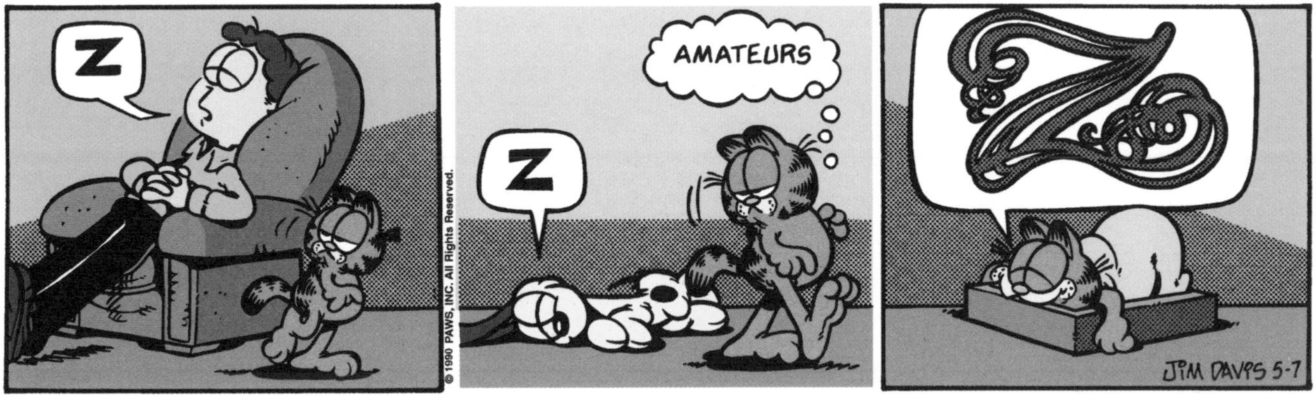
Z
© 1990 PAWS, INC. All Rights Reserved.
Z
AMATEURS
JIM DAVIS 5-7

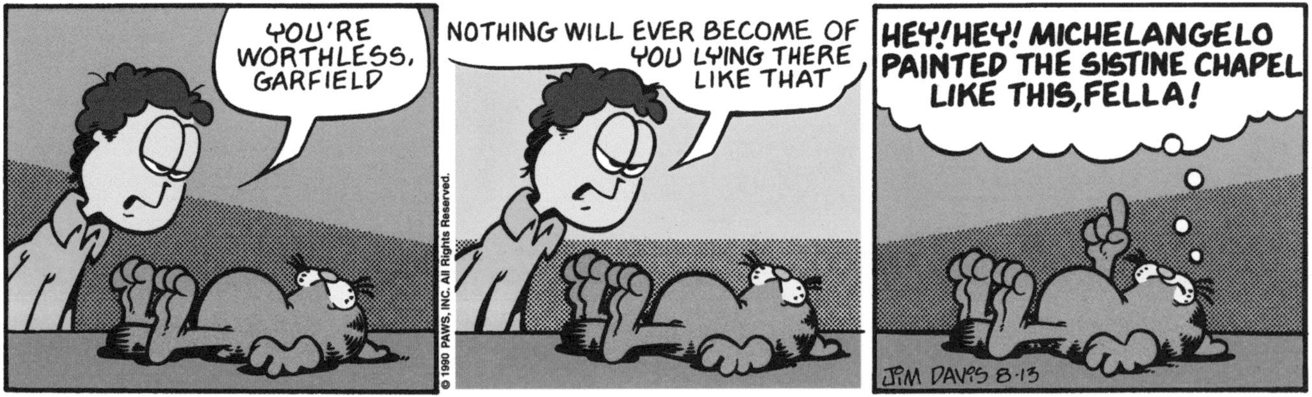
YOU'RE WORTHLESS, GARFIELD
© 1990 PAWS, INC. All Rights Reserved.
NOTHING WILL EVER BECOME OF YOU LYING THERE LIKE THAT
HEY! HEY! MICHELANGELO PAINTED THE SISTINE CHAPEL LIKE THIS, FELLA!
JIM DAVIS 8-13

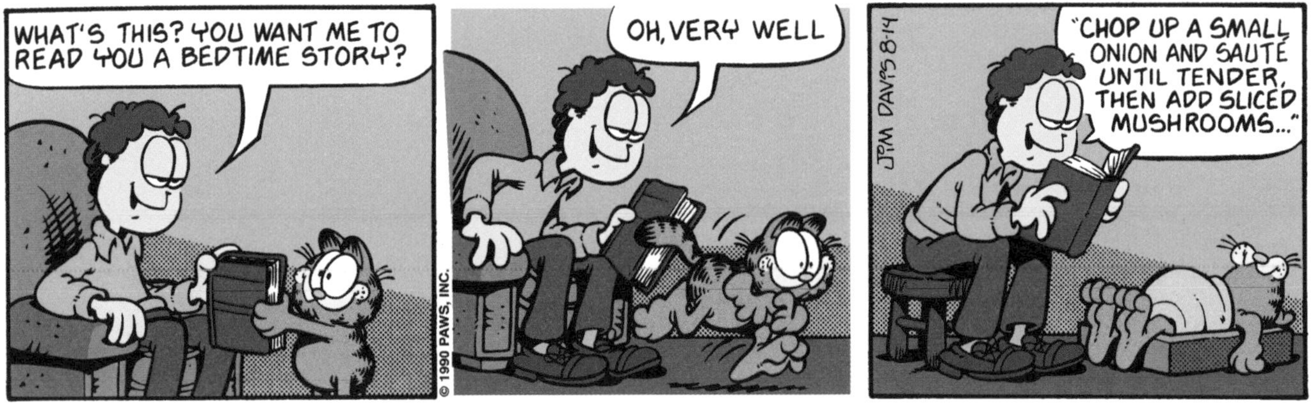
WHAT'S THIS? YOU WANT ME TO READ YOU A BEDTIME STORY?
© 1990 PAWS, INC.
OH, VERY WELL
JIM DAVIS 8-14
"CHOP UP A SMALL ONION AND SAUTÉ UNTIL TENDER, THEN ADD SLICED MUSHROOMS..."

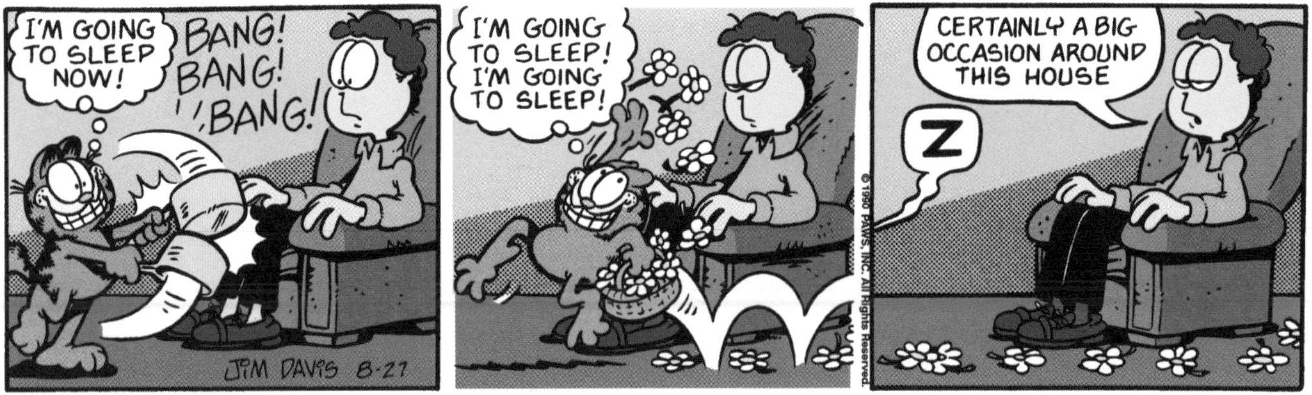
I'M GOING TO SLEEP NOW!
BANG! BANG! BANG!
JIM DAVIS 8-27
I'M GOING TO SLEEP! I'M GOING TO SLEEP!
© 1990 PAWS, INC. All Rights Reserved.
Z
CERTAINLY A BIG OCCASION AROUND THIS HOUSE

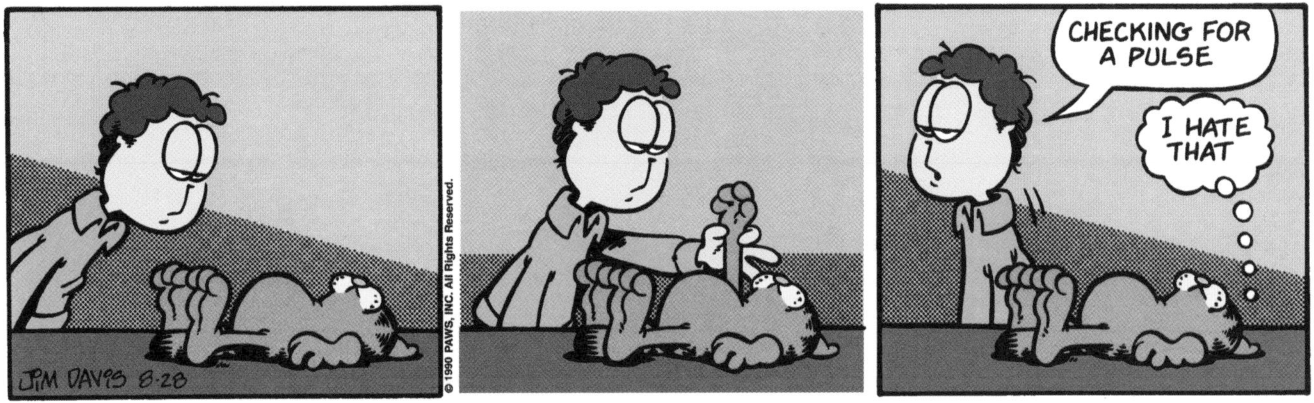
JIM DAVIS 8-28
© 1990 PAWS, INC. All Rights Reserved.
CHECKING FOR A PULSE
I HATE THAT

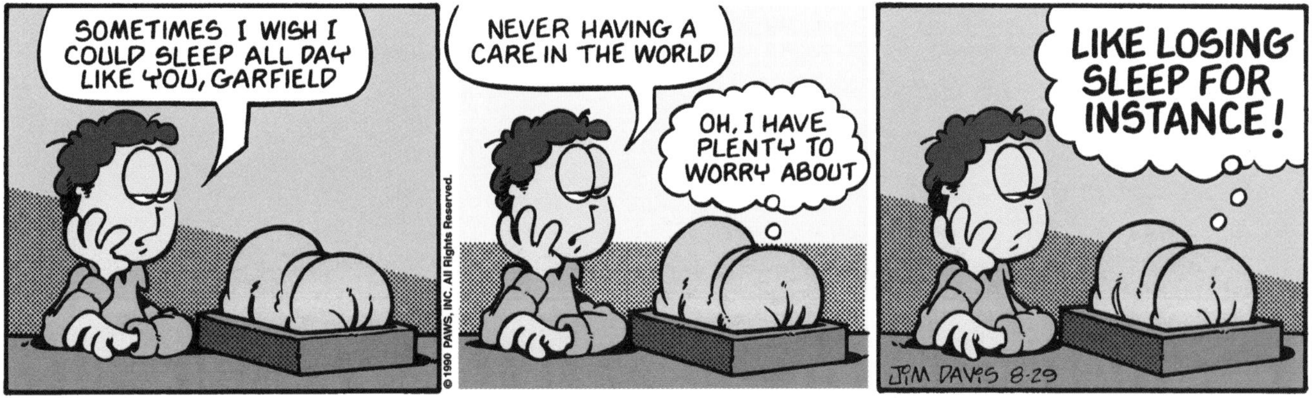
SOMETIMES I WISH I COULD SLEEP ALL DAY LIKE YOU, GARFIELD
© 1990 PAWS, INC. All Rights Reserved.
NEVER HAVING A CARE IN THE WORLD
OH, I HAVE PLENTY TO WORRY ABOUT
LIKE LOSING SLEEP FOR INSTANCE!
JIM DAVIS 8-29

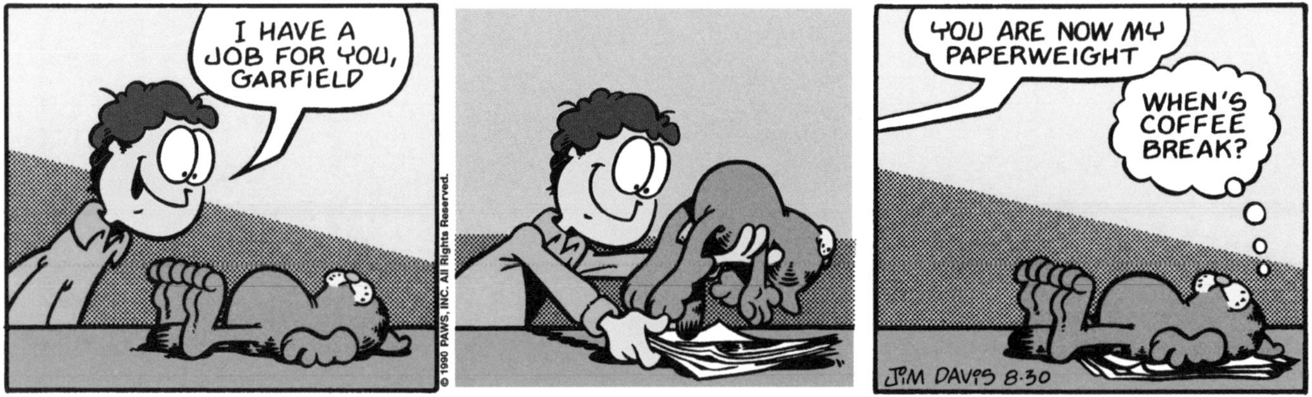
I HAVE A JOB FOR YOU, GARFIELD
YOU ARE NOW MY PAPERWEIGHT
WHEN'S COFFEE BREAK?
JIM DAVIS 8·30
© 1990 PAWS, INC. All Rights Reserved.

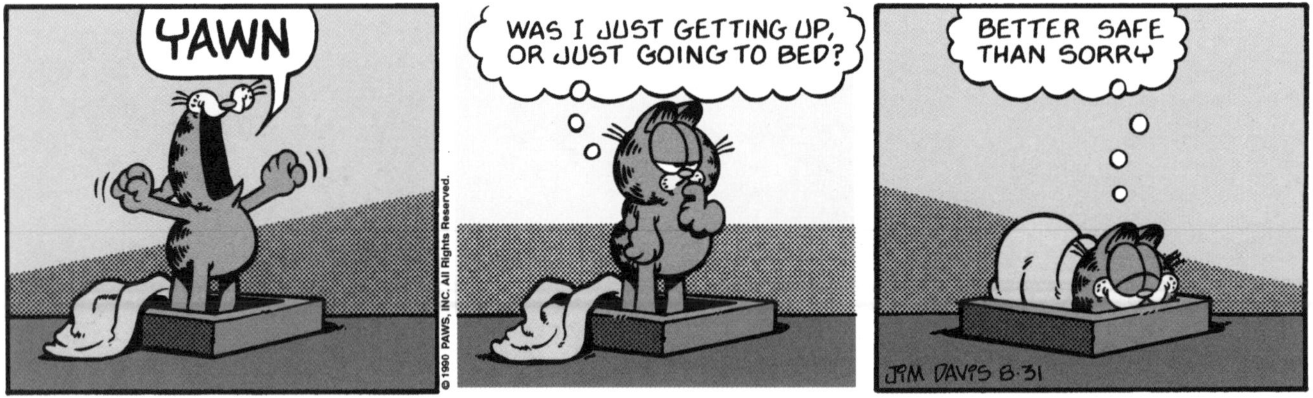
YAWN
WAS I JUST GETTING UP, OR JUST GOING TO BED?
BETTER SAFE THAN SORRY
JIM DAVIS 8·31
© 1990 PAWS, INC. All Rights Reserved.

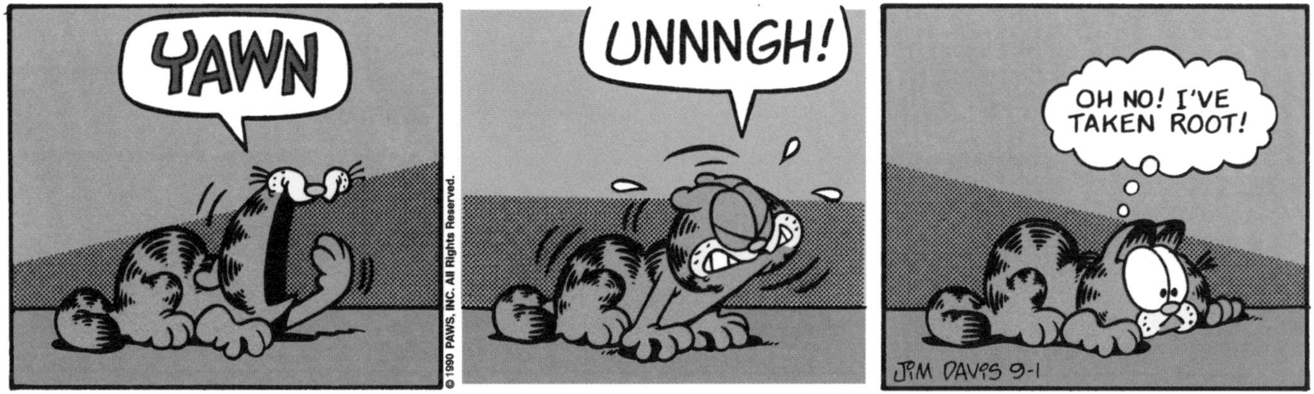
YAWN
UNNNGH!
OH NO! I'VE TAKEN ROOT!
JIM DAVIS 9-1
© 1990 PAWS, INC. All Rights Reserved.

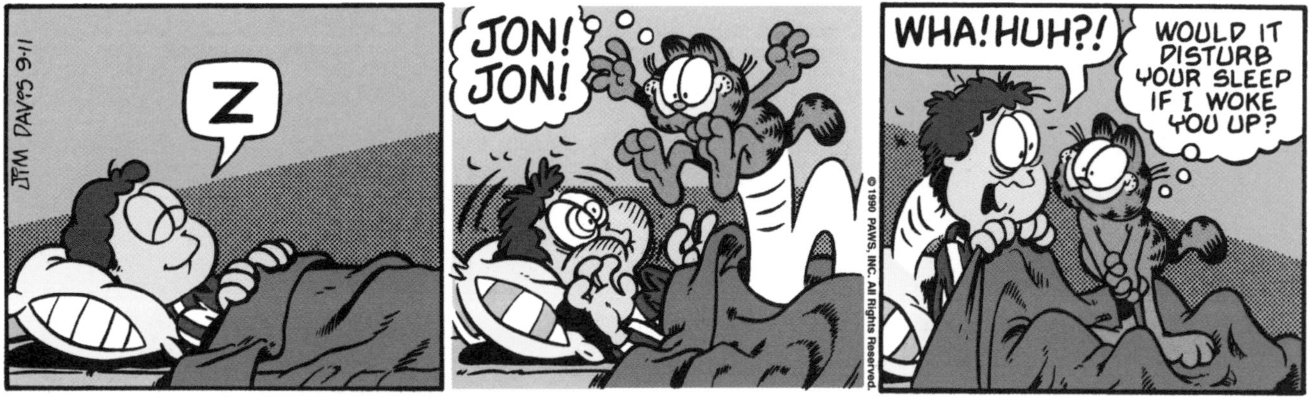
JIM DAVIS 9-11
Z
JON! JON!
WHA! HUH?!
WOULD IT DISTURB YOUR SLEEP IF I WOKE YOU UP?
© 1990 PAWS, INC. All Rights Reserved.

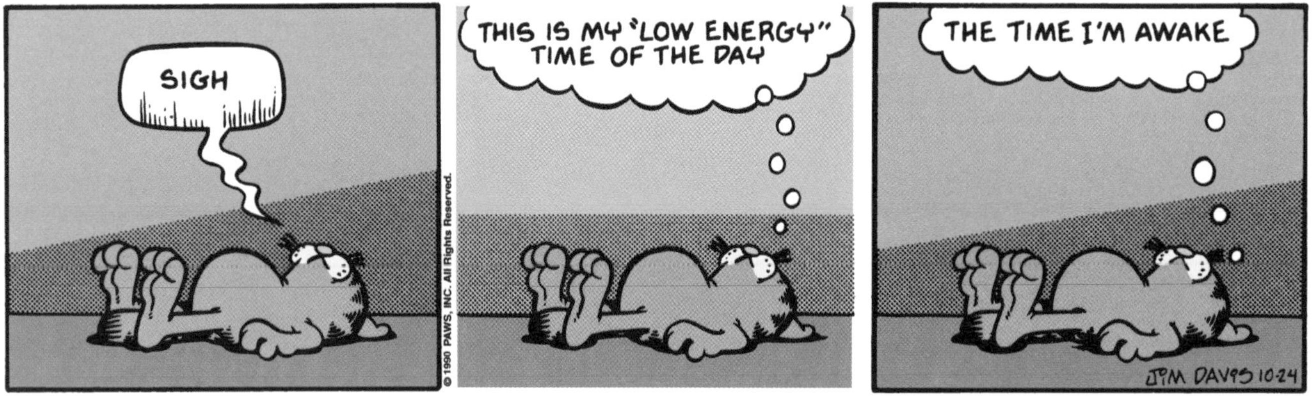
SIGH
THIS IS MY "LOW ENERGY" TIME OF THE DAY
THE TIME I'M AWAKE
JIM DAVIS 10-24
© 1990 PAWS, INC. All Rights Reserved.

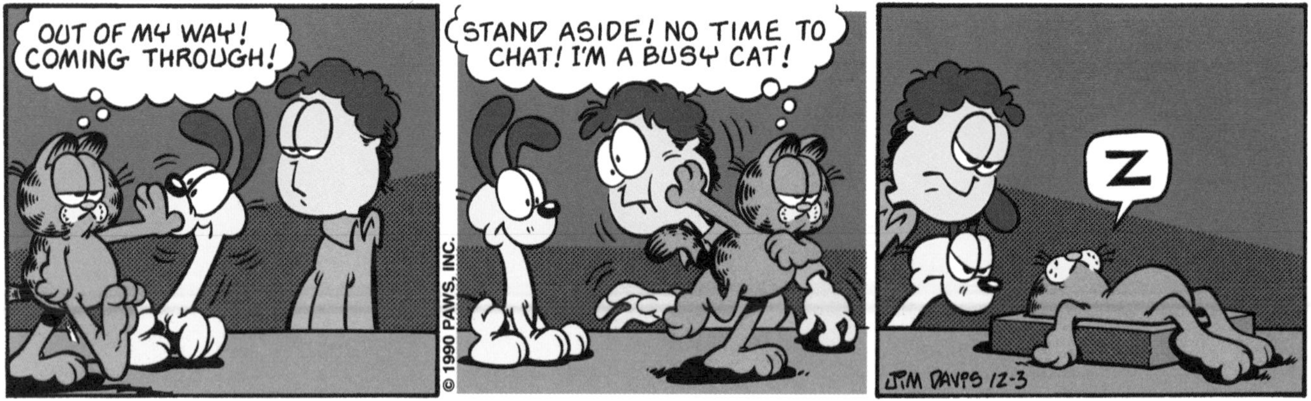
OUT OF MY WAY! COMING THROUGH!
STAND ASIDE! NO TIME TO CHAT! I'M A BUSY CAT!
Z
JIM DAVIS 12-3
© 1990 PAWS, INC.

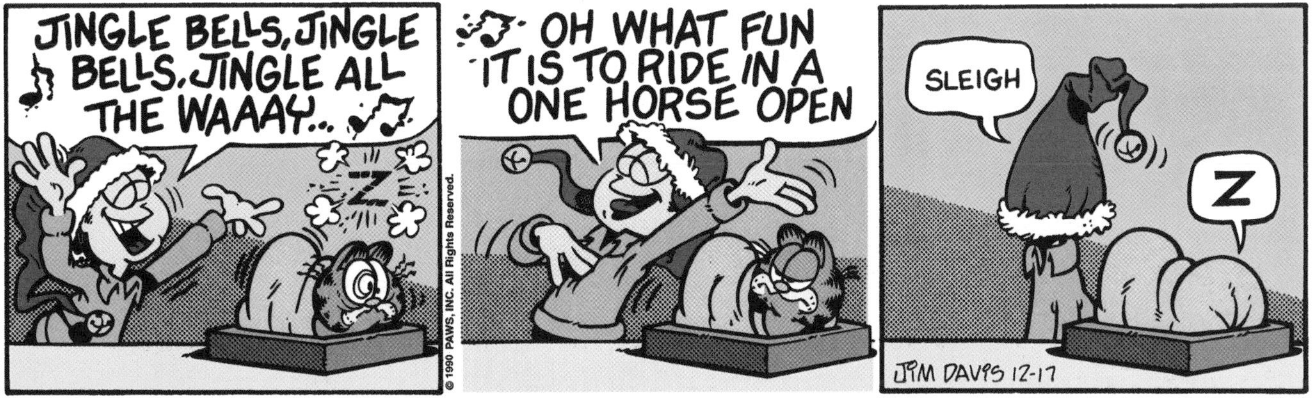
JINGLE BELLS, JINGLE BELLS, JINGLE ALL THE WAAAY...
Z
OH WHAT FUN IT IS TO RIDE IN A ONE HORSE OPEN
SLEIGH
Z
© 1990 PAWS, INC. All Rights Reserved.
JIM DAVIS 12-17

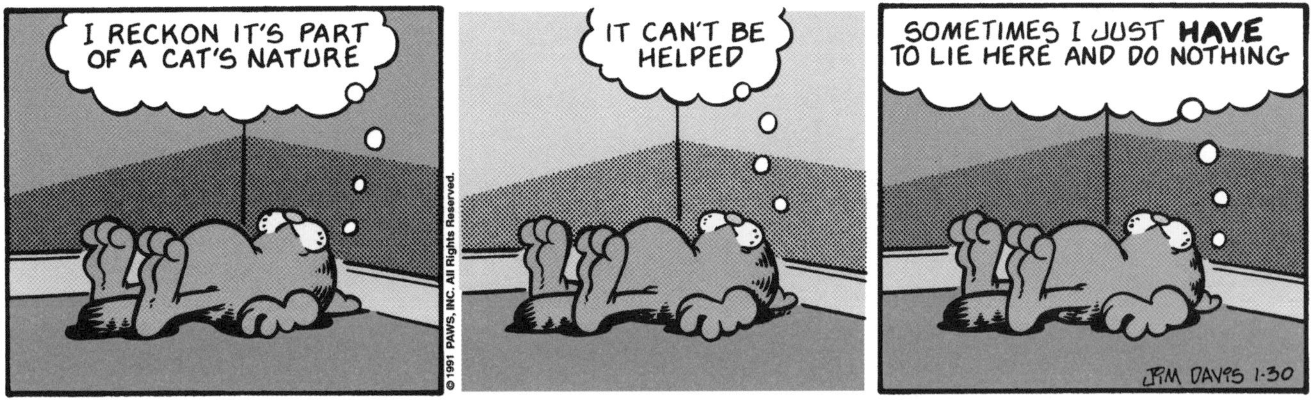
I RECKON IT'S PART OF A CAT'S NATURE
IT CAN'T BE HELPED
SOMETIMES I JUST **HAVE** TO LIE HERE AND DO NOTHING
© 1991 PAWS, INC. All Rights Reserved.
JIM DAVIS 1-30

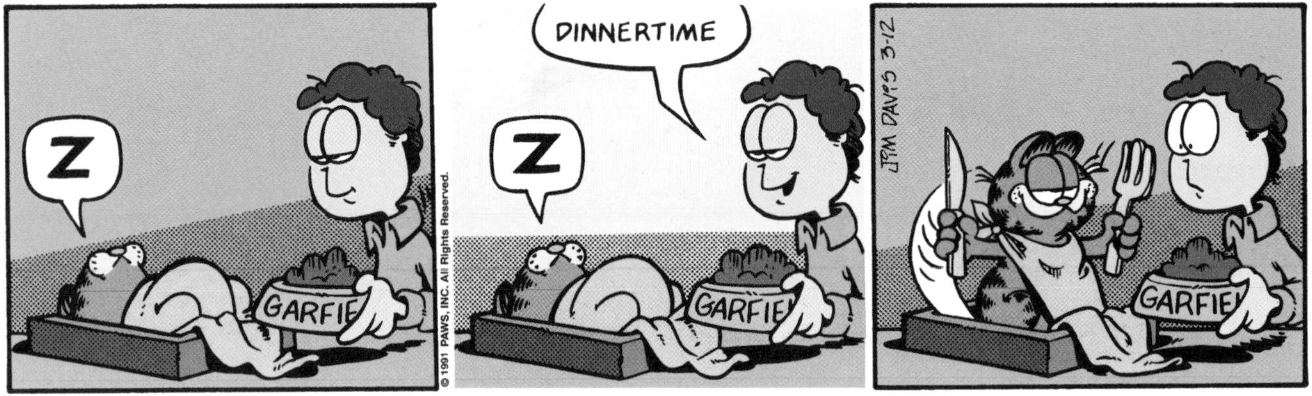
Z
Z
DINNERTIME
GARFIE
GARFIE
GARFIE
JIM DAVIS 3-12
© 1991 PAWS, INC. All Rights Reserved.

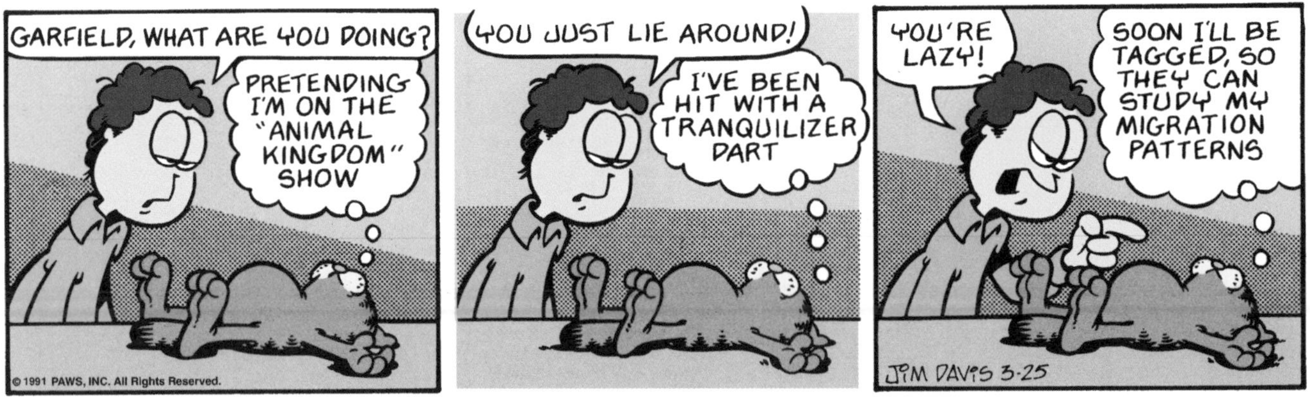
GARFIELD, WHAT ARE YOU DOING?
PRETENDING I'M ON THE "ANIMAL KINGDOM" SHOW
YOU JUST LIE AROUND!
I'VE BEEN HIT WITH A TRANQUILIZER DART
YOU'RE LAZY!
SOON I'LL BE TAGGED, SO THEY CAN STUDY MY MIGRATION PATTERNS
JIM DAVIS 3-25
© 1991 PAWS, INC. All Rights Reserved.

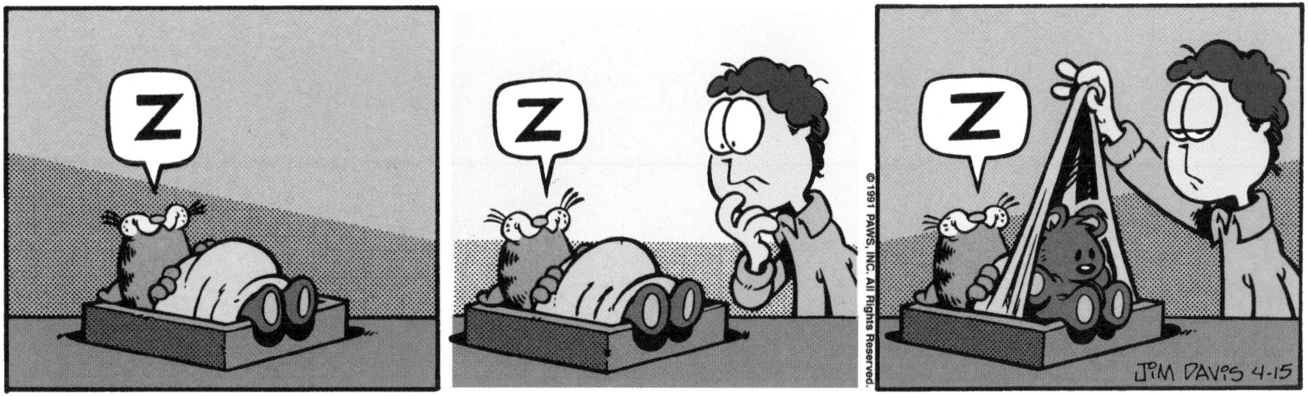
Z
Z
© 1991 PAWS, INC. All Rights Reserved.
Z
JIM DAVIS 4-15

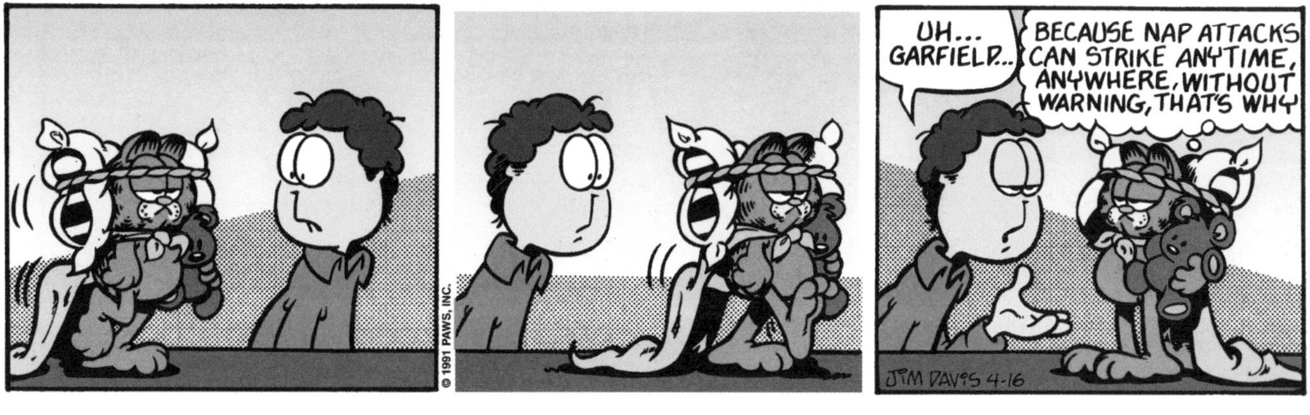
© 1991 PAWS, INC.
UH... GARFIELD...
BECAUSE NAP ATTACKS CAN STRIKE ANYTIME, ANYWHERE, WITHOUT WARNING, THAT'S WHY
JIM DAVIS 4-16

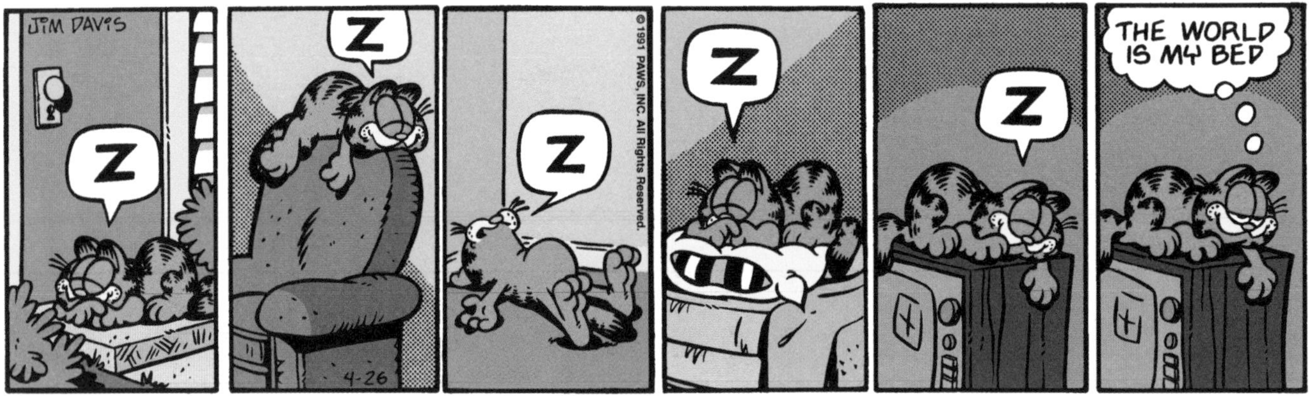
JIM DAVIS
Z
Z
4-26
Z
© 1991 PAWS, INC. All Rights Reserved.
Z
Z
THE WORLD IS MY BED

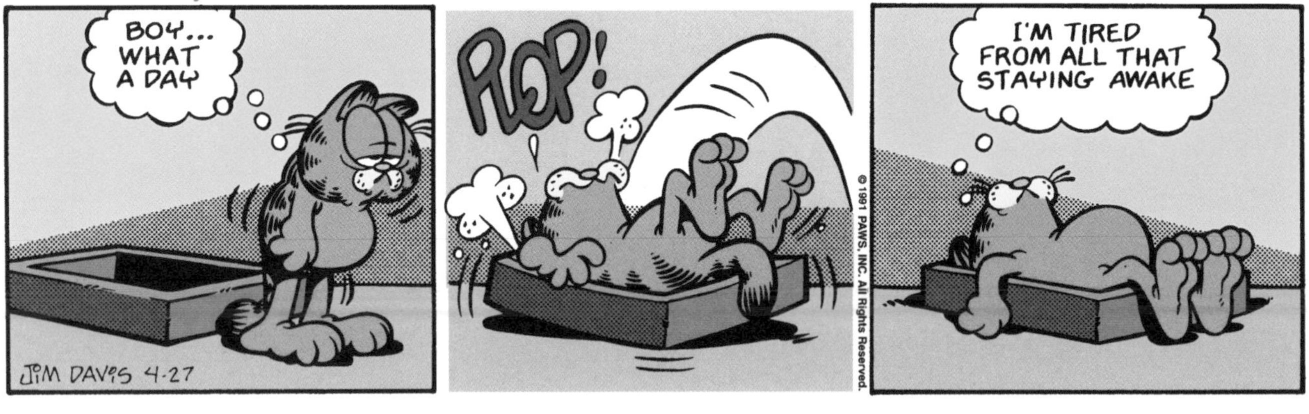
BOY... WHAT A DAY
JIM DAVIS 4-27
PLOP!
© 1991 PAWS, INC. All Rights Reserved.
I'M TIRED FROM ALL THAT STAYING AWAKE

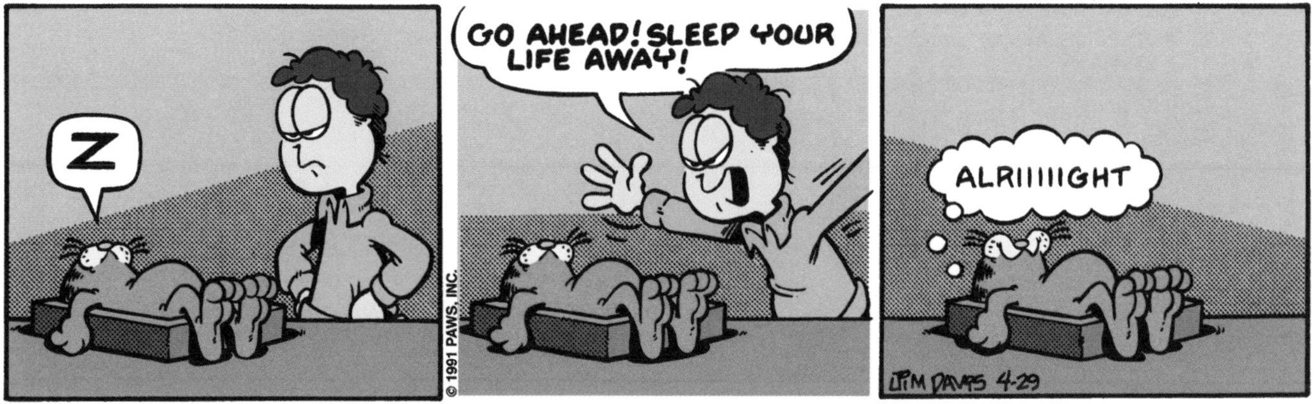
Z
GO AHEAD! SLEEP YOUR LIFE AWAY!
ALRIIIIIGHT
© 1991 PAWS, INC.
JIM DAVIS 4-29

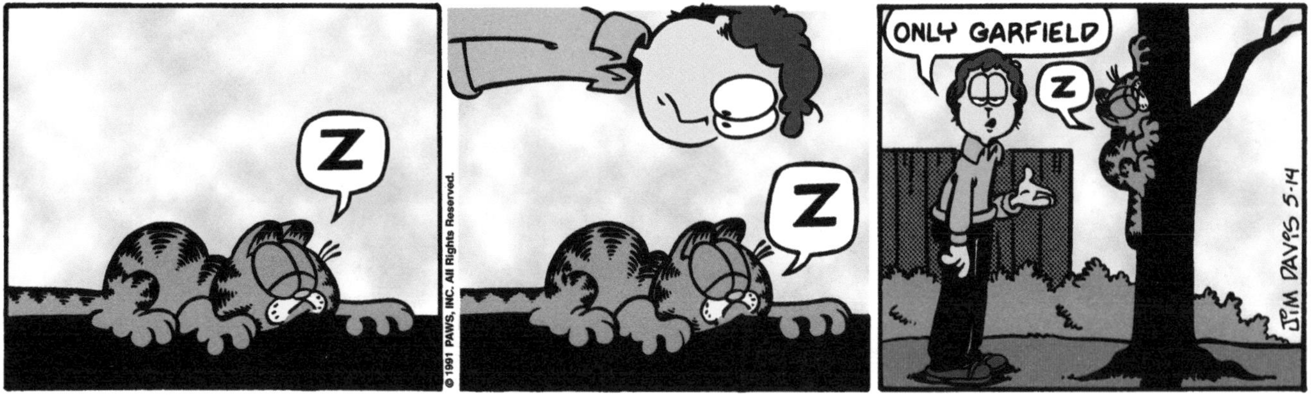
Z
Z
ONLY GARFIELD
Z
© 1991 PAWS, INC. All Rights Reserved.
JIM DAVIS 5-14

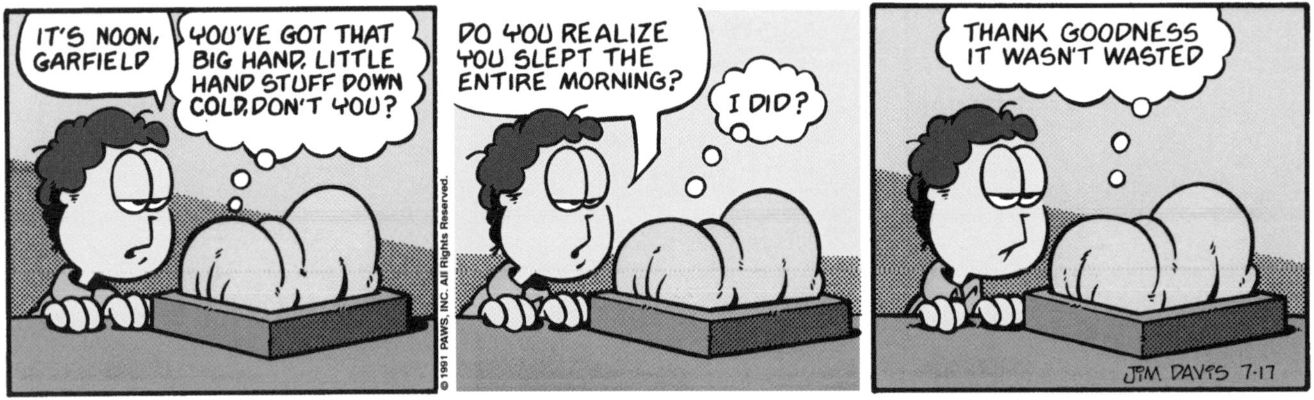
IT'S NOON, GARFIELD
YOU'VE GOT THAT BIG HAND, LITTLE HAND STUFF DOWN COLD, DON'T YOU?
DO YOU REALIZE YOU SLEPT THE ENTIRE MORNING?
I DID?
THANK GOODNESS IT WASN'T WASTED
JIM DAVIS 7-17

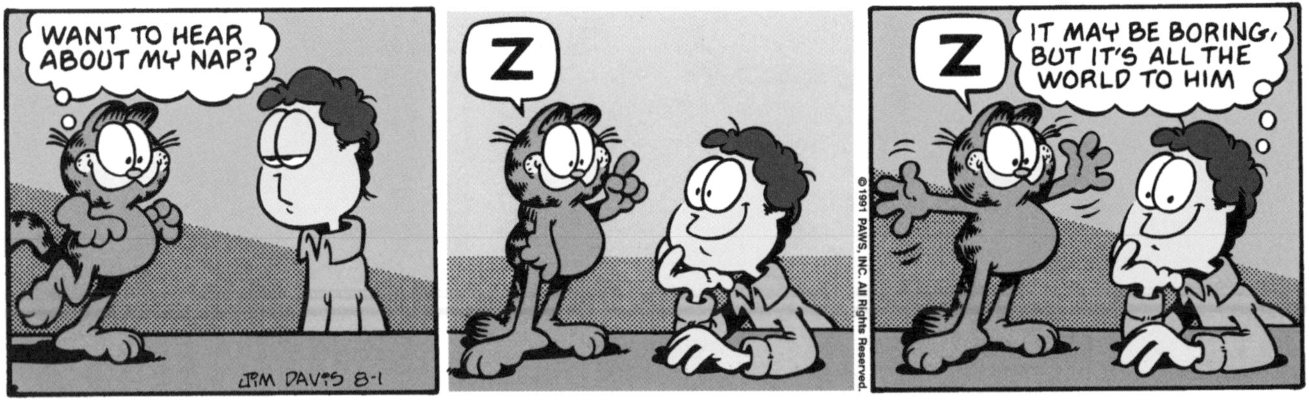
WANT TO HEAR ABOUT MY NAP?
JIM DAVIS 8-1
Z
Z
IT MAY BE BORING, BUT IT'S ALL THE WORLD TO HIM

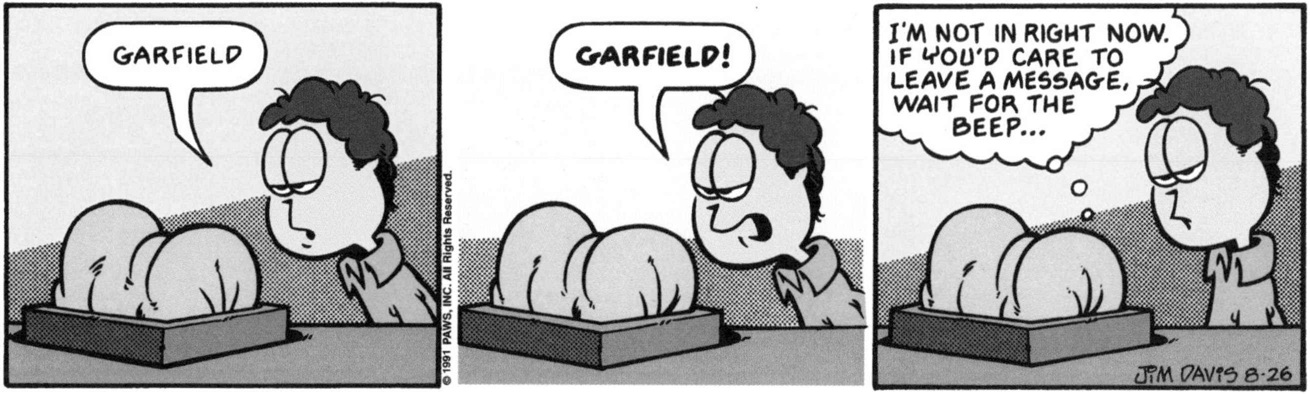
GARFIELD
GARFIELD!
I'M NOT IN RIGHT NOW. IF YOU'D CARE TO LEAVE A MESSAGE, WAIT FOR THE BEEP...
© 1991 PAWS, INC. All Rights Reserved.
JIM DAVIS 8-26

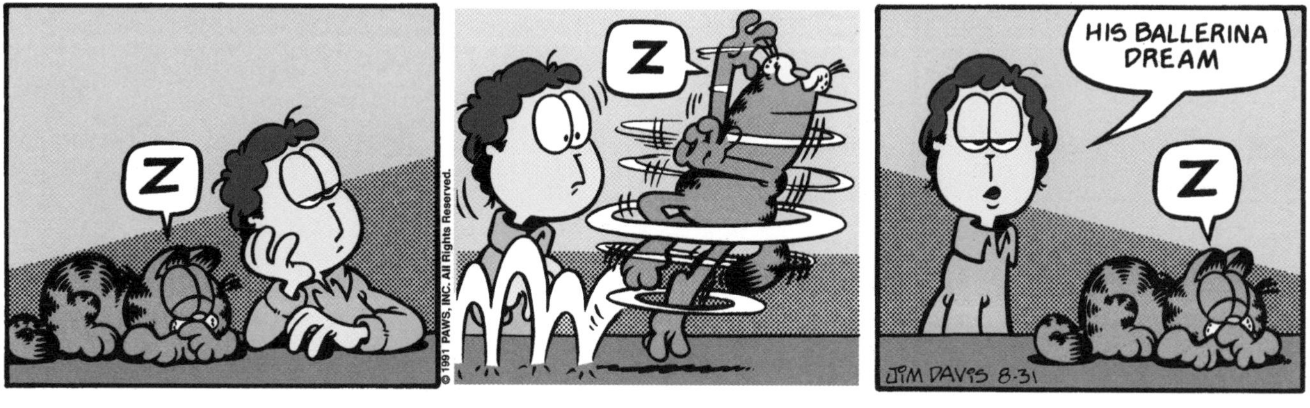
Z
© 1991 PAWS, INC. All Rights Reserved.
Z
HIS BALLERINA DREAM
Z
JIM DAVIS 8-31

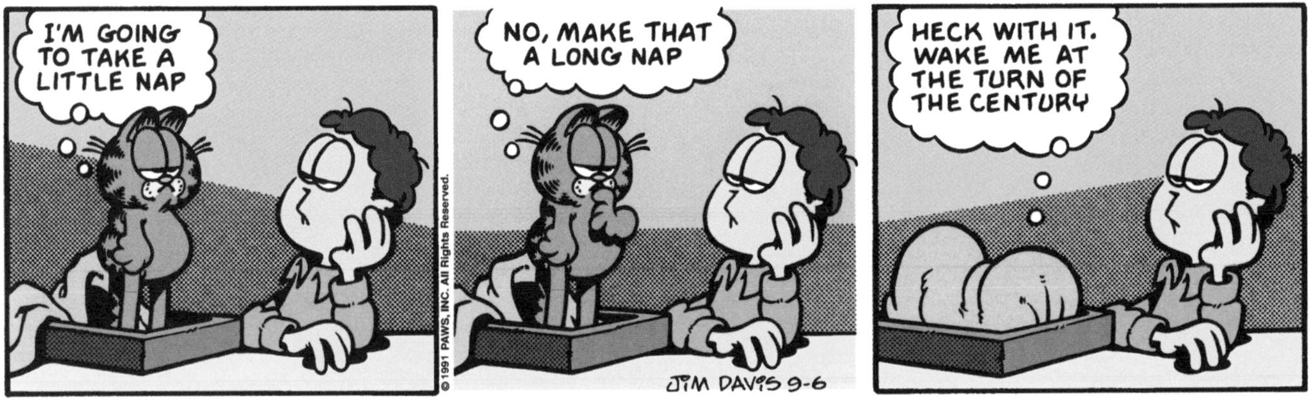
I'M GOING TO TAKE A LITTLE NAP
NO, MAKE THAT A LONG NAP
HECK WITH IT. WAKE ME AT THE TURN OF THE CENTURY
© 1991 PAWS, INC. All Rights Reserved.
JIM DAVIS 9-6

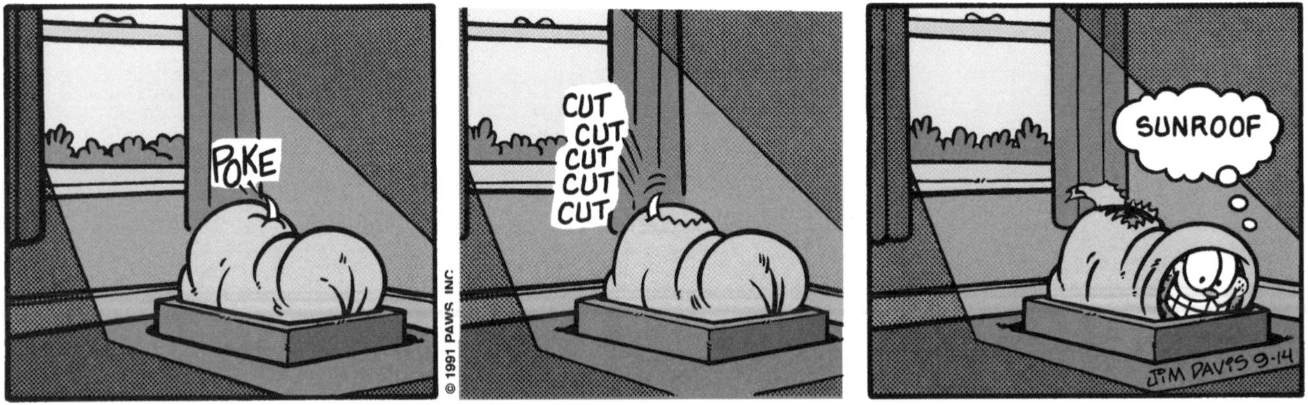
POKE
CUT CUT CUT CUT CUT
SUNROOF
© 1991 PAWS, INC.
JIM DAVIS 9-14

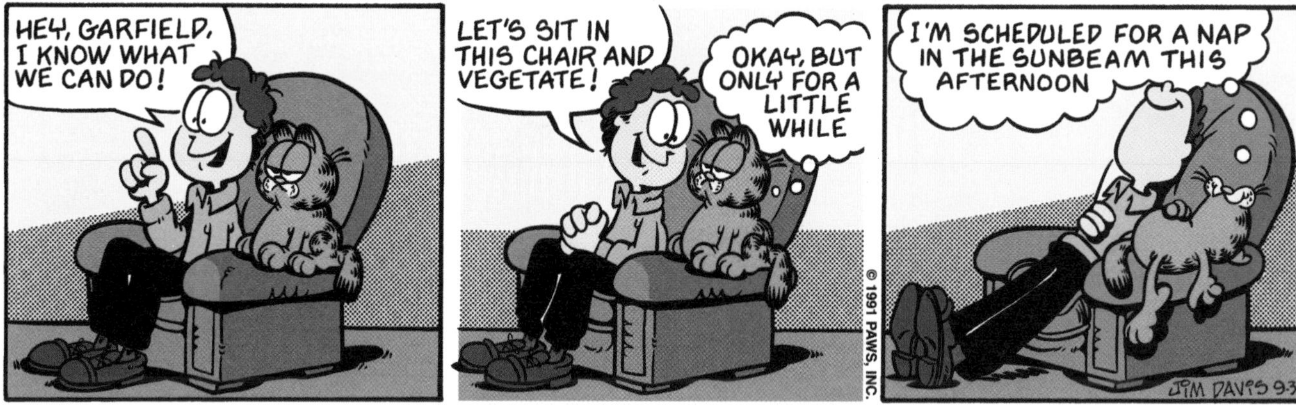
HEY, GARFIELD, I KNOW WHAT WE CAN DO!
LET'S SIT IN THIS CHAIR AND VEGETATE!
OKAY, BUT ONLY FOR A LITTLE WHILE
I'M SCHEDULED FOR A NAP IN THE SUNBEAM THIS AFTERNOON
© 1991 PAWS, INC.
JIM DAVIS 9-30

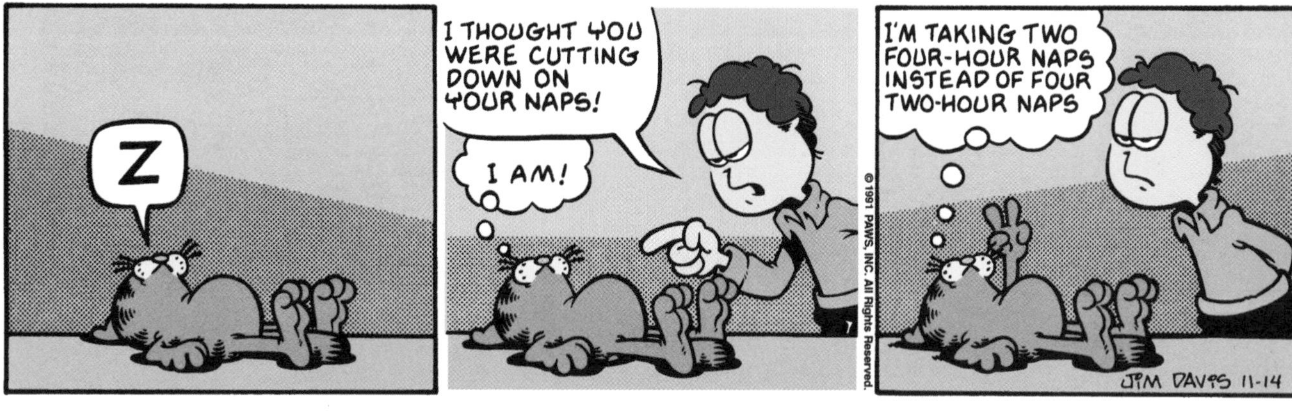
Z
I THOUGHT YOU WERE CUTTING DOWN ON YOUR NAPS!
I AM!
I'M TAKING TWO FOUR-HOUR NAPS INSTEAD OF FOUR TWO-HOUR NAPS
© 1991 PAWS, INC. All Rights Reserved.
JIM DAVIS 11-14

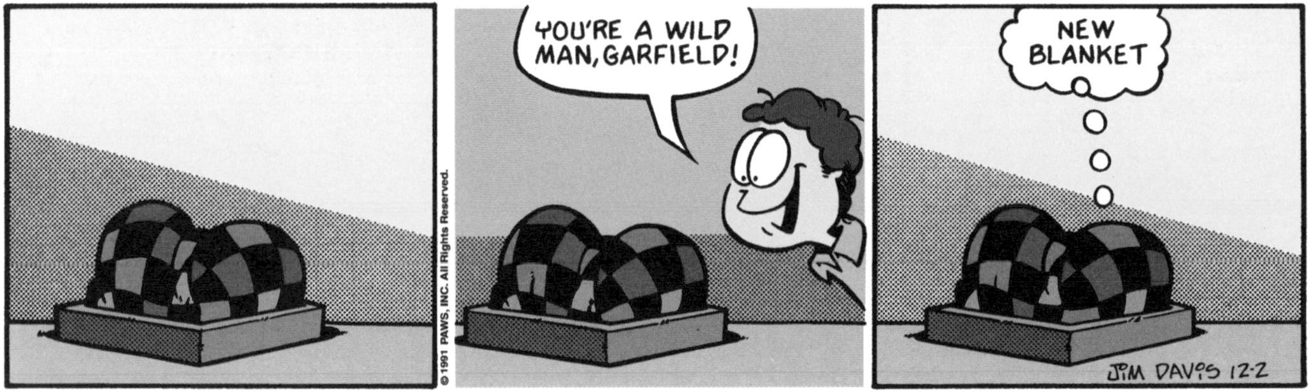
YOU'RE A WILD MAN, GARFIELD!
NEW BLANKET
© 1991 PAWS, INC. All Rights Reserved.
JIM DAVIS 12-2

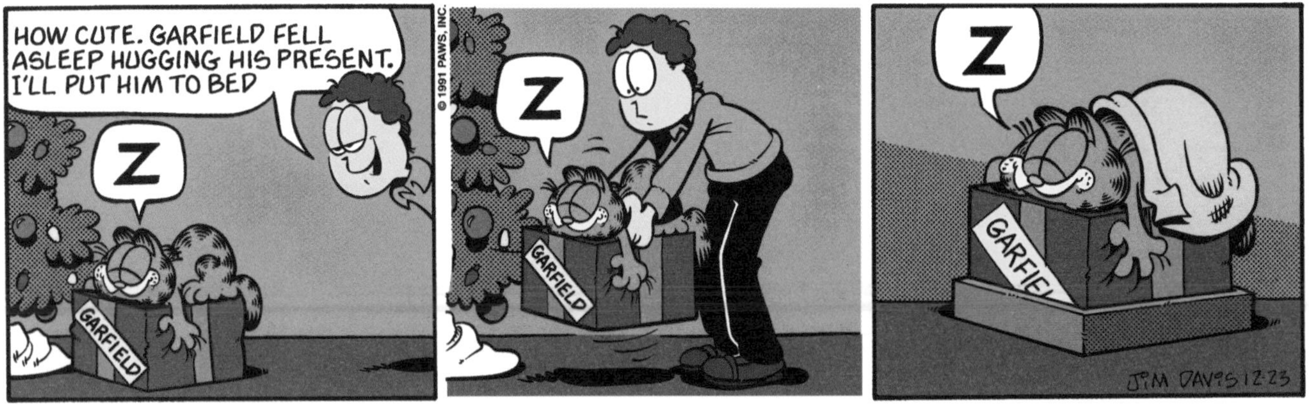
HOW CUTE. GARFIELD FELL ASLEEP HUGGING HIS PRESENT. I'LL PUT HIM TO BED
Z
GARFIELD
© 1991 PAWS, INC.
Z
GARFIELD
Z
GARFIEL
JIM DAVIS 12-23

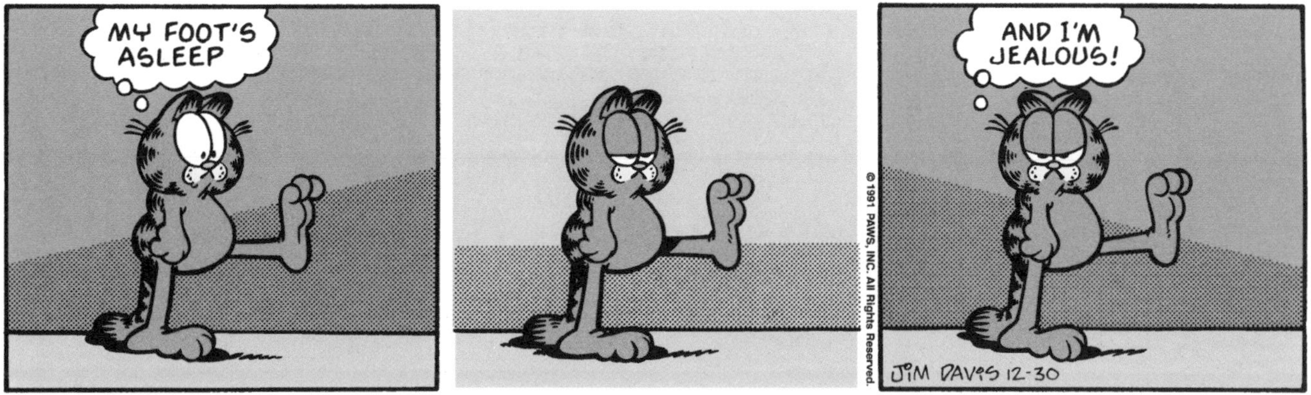
MY FOOT'S ASLEEP
AND I'M JEALOUS!
JIM DAVIS 12-30
© 1991 PAWS, INC. All Rights Reserved.

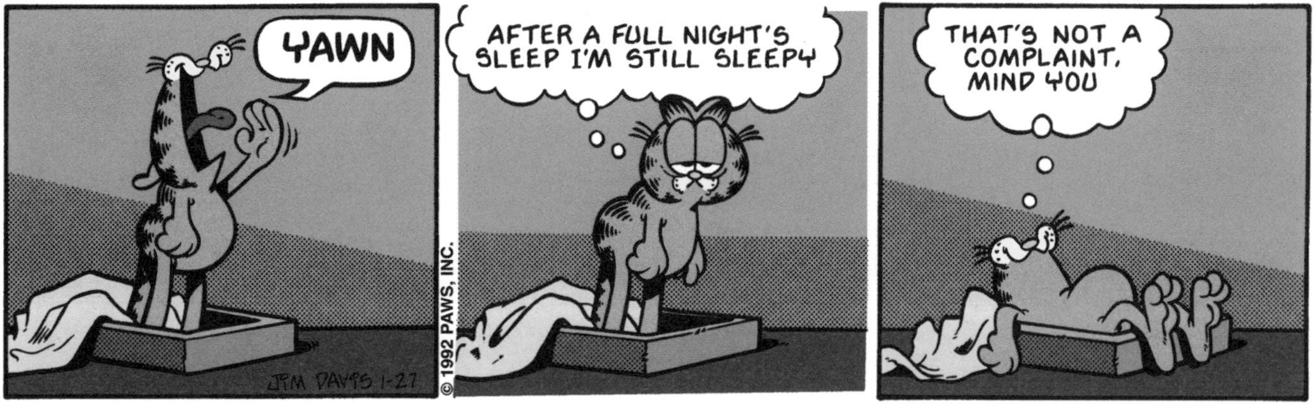
YAWN
JIM DAVIS 1-27
© 1992 PAWS, INC.
AFTER A FULL NIGHT'S SLEEP I'M STILL SLEEPY
THAT'S NOT A COMPLAINT, MIND YOU

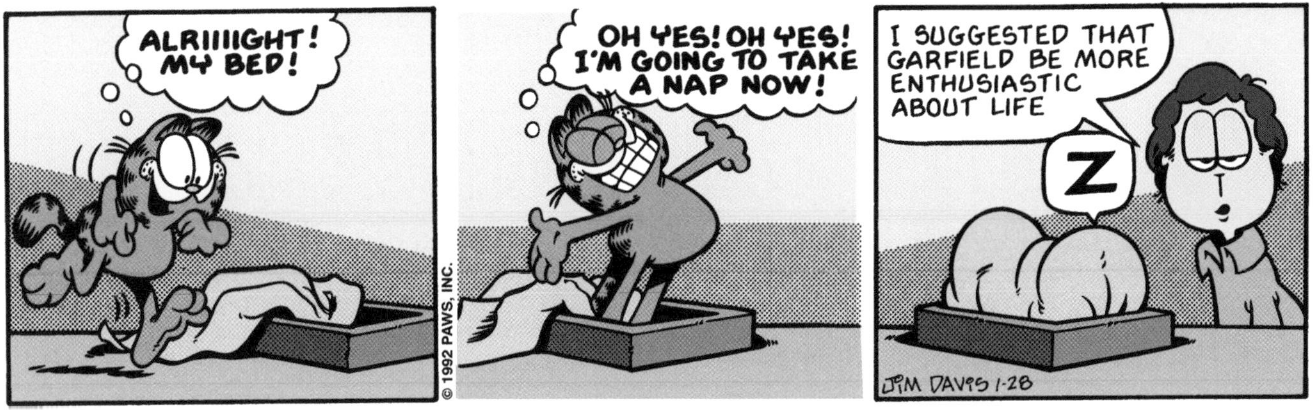
ALRIIIIGHT! MY BED!
OH YES! OH YES! I'M GOING TO TAKE A NAP NOW!
I SUGGESTED THAT GARFIELD BE MORE ENTHUSIASTIC ABOUT LIFE
Z
© 1992 PAWS, INC.
JIM DAVIS 1-28

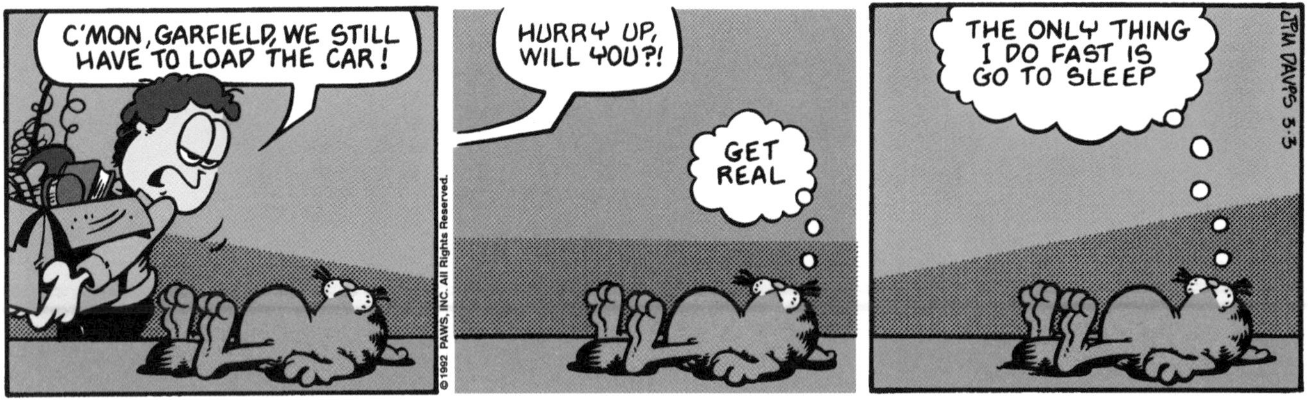
C'MON, GARFIELD, WE STILL HAVE TO LOAD THE CAR!
HURRY UP, WILL YOU?!
GET REAL
THE ONLY THING I DO FAST IS GO TO SLEEP
© 1992 PAWS, INC. All Rights Reserved.
JIM DAVIS 3-3

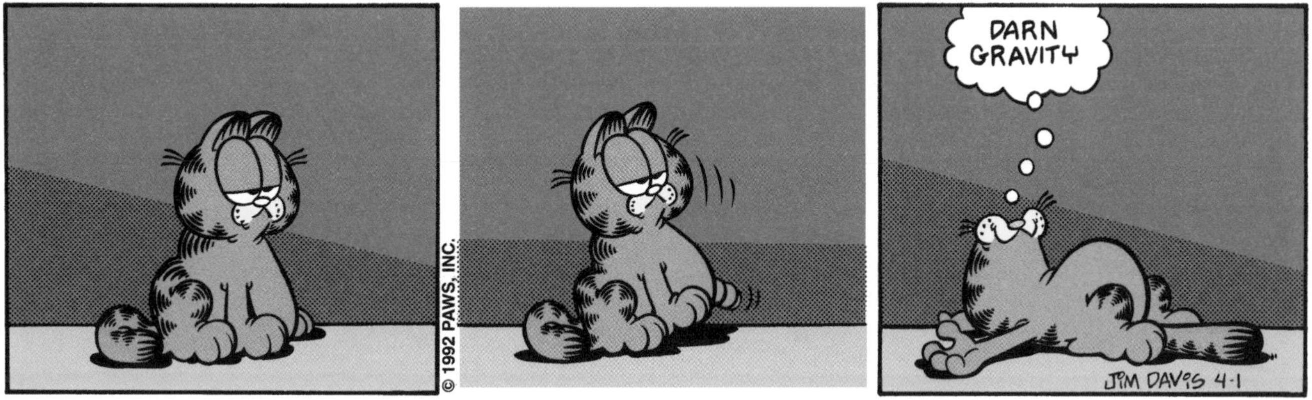
© 1992 PAWS, INC.
DARN GRAVITY
JIM DAVIS 4-1

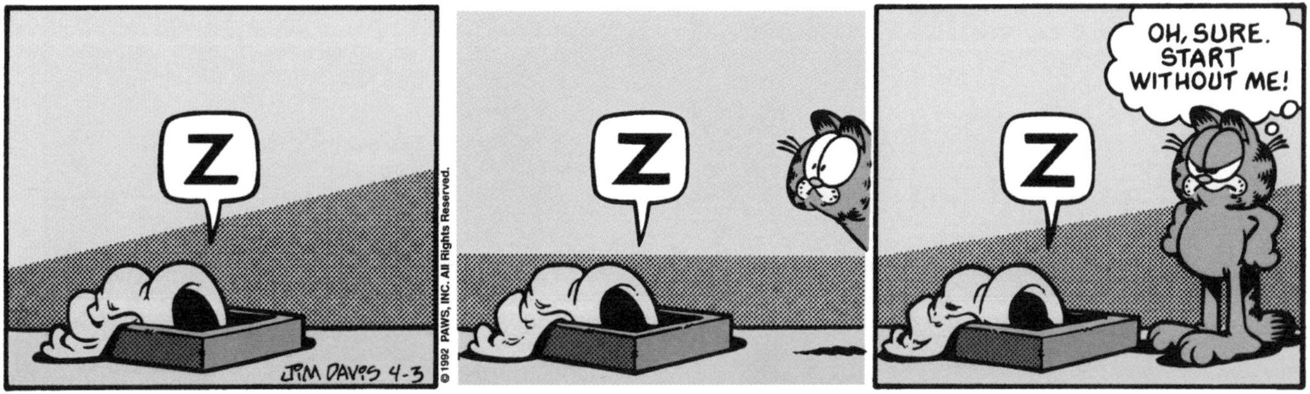
Z
© 1992 PAWS, INC. All Rights Reserved.
JIM DAVIS 4-3
Z
Z
OH, SURE. START WITHOUT ME!

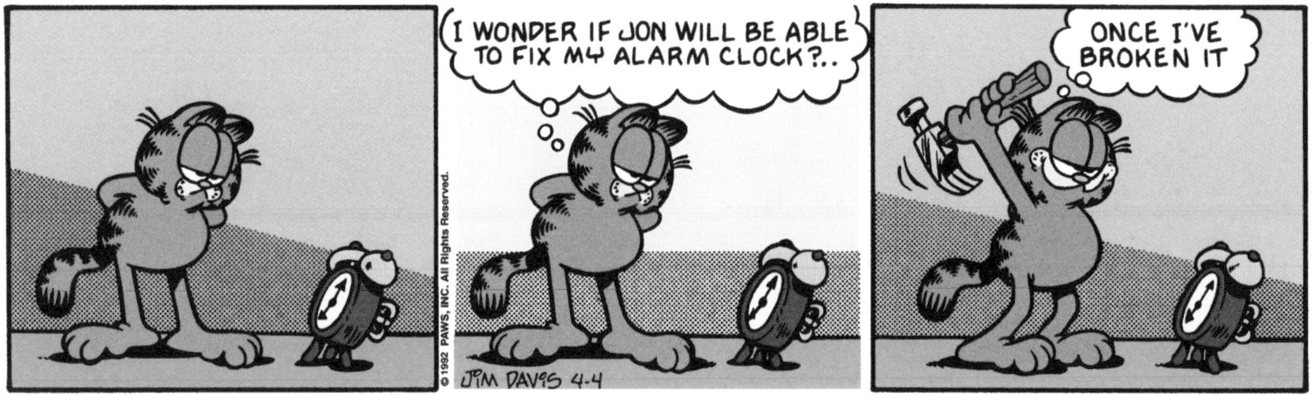
I WONDER IF JON WILL BE ABLE TO FIX MY ALARM CLOCK?..
ONCE I'VE BROKEN IT
© 1992 PAWS, INC. All Rights Reserved.
JIM DAVIS 4-4

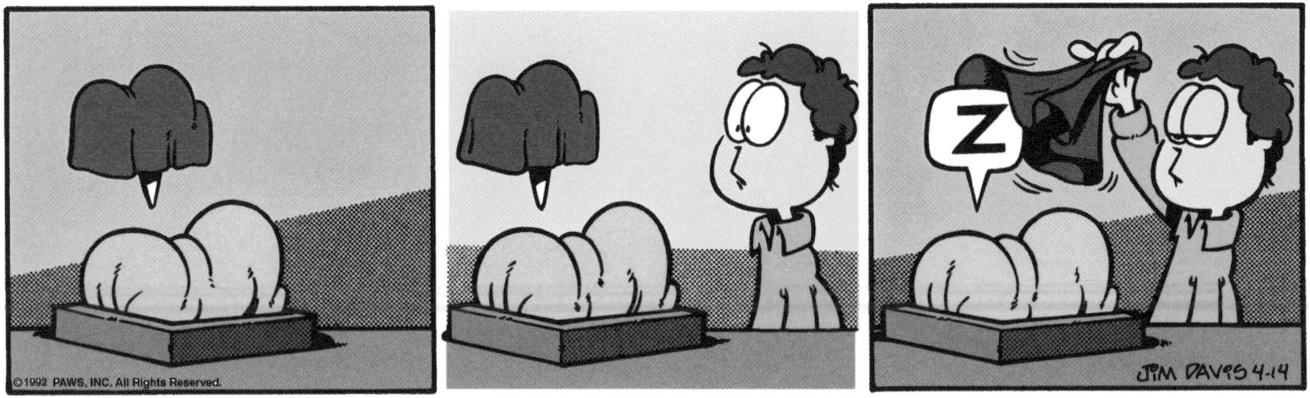
Z
©1992 PAWS, INC. All Rights Reserved.
JIM DAVIS 4-14

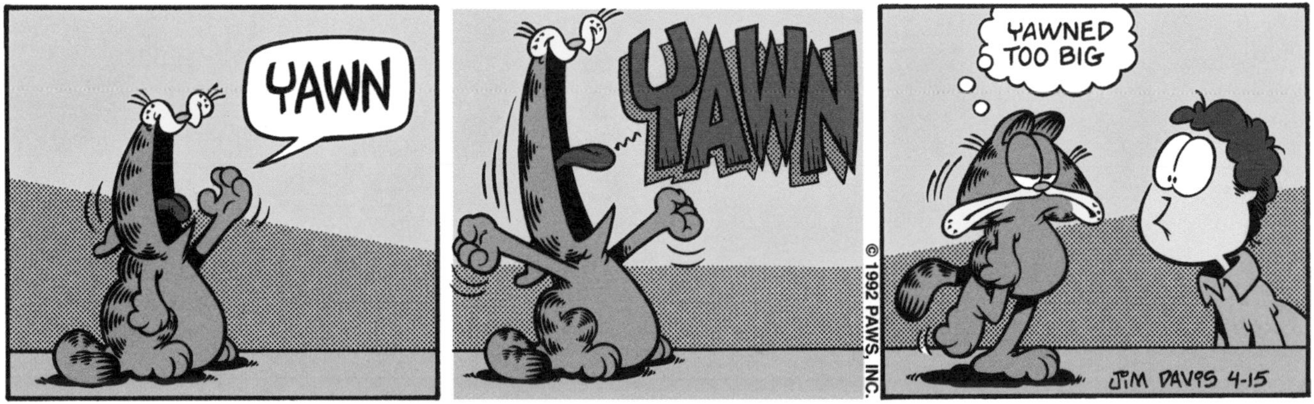
YAWN
YAWN
© 1992 PAWS, INC.
YAWNED TOO BIG
JIM DAVIS 4-15

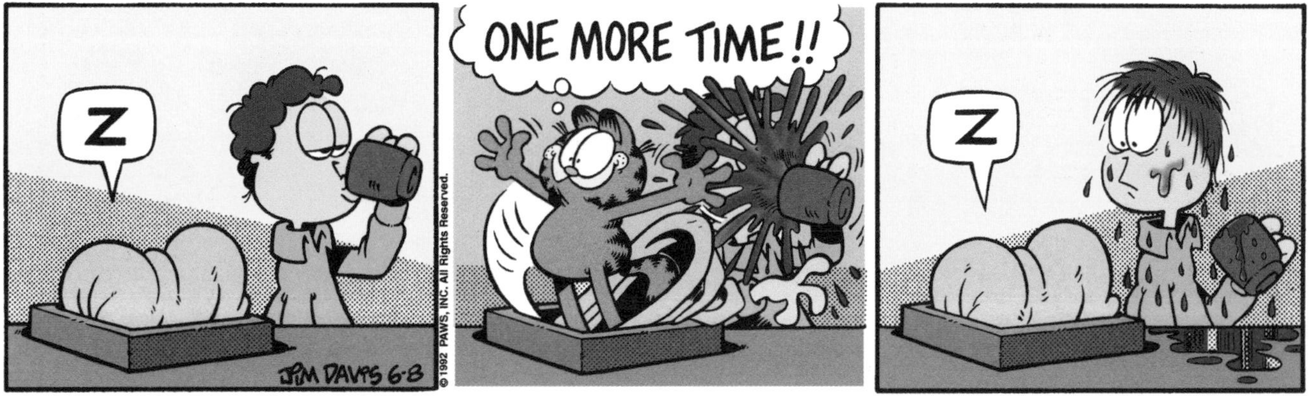
Z
JIM DAVIS 6-8
©1992 PAWS, INC. All Rights Reserved.
ONE MORE TIME!!
Z

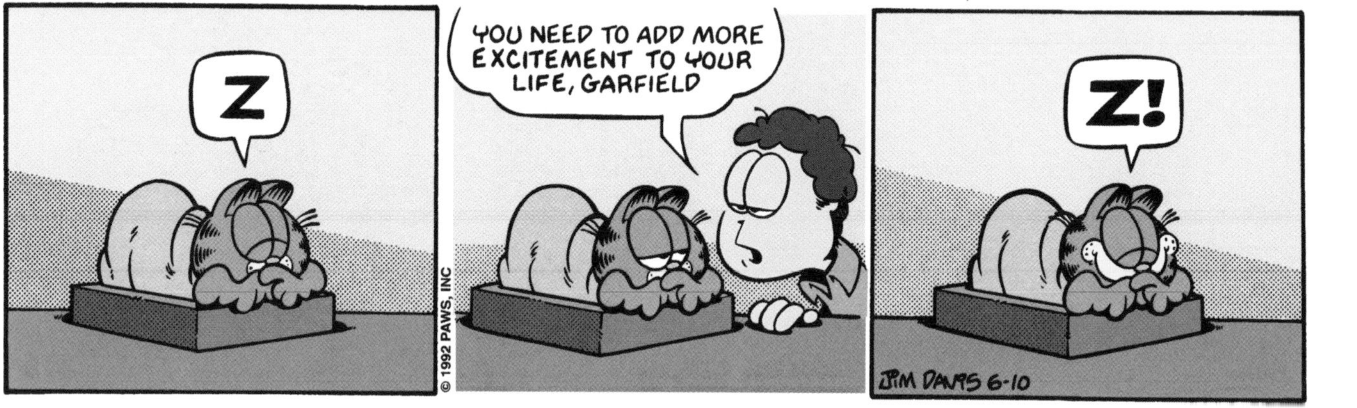
Z
YOU NEED TO ADD MORE EXCITEMENT TO YOUR LIFE, GARFIELD
Z!
© 1992 PAWS, INC
JIM DAVIS 6-10

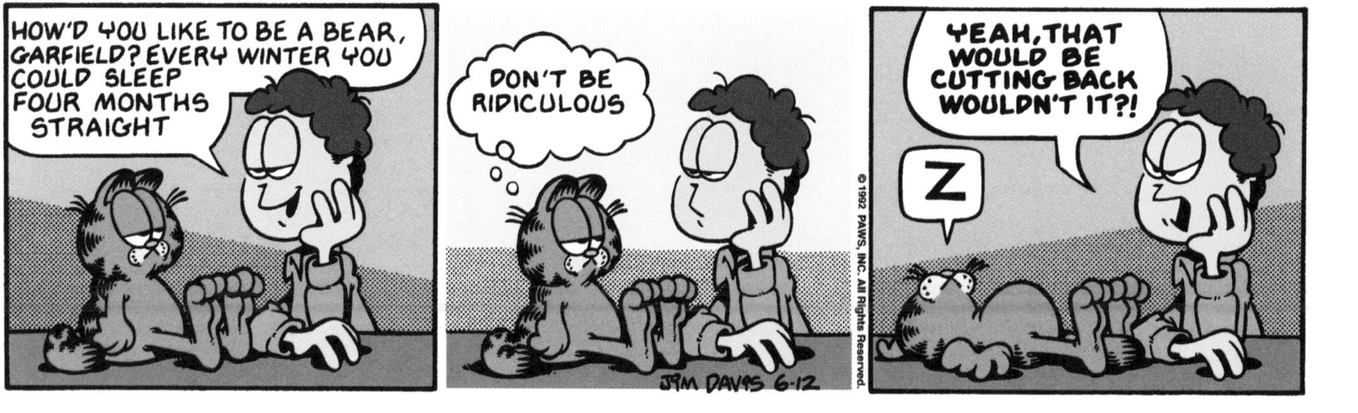
HOW'D YOU LIKE TO BE A BEAR, GARFIELD? EVERY WINTER YOU COULD SLEEP FOUR MONTHS STRAIGHT
DON'T BE RIDICULOUS
Z
YEAH, THAT WOULD BE CUTTING BACK WOULDN'T IT?!
JIM DAVIS 6-12
© 1992 PAWS, INC. All Rights Reserved.

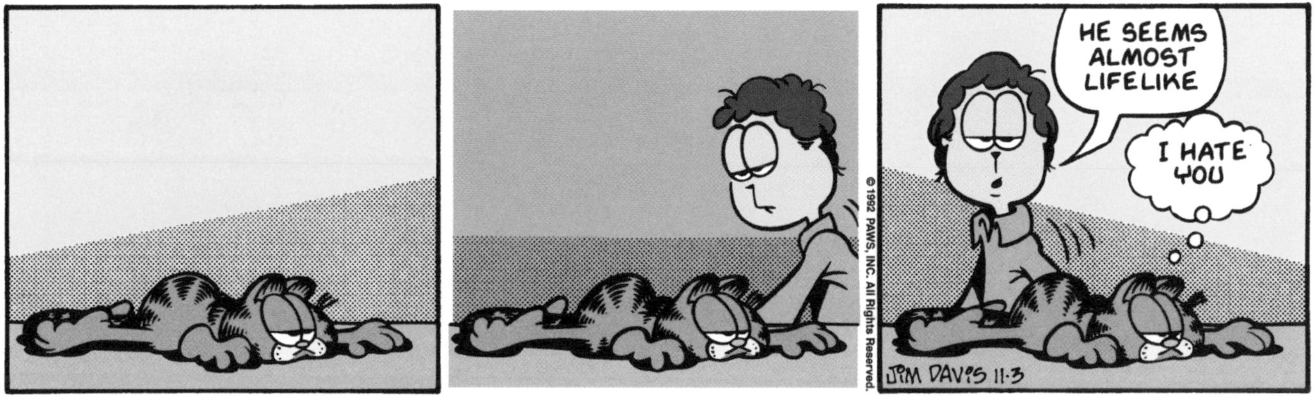
© 1992 PAWS, INC. All Rights Reserved.
HE SEEMS ALMOST LIFELIKE
I HATE YOU
JIM DAVIS 11-3

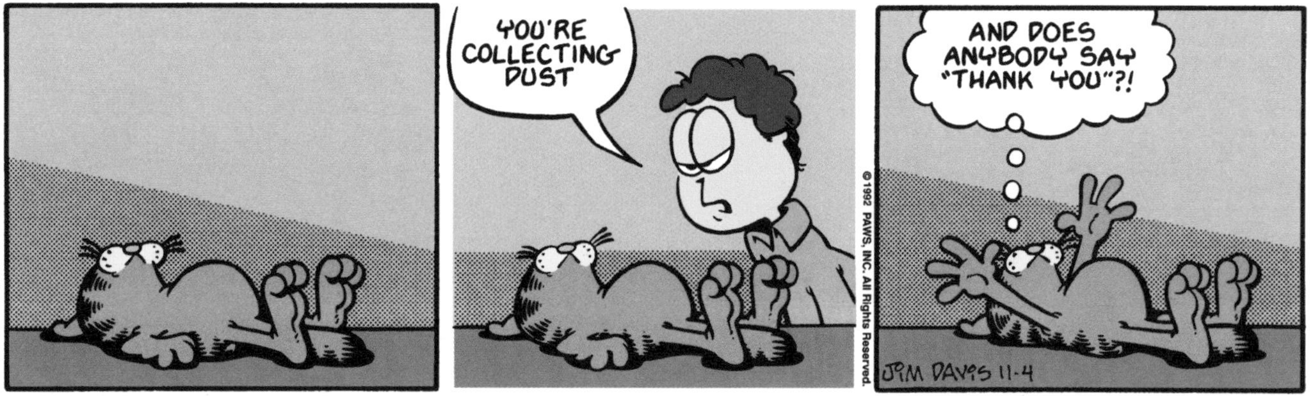
YOU'RE COLLECTING DUST
© 1992 PAWS, INC. All Rights Reserved.
AND DOES ANYBODY SAY "THANK YOU"?!
JIM DAVIS 11-4

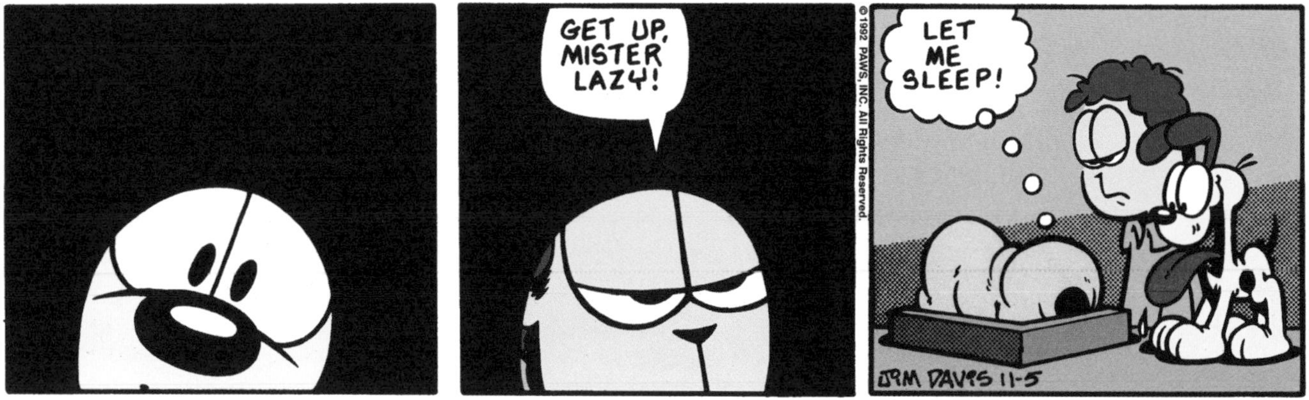
GET UP, MISTER LAZY!
© 1992 PAWS, INC. All Rights Reserved.
LET ME SLEEP!
JIM DAVIS 11-5

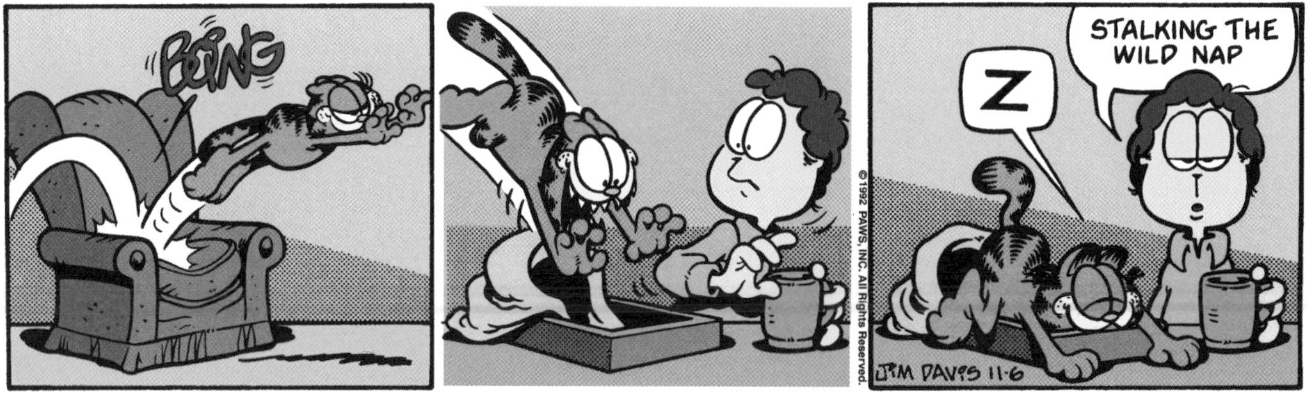
BOING
© 1992 PAWS, INC. All Rights Reserved.
Z
STALKING THE WILD NAP
JIM DAVIS 11-6

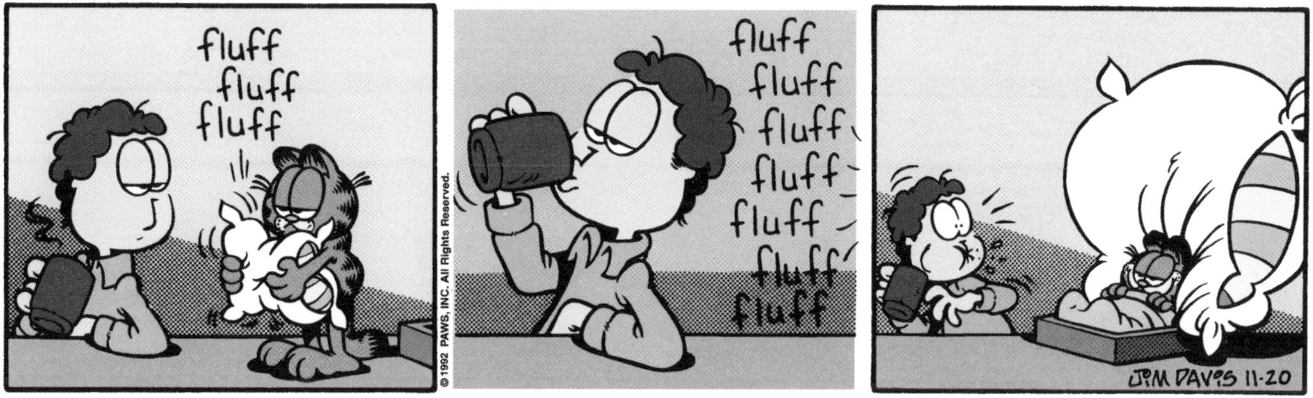
fluff
fluff
fluff
fluff
fluff
fluff
fluff
fluff
fluff
fluff
© 1992 PAWS, INC. All Rights Reserved.
JIM DAVIS 11-20

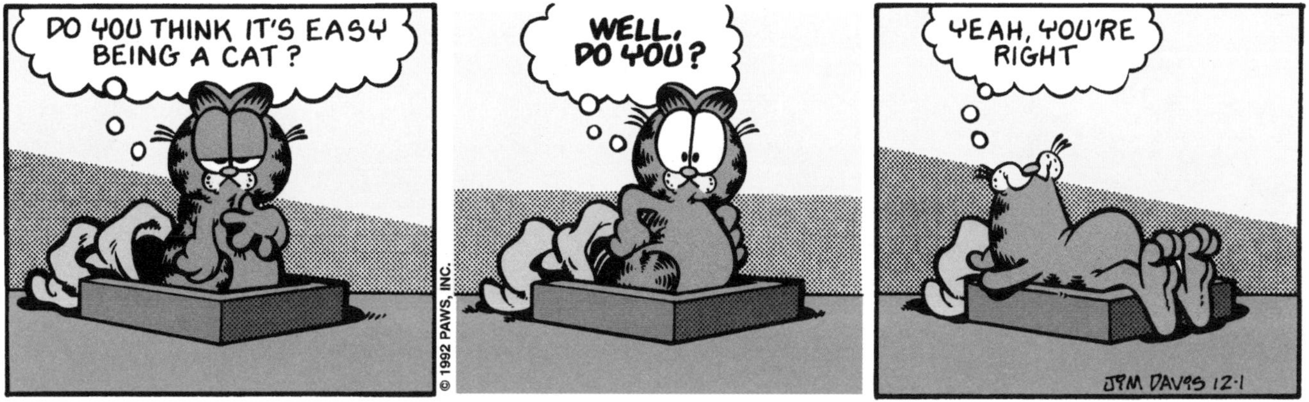
DO YOU THINK IT'S EASY BEING A CAT?
WELL, DO YOU?
YEAH, YOU'RE RIGHT
© 1992 PAWS, INC.
JIM DAVIS 12-1

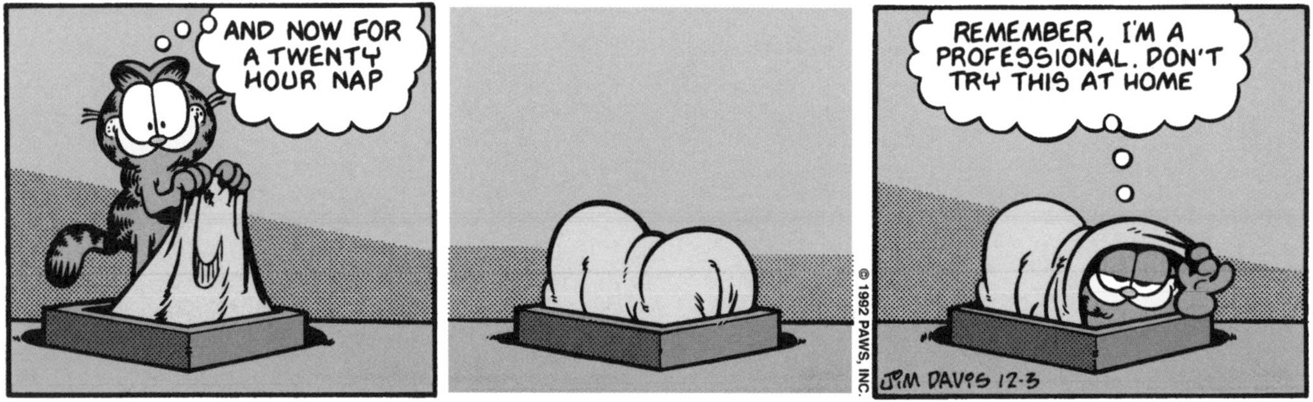
AND NOW FOR A TWENTY HOUR NAP
REMEMBER, I'M A PROFESSIONAL. DON'T TRY THIS AT HOME
JIM DAVIS 12-3

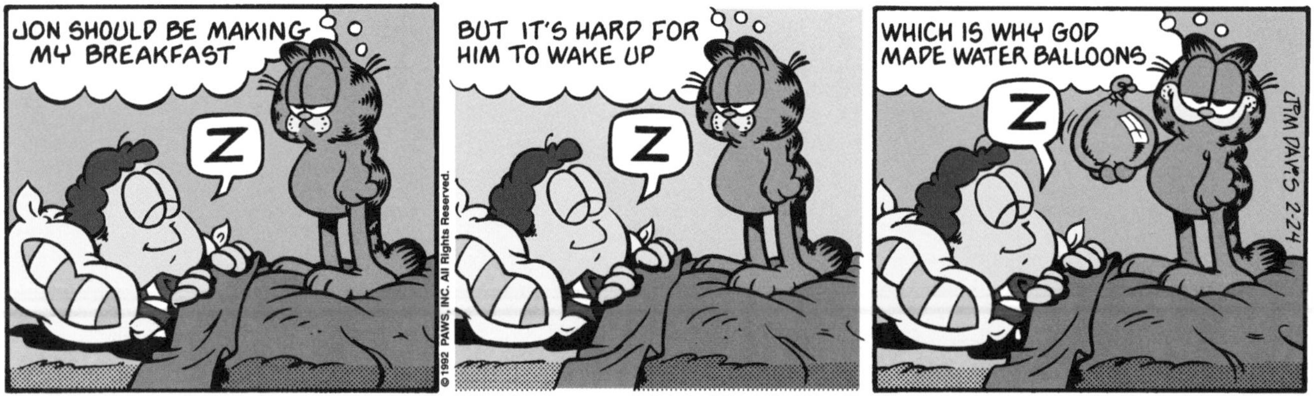
JON SHOULD BE MAKING MY BREAKFAST
Z
BUT IT'S HARD FOR HIM TO WAKE UP
Z
WHICH IS WHY GOD MADE WATER BALLOONS
Z
JIM DAVIS 2-24

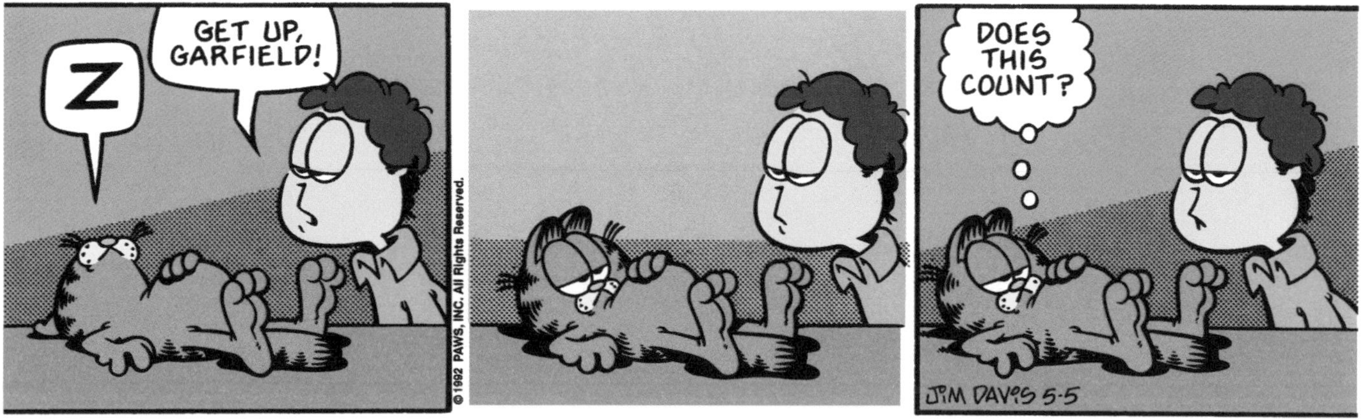
Z
GET UP, GARFIELD!
© 1992 PAWS, INC. All Rights Reserved.
DOES THIS COUNT?
JIM DAVIS 5-5

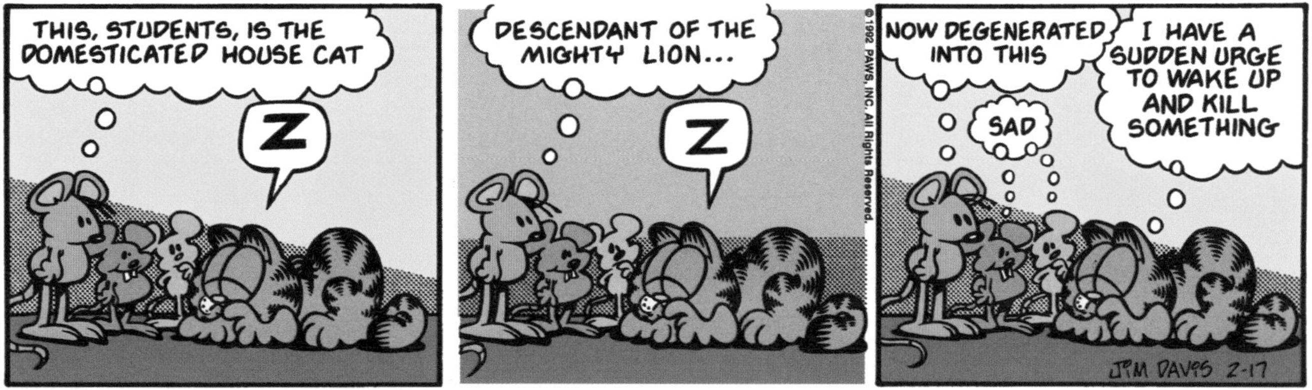
THIS, STUDENTS, IS THE DOMESTICATED HOUSE CAT
Z
DESCENDANT OF THE MIGHTY LION...
Z
© 1992 PAWS, INC. All Rights Reserved.
NOW DEGENERATED INTO THIS
SAD
I HAVE A SUDDEN URGE TO WAKE UP AND KILL SOMETHING
JIM DAVIS 2-17

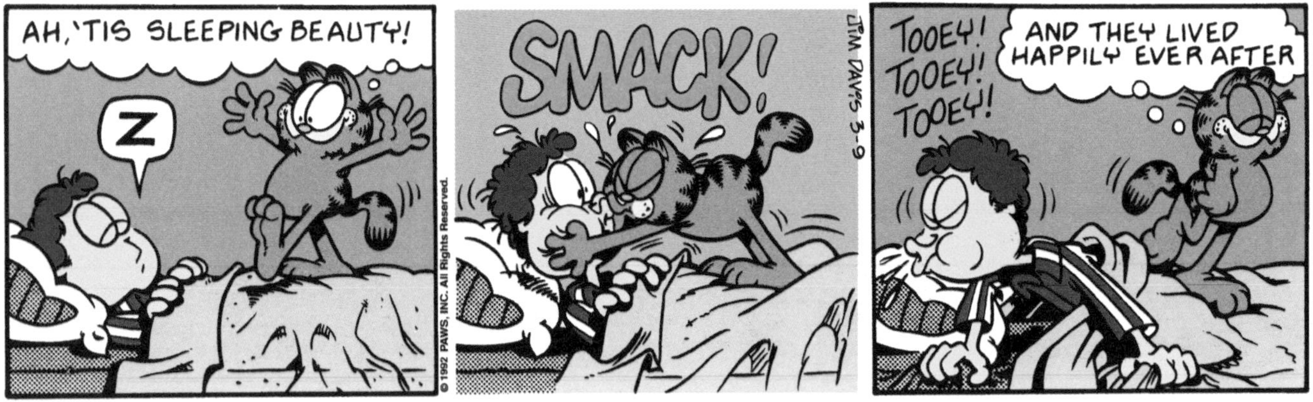
AH, 'TIS SLEEPING BEAUTY!
Z
© 1992 PAWS, INC. All Rights Reserved.
SMACK!
JIM DAVIS 3-9
TOOEY! TOOEY! TOOEY!
AND THEY LIVED HAPPILY EVER AFTER

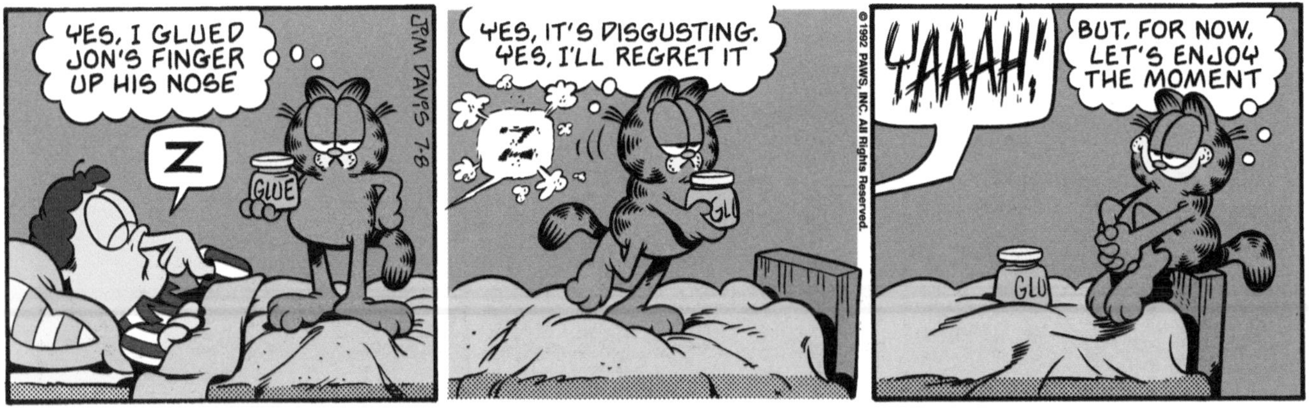
YES, I GLUED JON'S FINGER UP HIS NOSE
Z
GLUE
JIM DAVIS 7-8
YES, IT'S DISGUSTING. YES, I'LL REGRET IT
Z
GLU
© 1992 PAWS, INC. All Rights Reserved.
YAAAH!
BUT, FOR NOW, LET'S ENJOY THE MOMENT
GLU

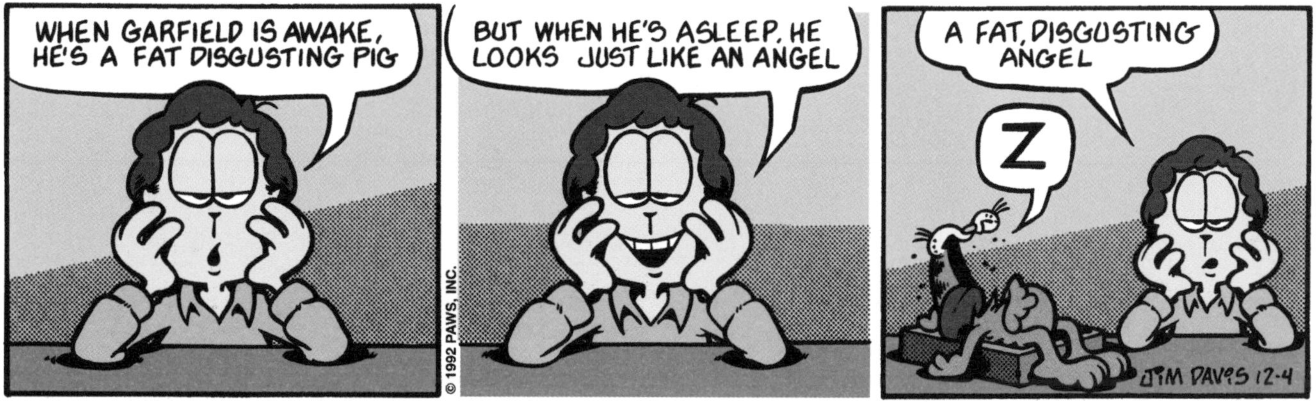
WHEN GARFIELD IS AWAKE, HE'S A FAT DISGUSTING PIG
BUT WHEN HE'S ASLEEP, HE LOOKS JUST LIKE AN ANGEL
Z
A FAT, DISGUSTING ANGEL
JIM DAVIS 12-4

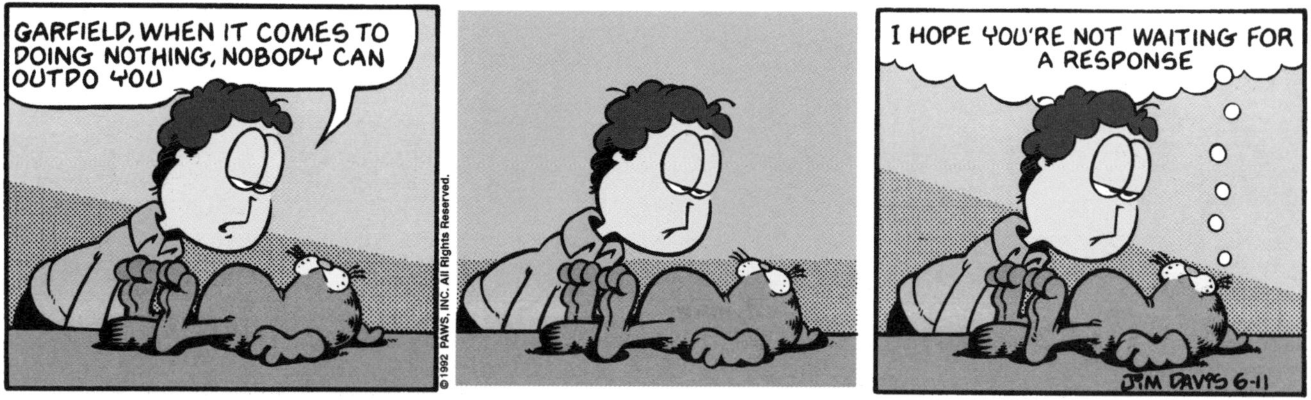
GARFIELD, WHEN IT COMES TO DOING NOTHING, NOBODY CAN OUTDO YOU
I HOPE YOU'RE NOT WAITING FOR A RESPONSE
JIM DAVIS 6-11

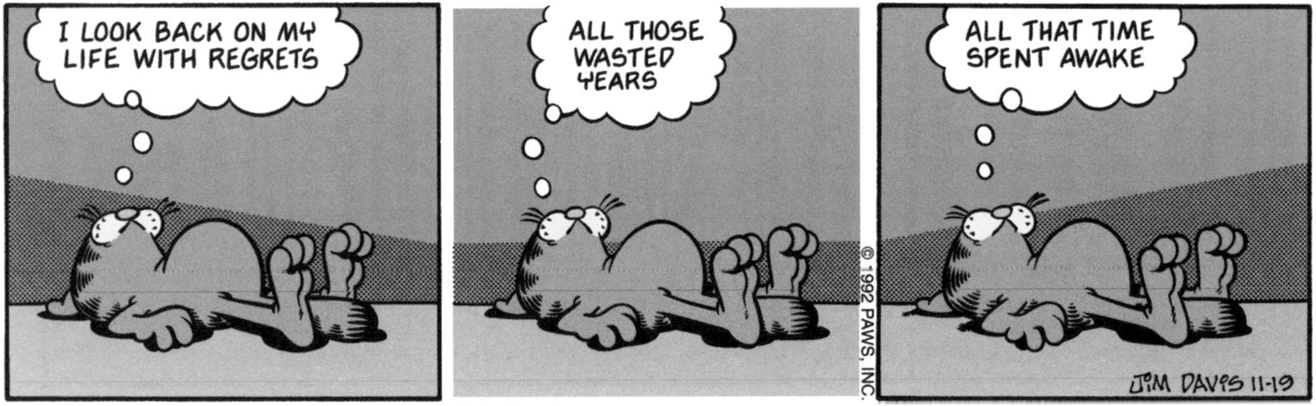
I LOOK BACK ON MY LIFE WITH REGRETS
ALL THOSE WASTED YEARS
© 1992 PAWS, INC.
ALL THAT TIME SPENT AWAKE
JIM DAVIS 11-19

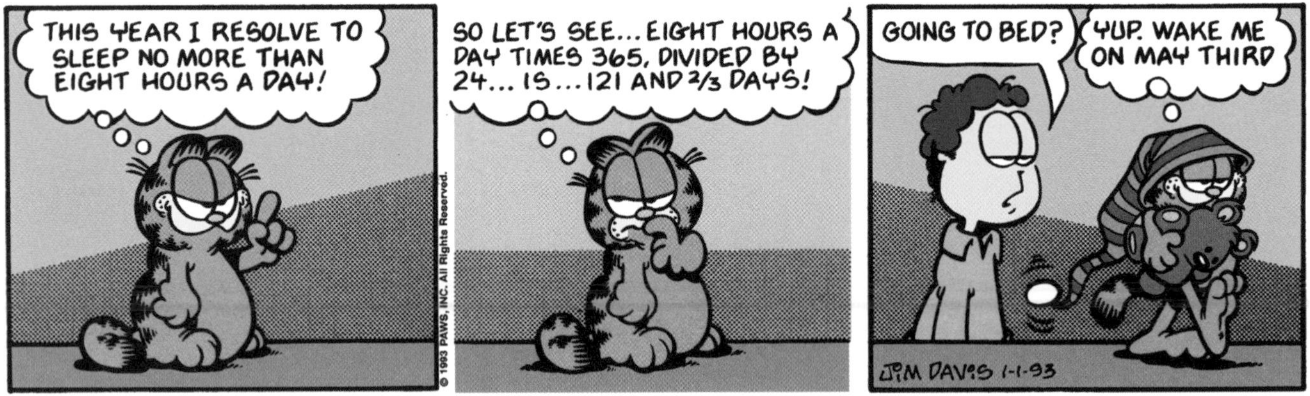
THIS YEAR I RESOLVE TO SLEEP NO MORE THAN EIGHT HOURS A DAY!
© 1993 PAWS, INC. All Rights Reserved.
SO LET'S SEE... EIGHT HOURS A DAY TIMES 365, DIVIDED BY 24... IS... 121 AND 2/3 DAYS!
GOING TO BED?
YUP. WAKE ME ON MAY THIRD
JIM DAVIS 1-1-93

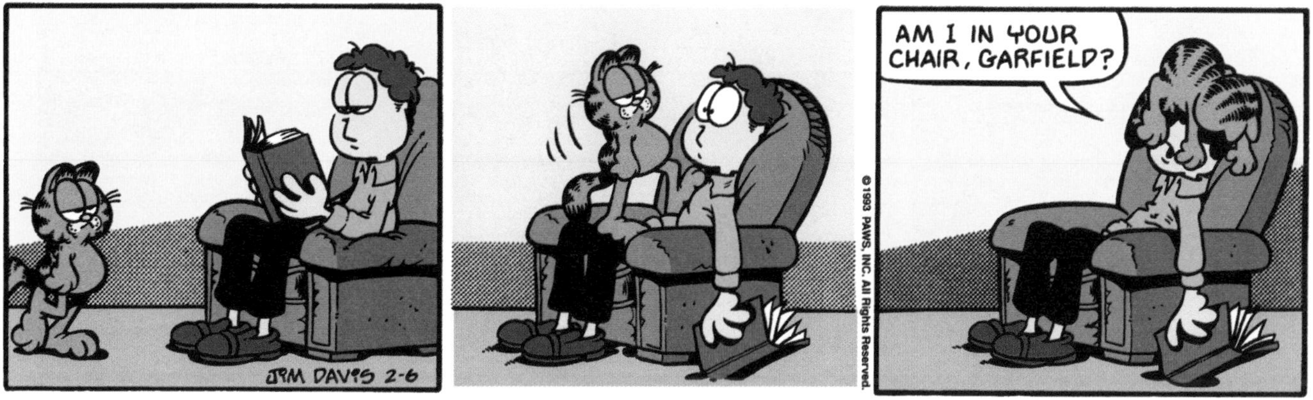
JIM DAVIS 2-6
© 1993 PAWS, INC. All Rights Reserved.
AM I IN YOUR CHAIR, GARFIELD?

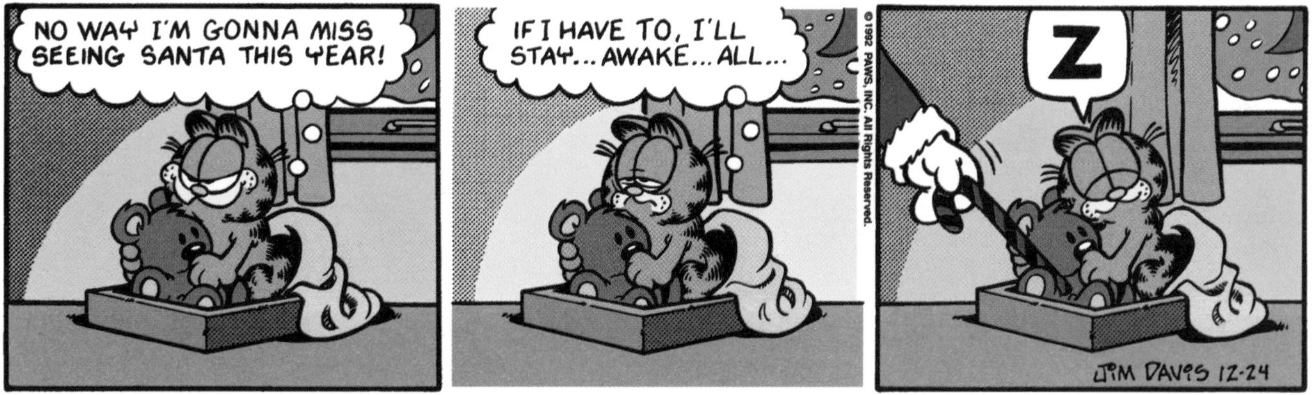
NO WAY I'M GONNA MISS SEEING SANTA THIS YEAR!
IF I HAVE TO, I'LL STAY... AWAKE... ALL...
© 1992 PAWS, INC. All Rights Reserved.
Z
JIM DAVIS 12-24

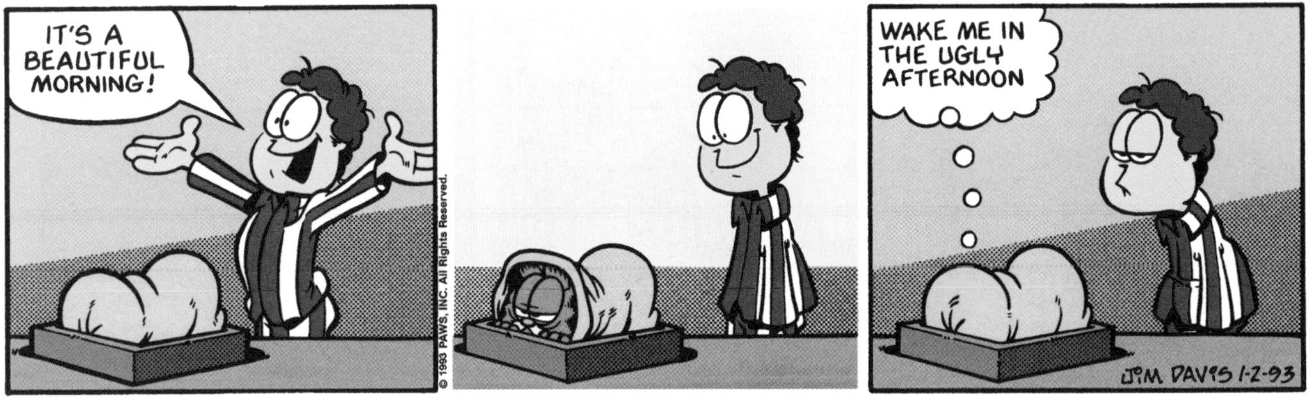
IT'S A BEAUTIFUL MORNING!
© 1993 PAWS, INC. All Rights Reserved.
WAKE ME IN THE UGLY AFTERNOON
JIM DAVIS 1-2-93

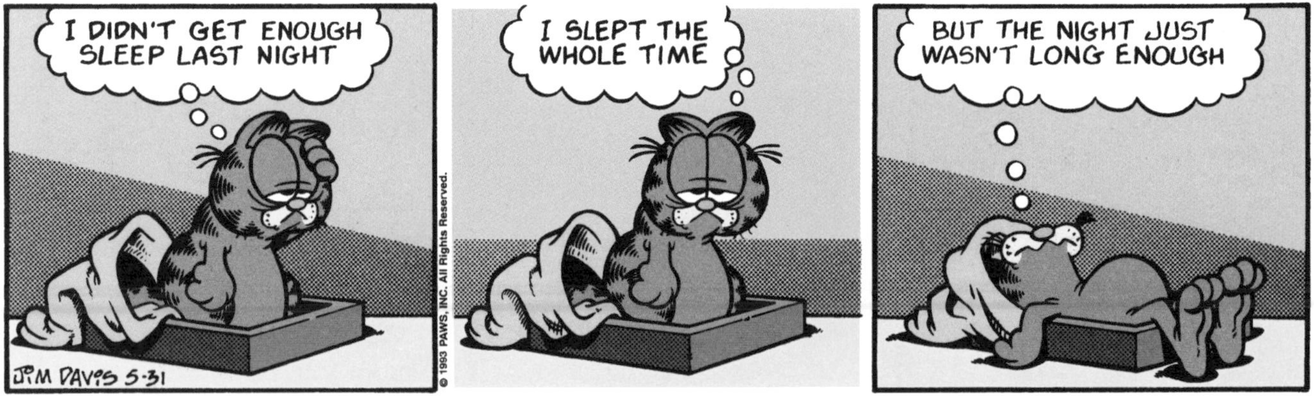
I DIDN'T GET ENOUGH SLEEP LAST NIGHT
JIM DAVIS 5-31
© 1993 PAWS, INC. All Rights Reserved.
I SLEPT THE WHOLE TIME
BUT THE NIGHT JUST WASN'T LONG ENOUGH

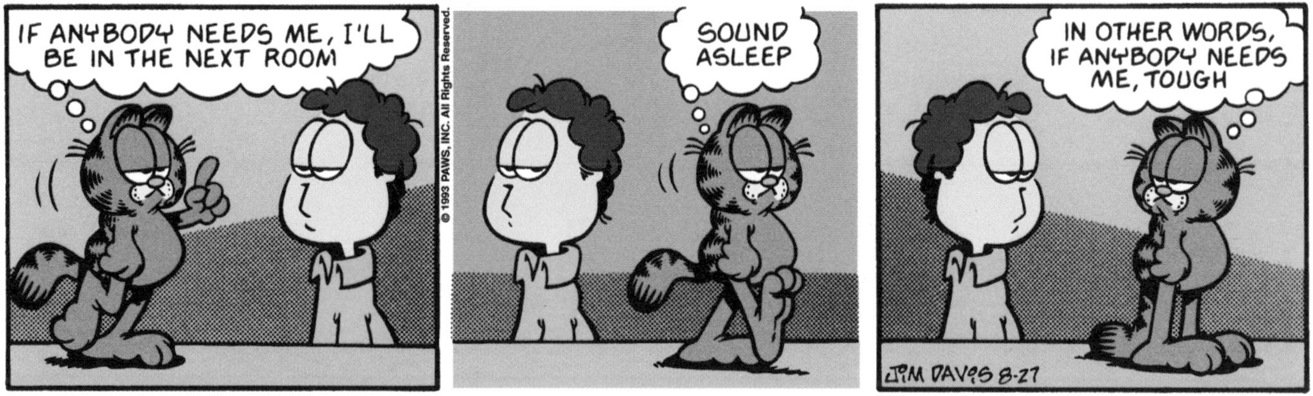
IF ANYBODY NEEDS ME, I'LL BE IN THE NEXT ROOM
SOUND ASLEEP
IN OTHER WORDS, IF ANYBODY NEEDS ME, TOUGH
JIM DAVIS 8-27

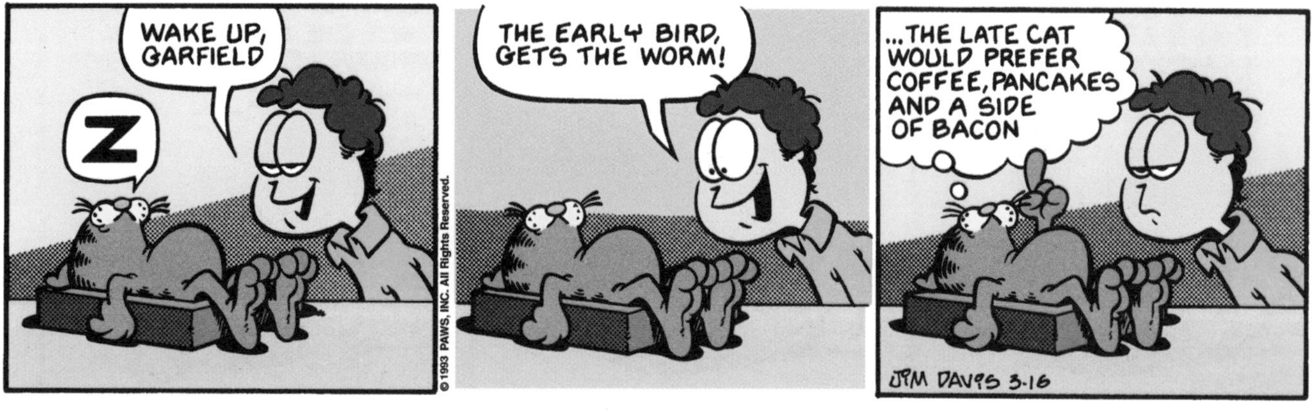
WAKE UP, GARFIELD
Z
THE EARLY BIRD, GETS THE WORM!
...THE LATE CAT WOULD PREFER COFFEE, PANCAKES AND A SIDE OF BACON
JIM DAVIS 3-16

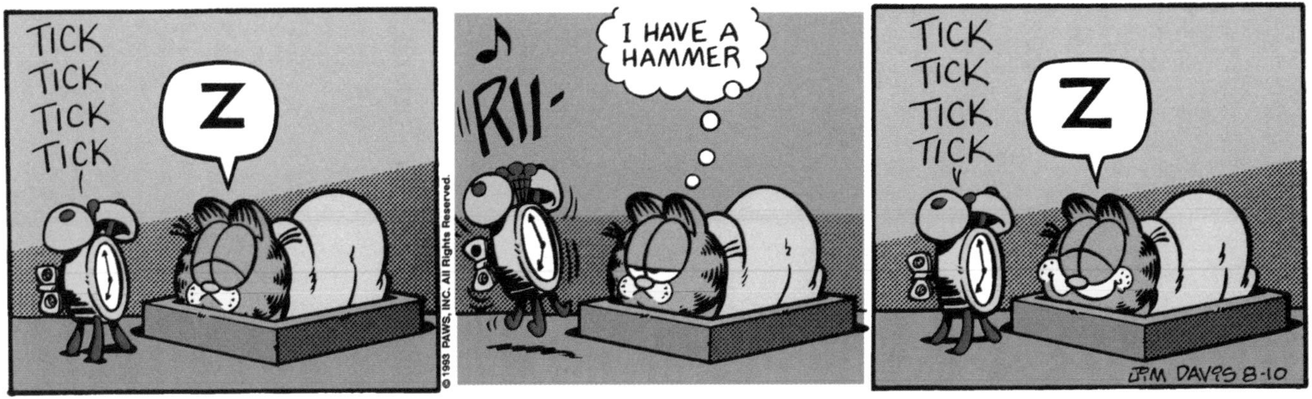
TICK TICK TICK TICK
Z
RII-
I HAVE A HAMMER
TICK TICK TICK TICK
Z
JIM DAVIS 8-10

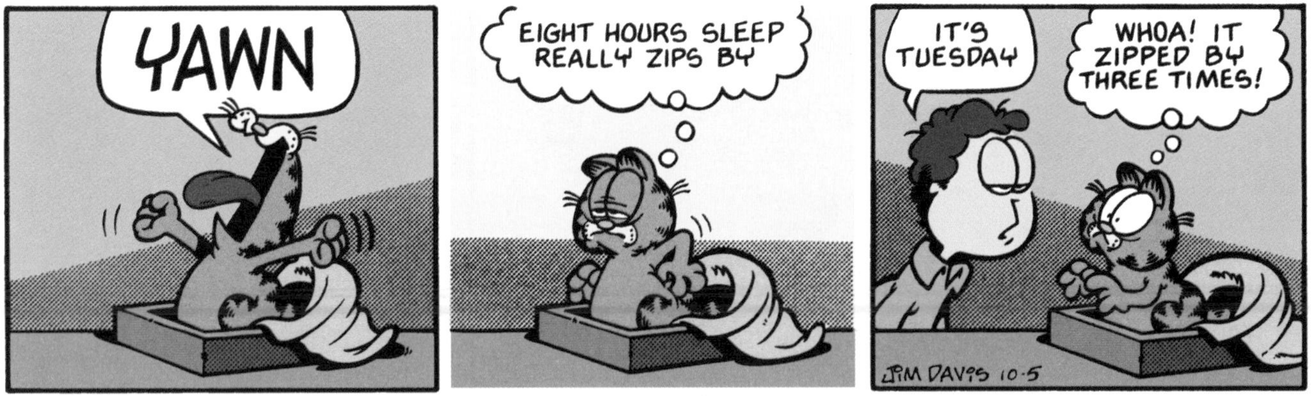
YAWN
EIGHT HOURS SLEEP REALLY ZIPS BY
IT'S TUESDAY
WHOA! IT ZIPPED BY THREE TIMES!
JIM DAVIS 10-5

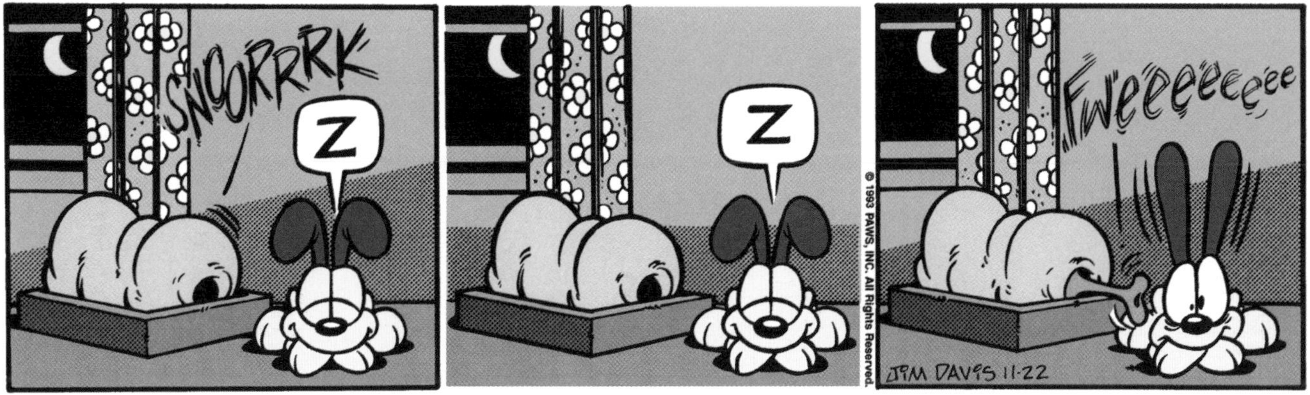
SNOORRRK
Z
Z
Fweeeeeeee
© 1993 PAWS, INC. All Rights Reserved.
JIM DAVIS 11-22

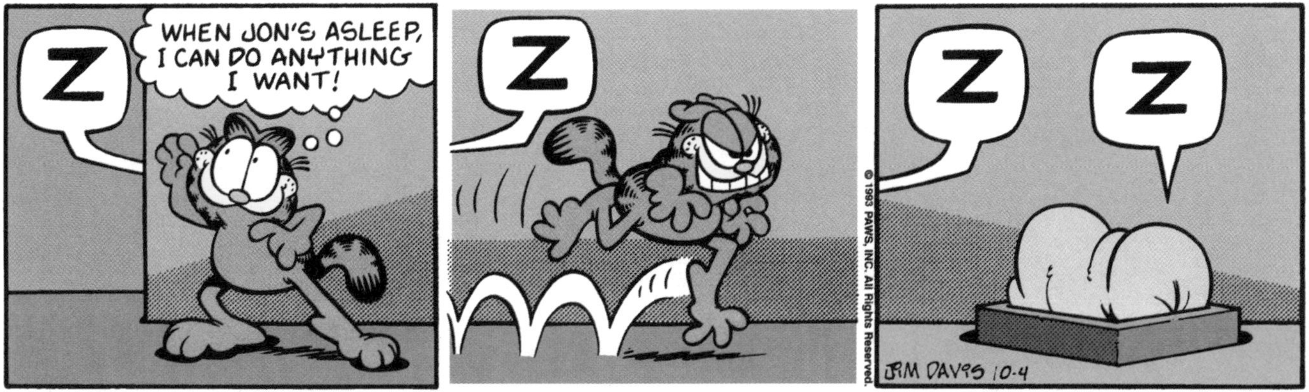
Z
WHEN JON'S ASLEEP, I CAN DO ANYTHING I WANT!
Z
Z
Z
© 1993 PAWS, INC. All Rights Reserved.
JIM DAVIS 10-4

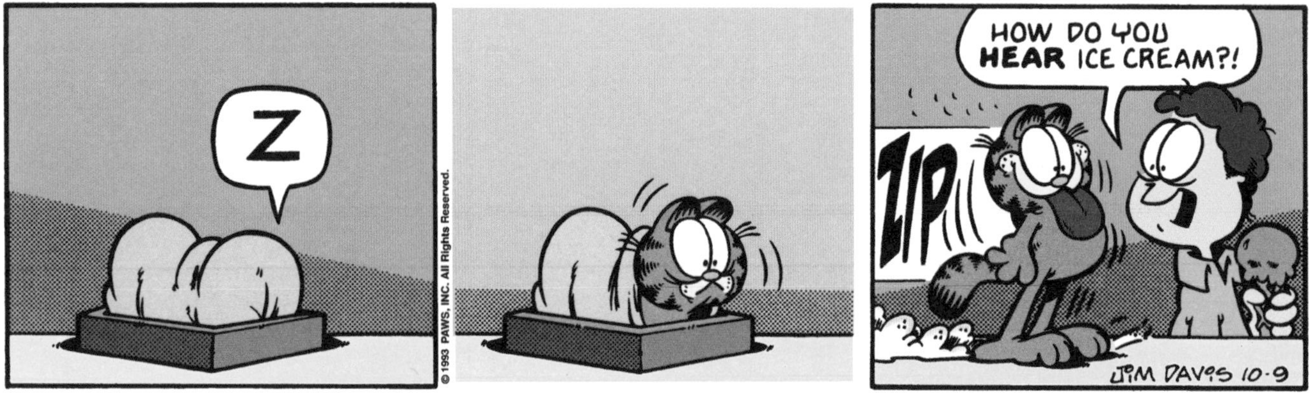
Z
© 1993 PAWS, INC. All Rights Reserved.
ZIP
HOW DO YOU **HEAR** ICE CREAM?!
JIM DAVIS 10-9

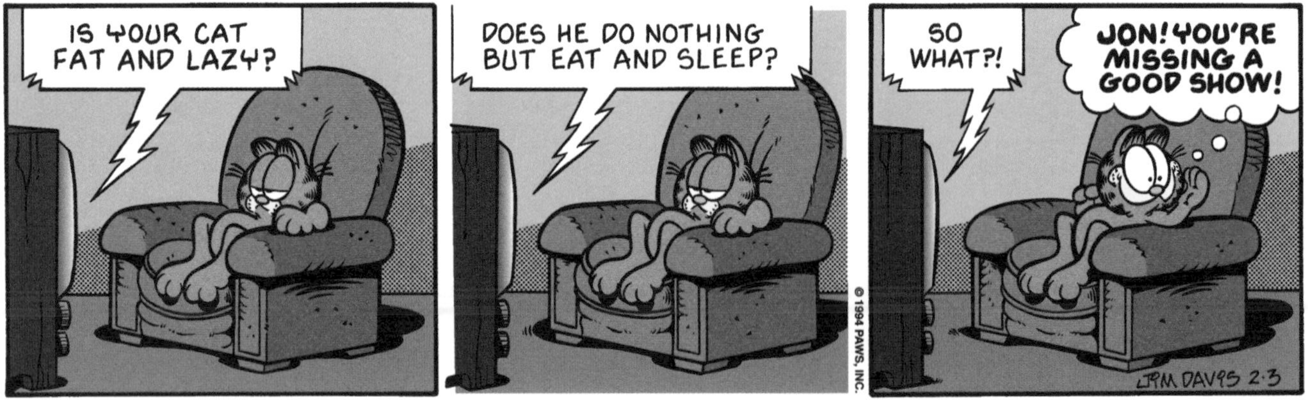
IS YOUR CAT FAT AND LAZY?
DOES HE DO NOTHING BUT EAT AND SLEEP?
© 1994 PAWS, INC.
SO WHAT?!
JON! YOU'RE MISSING A GOOD SHOW!
JIM DAVIS 2-3

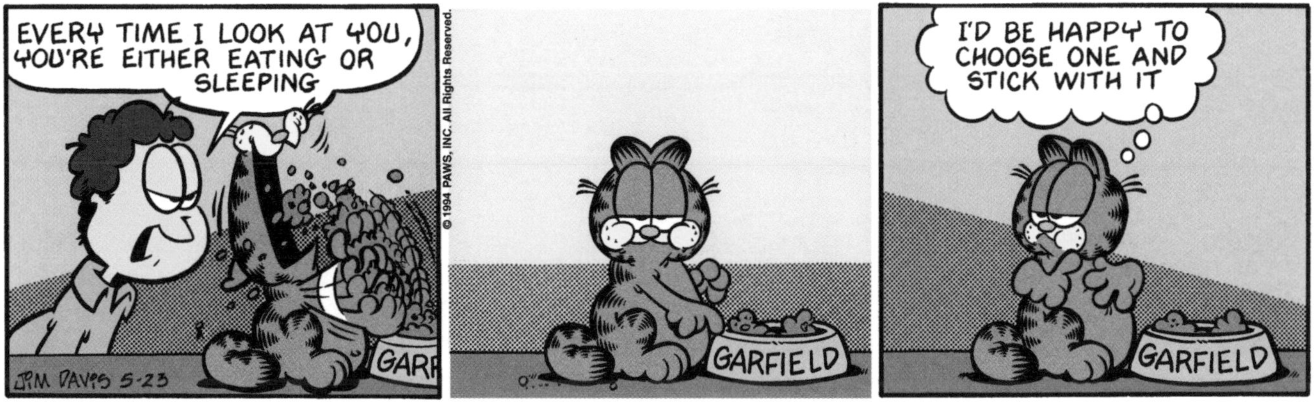
EVERY TIME I LOOK AT YOU, YOU'RE EITHER EATING OR SLEEPING
GARF
JIM DAVIS 5-23
© 1994 PAWS, INC. All Rights Reserved.
GARFIELD
I'D BE HAPPY TO CHOOSE ONE AND STICK WITH IT
GARFIELD

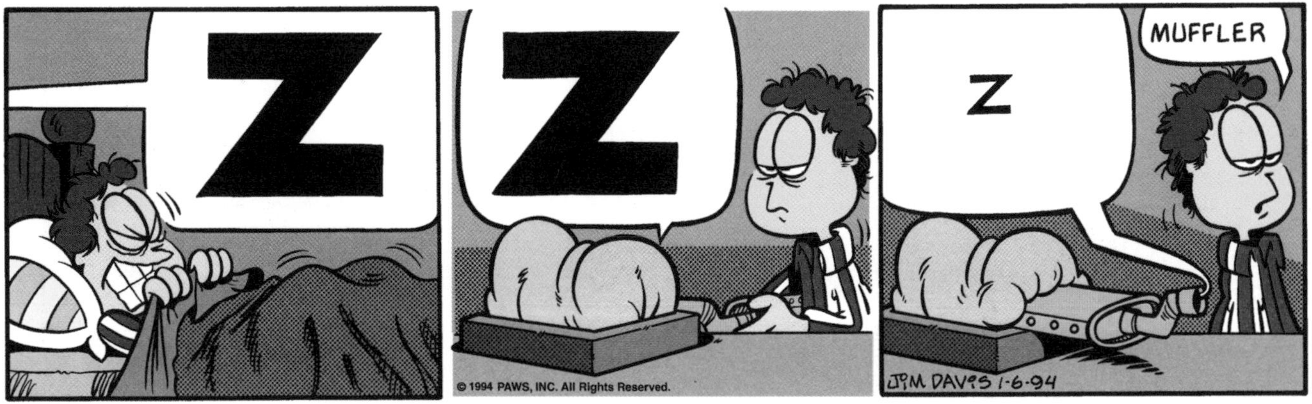
Z
Z
© 1994 PAWS, INC. All Rights Reserved.
Z
MUFFLER
JIM DAVIS 1-6-94

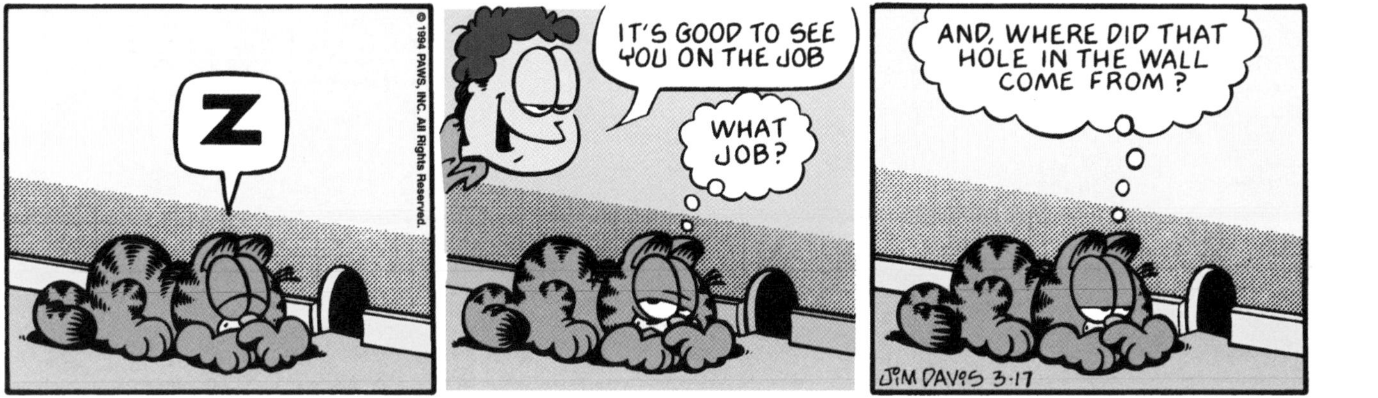
Z
© 1994 PAWS, INC. All Rights Reserved.
IT'S GOOD TO SEE YOU ON THE JOB
WHAT JOB?
AND, WHERE DID THAT HOLE IN THE WALL COME FROM?
JIM DAVIS 3-17

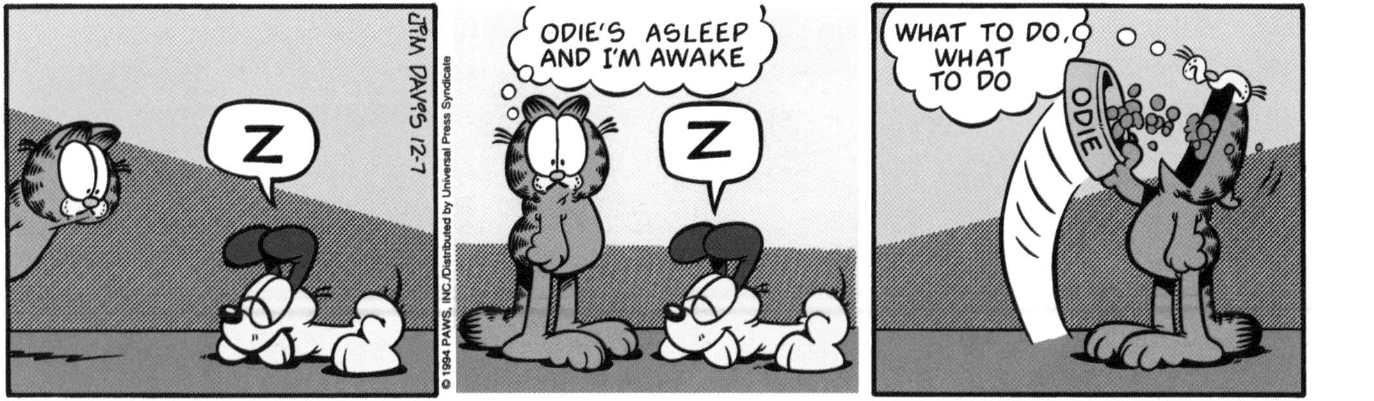
Z
JIM DAVIS 12-7
© 1994 PAWS, INC./Distributed by Universal Press Syndicate
ODIE'S ASLEEP AND I'M AWAKE
Z
WHAT TO DO, WHAT TO DO
ODIE

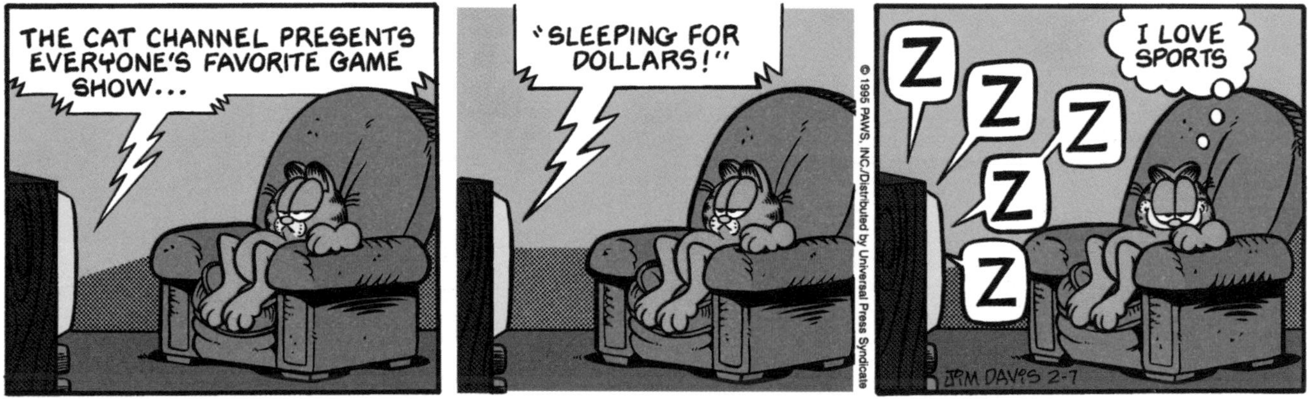
THE CAT CHANNEL PRESENTS EVERYONE'S FAVORITE GAME SHOW...
"SLEEPING FOR DOLLARS!"
Z
Z
Z
Z
Z
I LOVE SPORTS
JIM DAVIS 2-7
© 1995 PAWS, INC./Distributed by Universal Press Syndicate

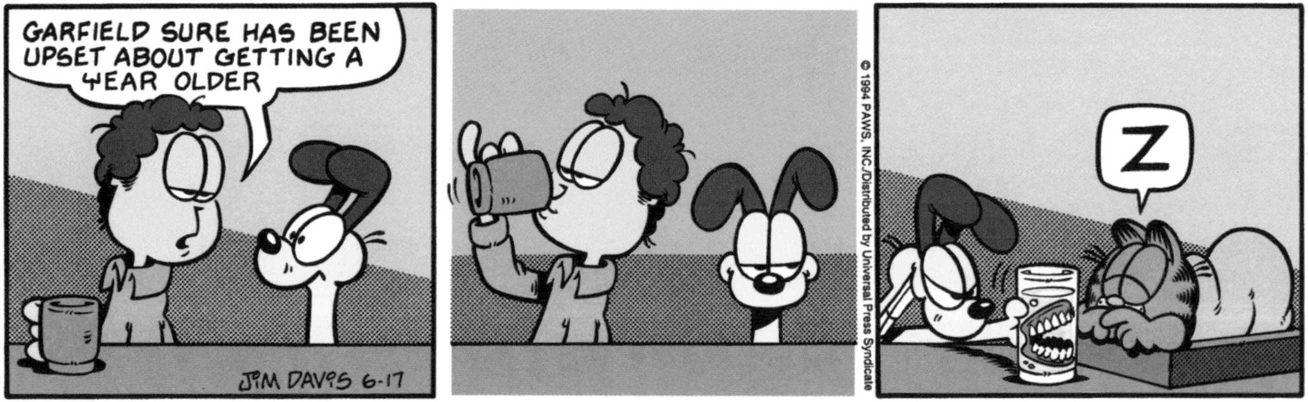
GARFIELD SURE HAS BEEN UPSET ABOUT GETTING A YEAR OLDER
JIM DAVIS 6-17
Z
© 1994 PAWS, INC./Distributed by Universal Press Syndicate

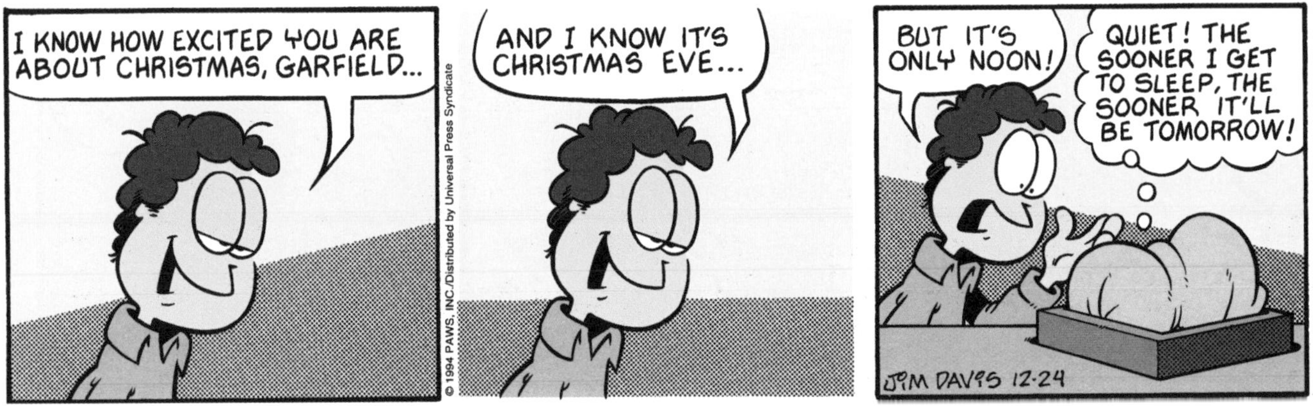
I KNOW HOW EXCITED YOU ARE ABOUT CHRISTMAS, GARFIELD...
© 1994 PAWS, INC./Distributed by Universal Press Syndicate
AND I KNOW IT'S CHRISTMAS EVE...
BUT IT'S ONLY NOON!
QUIET! THE SOONER I GET TO SLEEP, THE SOONER IT'LL BE TOMORROW!
JIM DAVIS 12-24

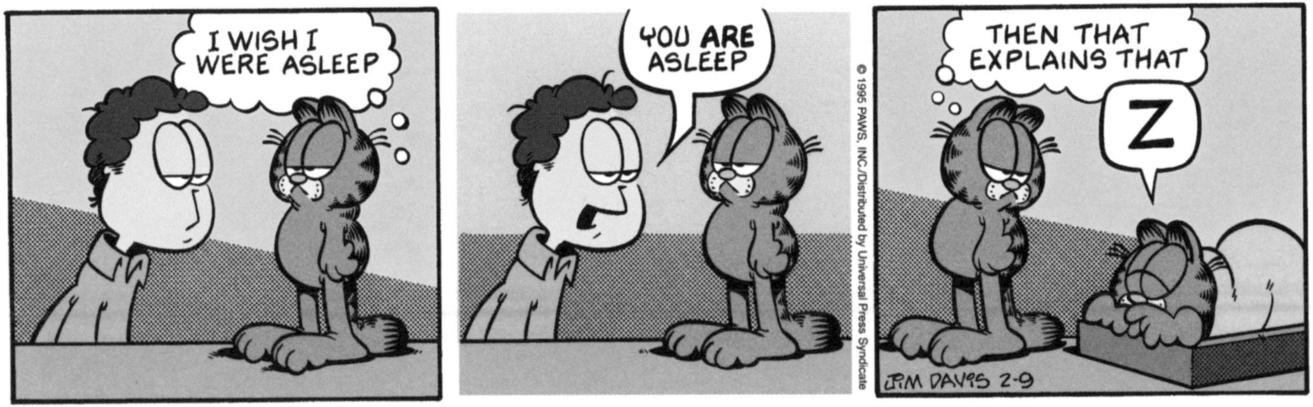
I WISH I WERE ASLEEP
YOU **ARE** ASLEEP
© 1995 PAWS, INC./Distributed by Universal Press Syndicate
THEN THAT EXPLAINS THAT
Z
JIM DAVIS 2-9

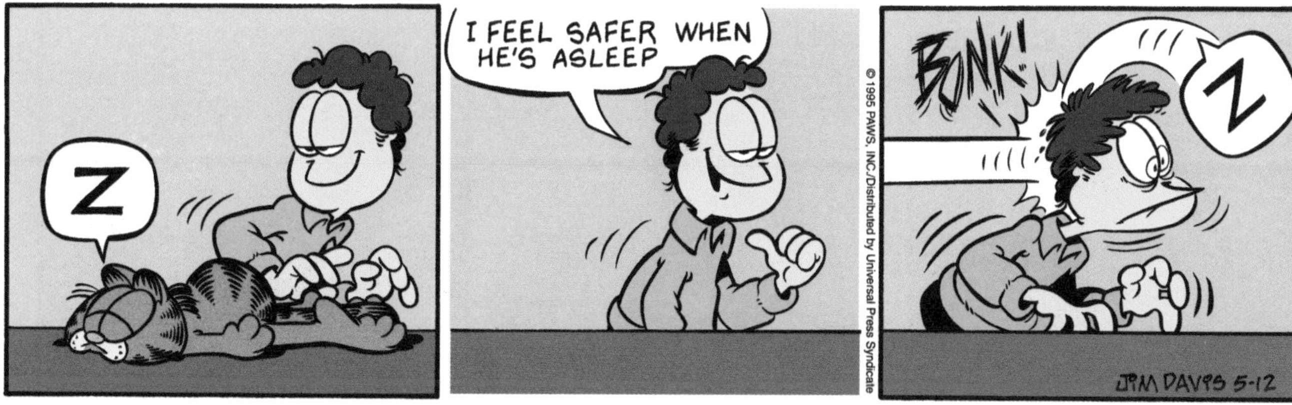
Z
I FEEL SAFER WHEN HE'S ASLEEP
© 1995 PAWS, INC./Distributed by Universal Press Syndicate
BONK!
Z
JIM DAVIS 5-12

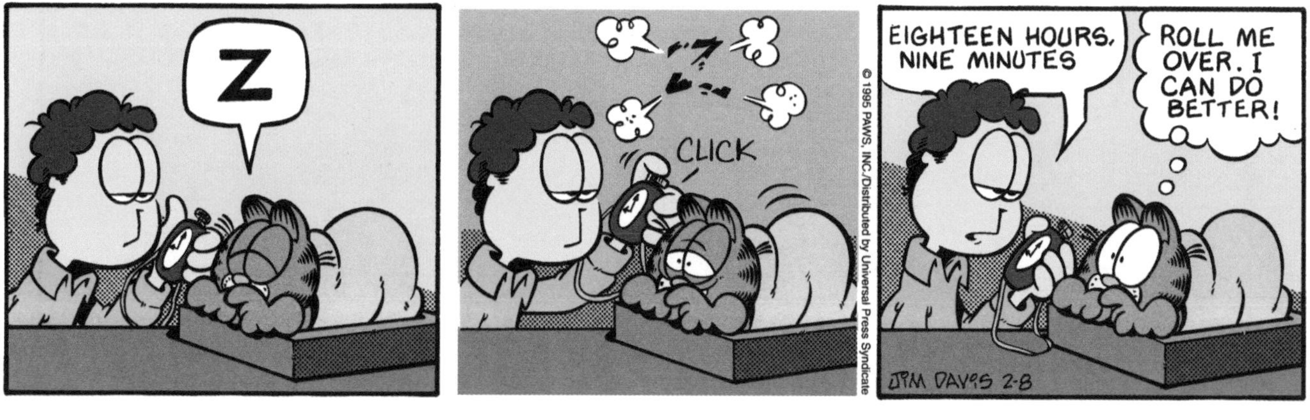
Z
CLICK
© 1995 PAWS, INC./Distributed by Universal Press Syndicate
EIGHTEEN HOURS, NINE MINUTES
ROLL ME OVER. I CAN DO BETTER!
JIM DAVIS 2-8

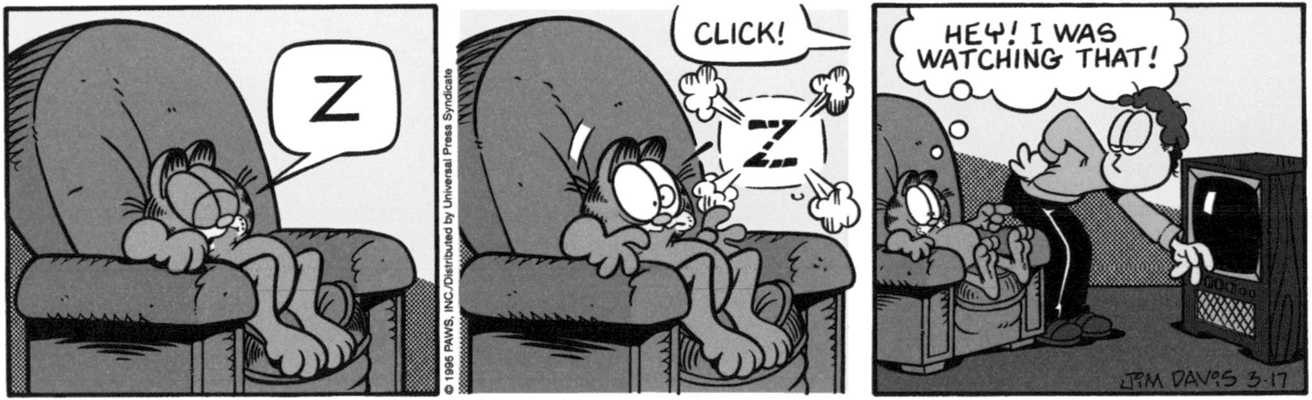
Z
CLICK!
Z
HEY! I WAS WATCHING THAT!
© 1995 PAWS, INC./Distributed by Universal Press Syndicate
JIM DAVIS 3-17

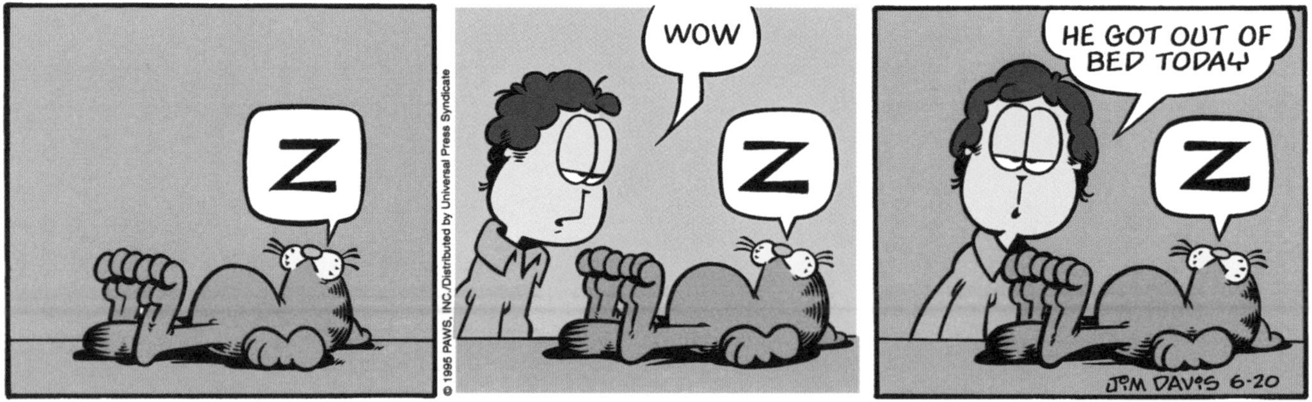
Z
WOW
Z
HE GOT OUT OF BED TODAY
Z
© 1995 PAWS, INC./Distributed by Universal Press Syndicate
JIM DAVIS 6-20

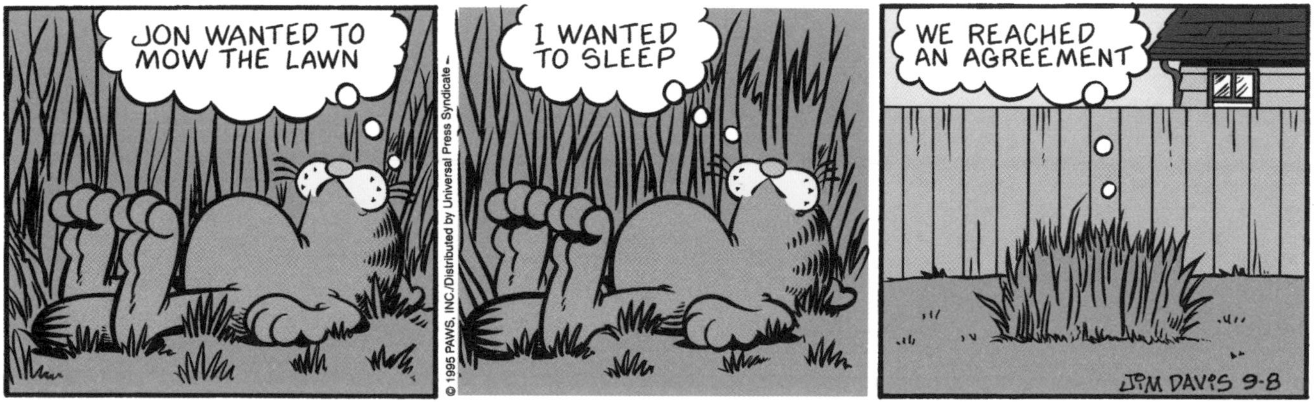
JON WANTED TO MOW THE LAWN
I WANTED TO SLEEP
WE REACHED AN AGREEMENT
JIM DAVIS 9-8

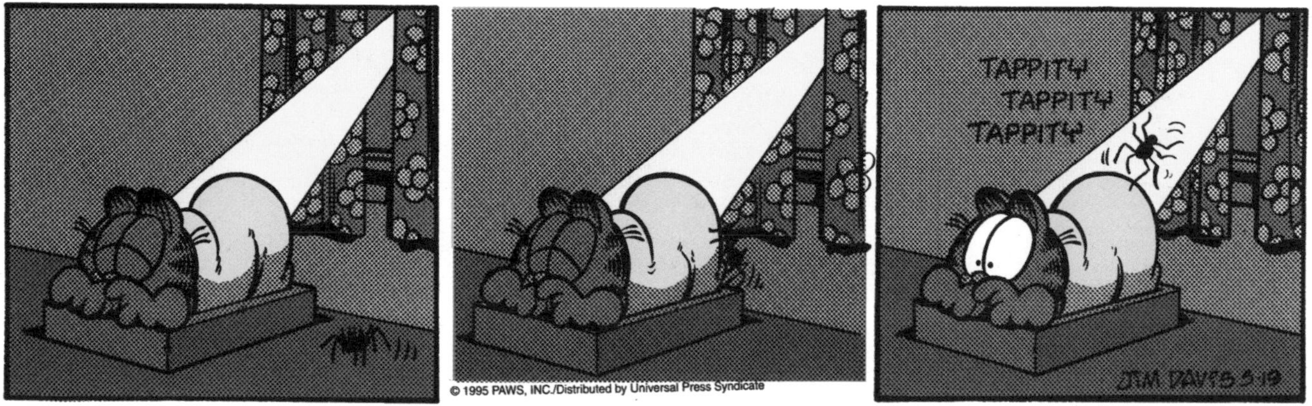
TAPPITY
TAPPITY
TAPPITY
JIM DAVIS 9-19

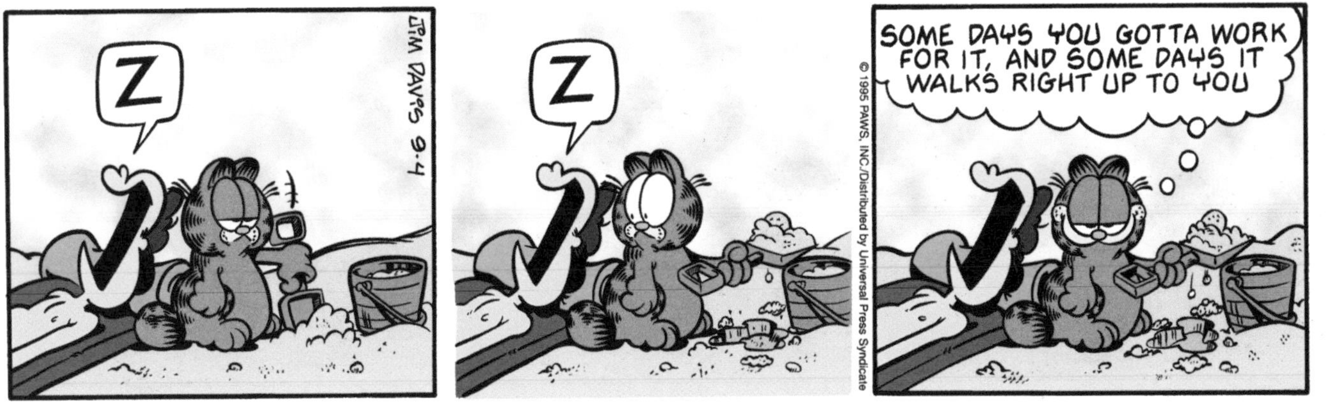
JIM DAVIS 9-4
Z
Z
SOME DAYS YOU GOTTA WORK FOR IT, AND SOME DAYS IT WALKS RIGHT UP TO YOU
© 1995 PAWS, INC./Distributed by Universal Press Syndicate

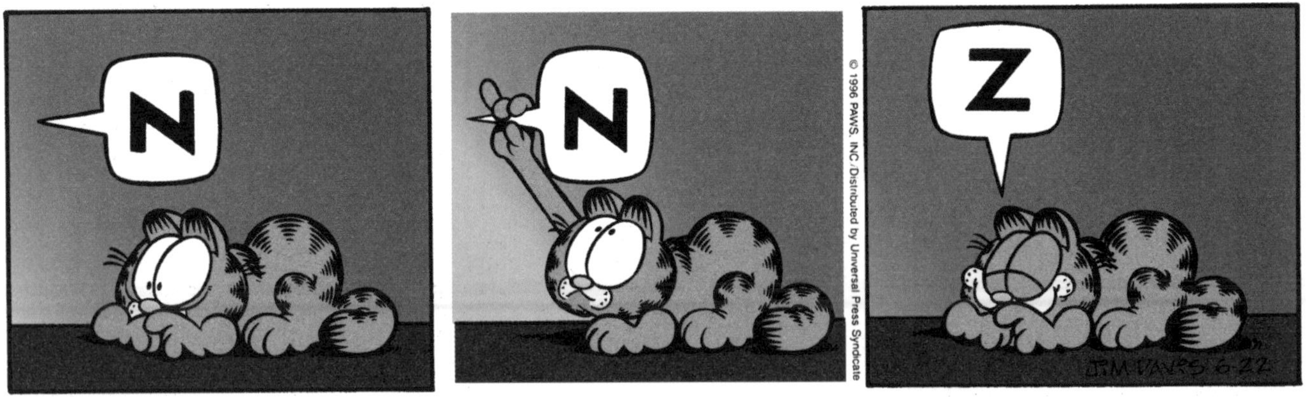
N
N
Z
JIM DAVIS 6-22
© 1996 PAWS, INC./Distributed by Universal Press Syndicate

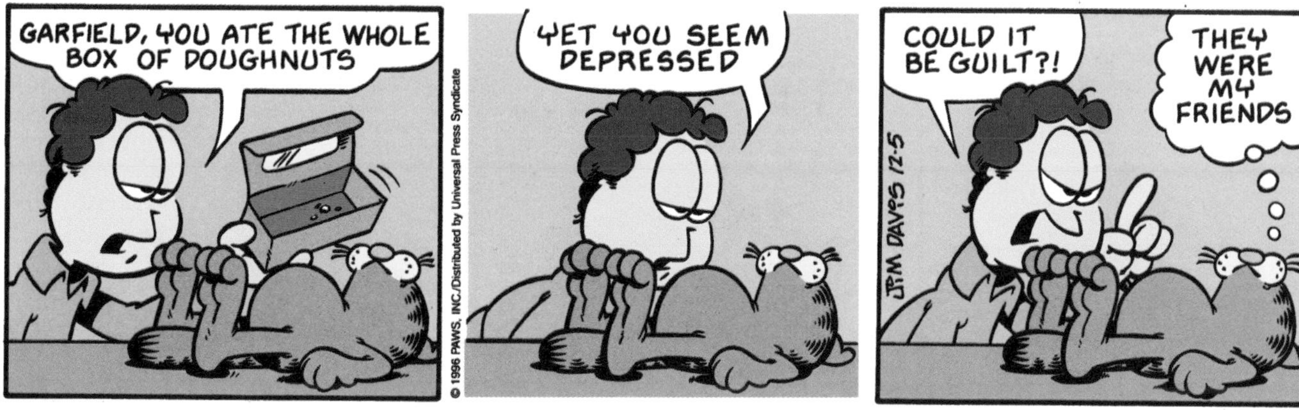
GARFIELD, YOU ATE THE WHOLE BOX OF DOUGHNUTS
YET YOU SEEM DEPRESSED
COULD IT BE GUILT?!
THEY WERE MY FRIENDS
JIM DAVIS 12-5

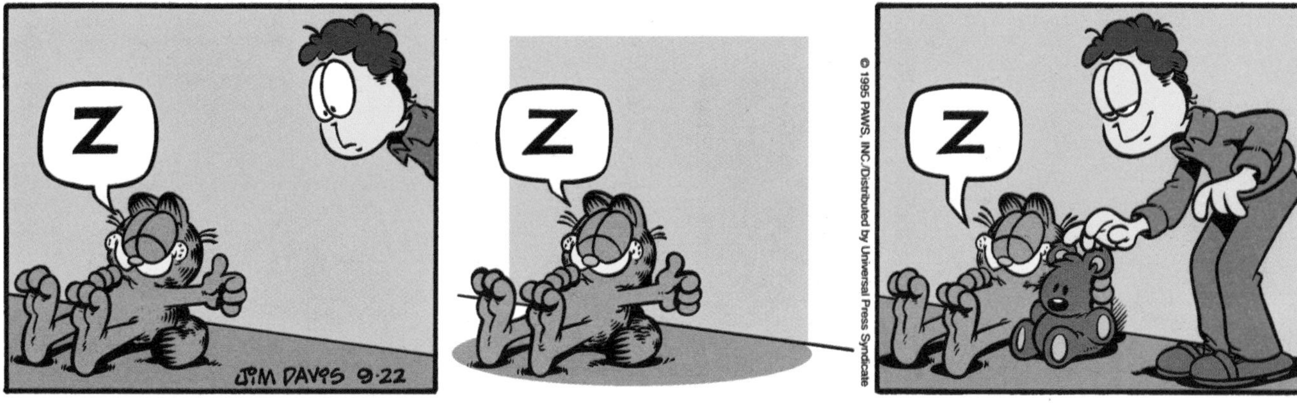
Z
JIM DAVIS 9-22
Z
Z

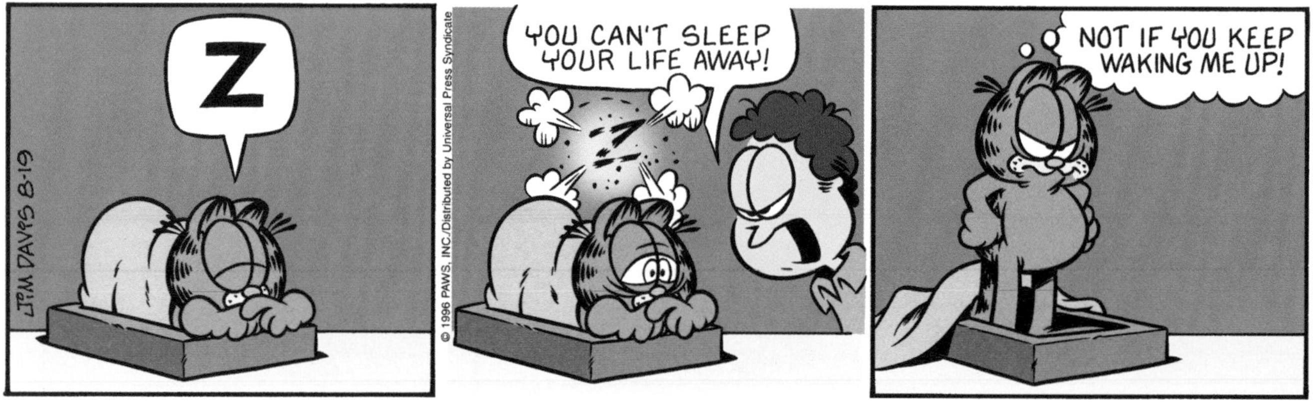
Z
JIM DAVIS 8-19
© 1996 PAWS, INC./Distributed by Universal Press Syndicate
YOU CAN'T SLEEP YOUR LIFE AWAY!
NOT IF YOU KEEP WAKING ME UP!

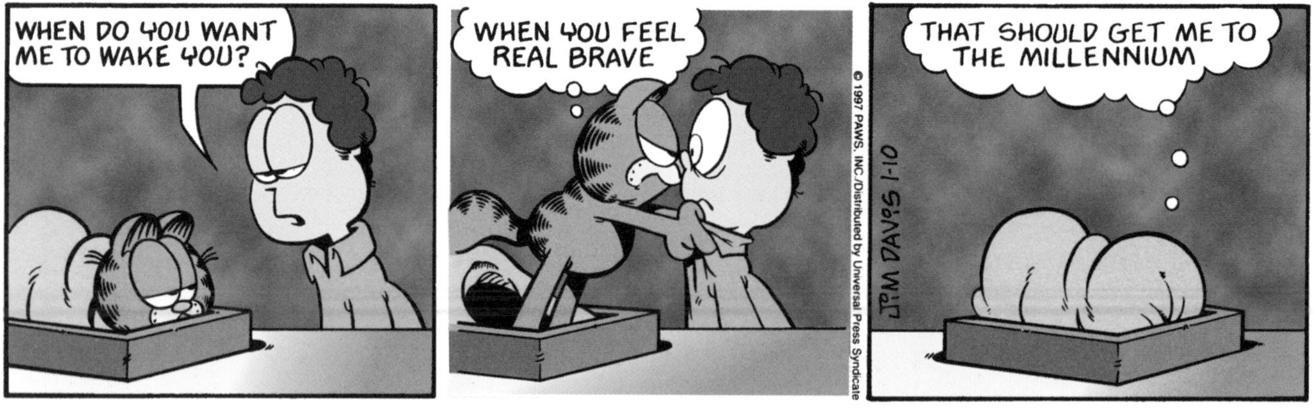
WHEN DO YOU WANT ME TO WAKE YOU?
WHEN YOU FEEL REAL BRAVE
© 1997 PAWS, INC./Distributed by Universal Press Syndicate
JIM DAVIS 1-10
THAT SHOULD GET ME TO THE MILLENNIUM

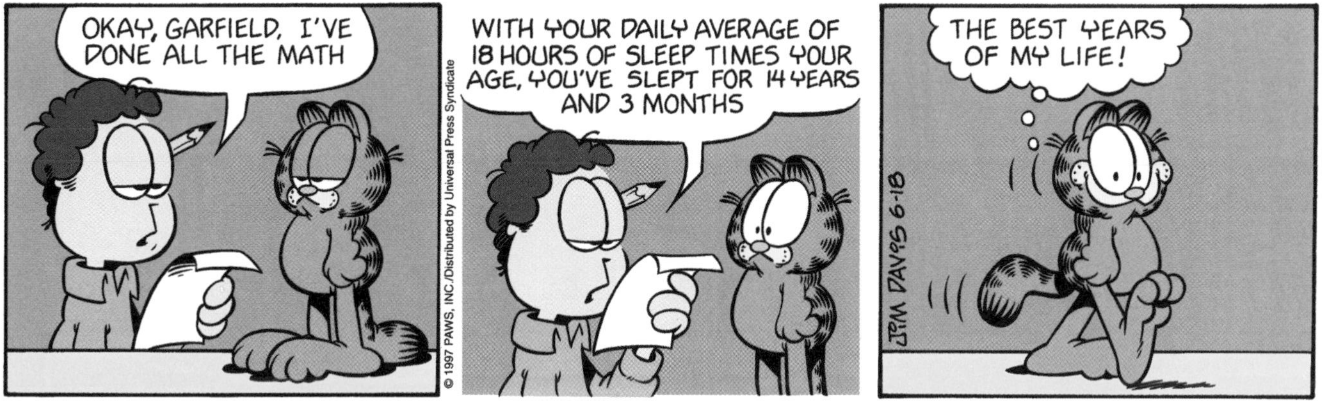
OKAY, GARFIELD, I'VE DONE ALL THE MATH
WITH YOUR DAILY AVERAGE OF 18 HOURS OF SLEEP TIMES YOUR AGE, YOU'VE SLEPT FOR 14 YEARS AND 3 MONTHS
THE BEST YEARS OF MY LIFE!
JIM DAVIS 6-18
© 1997 PAWS, INC./Distributed by Universal Press Syndicate

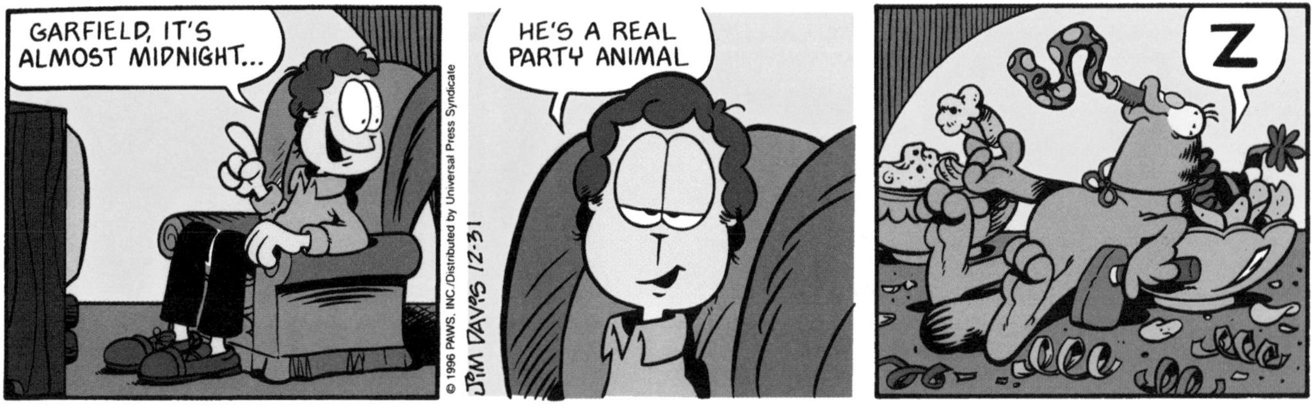
GARFIELD, IT'S ALMOST MIDNIGHT...
HE'S A REAL PARTY ANIMAL
Z
JIM DAVIS 12-31
© 1996 PAWS, INC./Distributed by Universal Press Syndicate

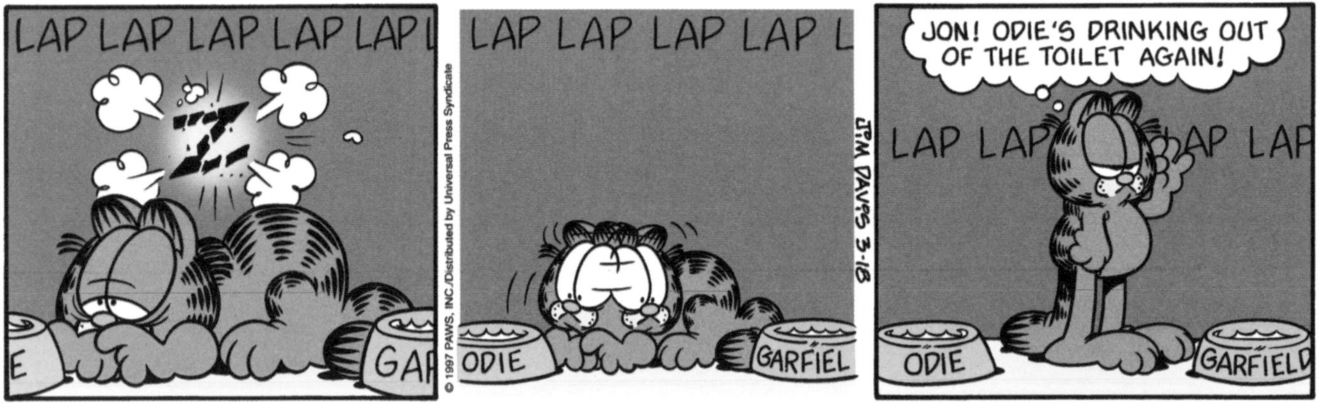
LAP LAP LAP LAP LAP L
LAP LAP LAP LAP L
JON! ODIE'S DRINKING OUT OF THE TOILET AGAIN!
LAP LAP LAP LAP
ODIE
GARFIELD
JIM DAVIS 3-18

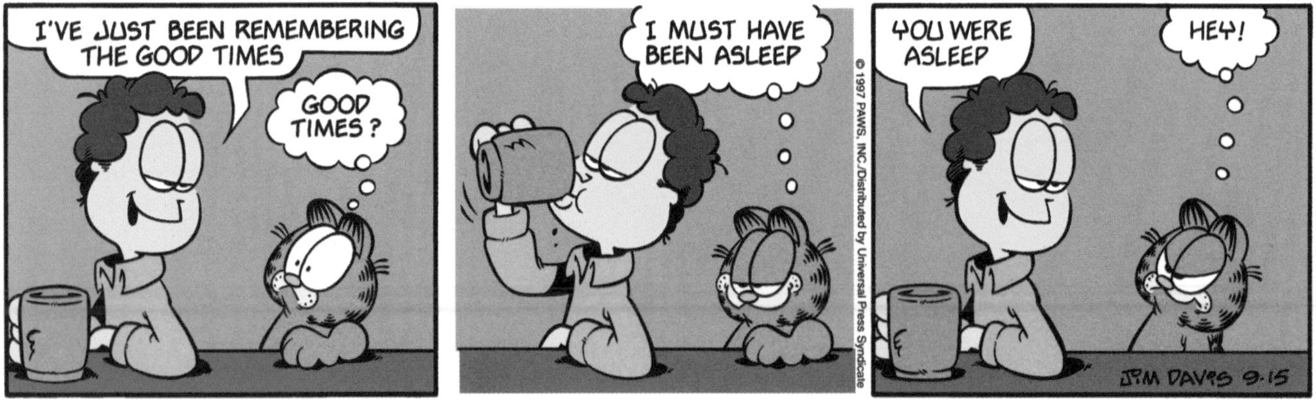
I'VE JUST BEEN REMEMBERING THE GOOD TIMES
GOOD TIMES?
I MUST HAVE BEEN ASLEEP
YOU WERE ASLEEP
HEY!
JIM DAVIS 9-15

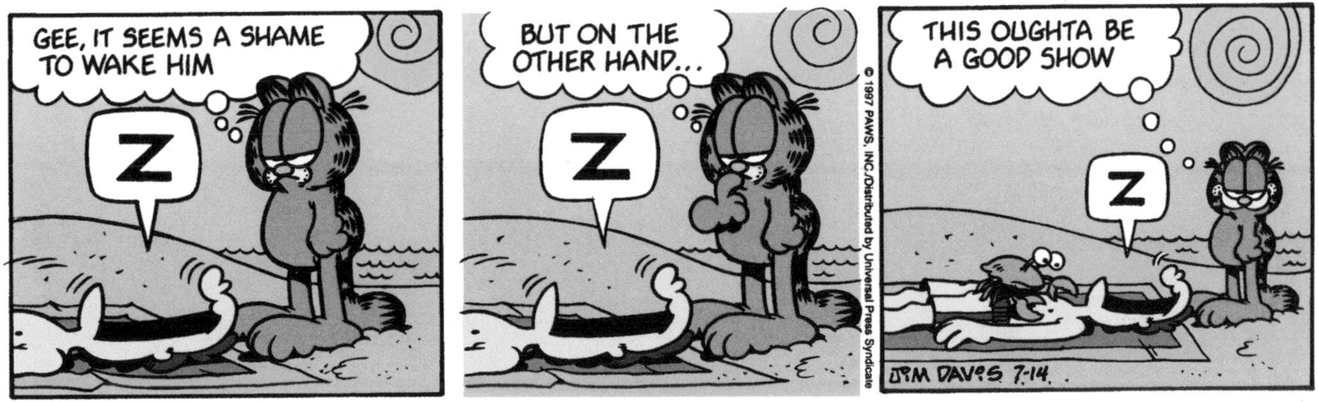
GEE, IT SEEMS A SHAME TO WAKE HIM
Z
BUT ON THE OTHER HAND...
Z
© 1997 PAWS, INC./Distributed by Universal Press Syndicate
THIS OUGHTA BE A GOOD SHOW
Z
JIM DAVIS 7-14

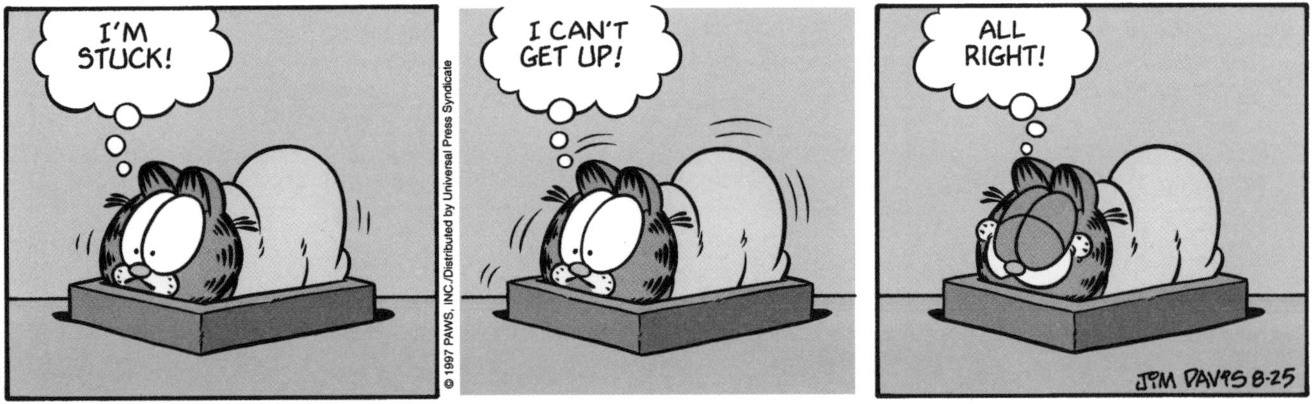
I'M STUCK!
© 1997 PAWS, INC./Distributed by Universal Press Syndicate
I CAN'T GET UP!
ALL RIGHT!
JIM DAVIS 8-25

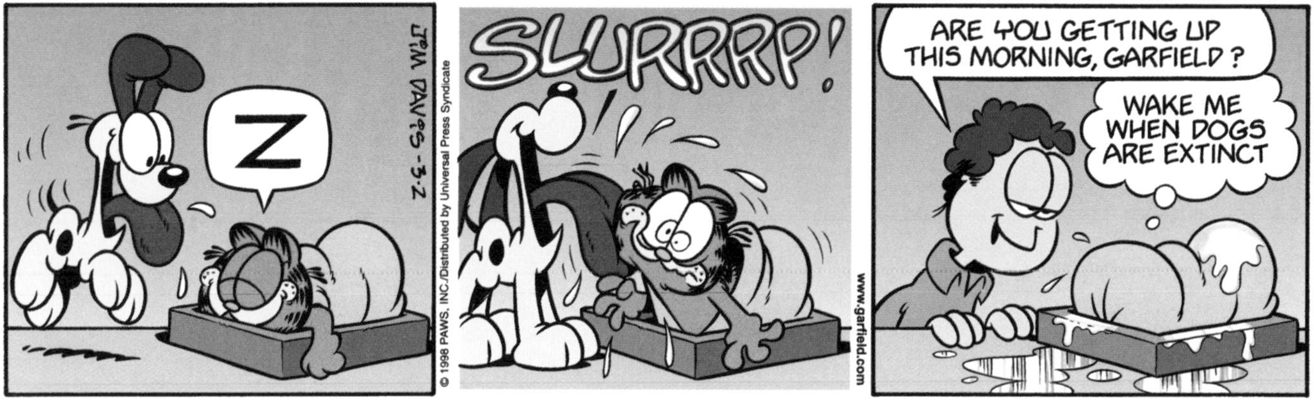
JIM DAVIS 5-2
Z
SLURRRP!
ARE YOU GETTING UP THIS MORNING, GARFIELD ?
WAKE ME WHEN DOGS ARE EXTINCT
© 1998 PAWS, INC./Distributed by Universal Press Syndicate
www.garfield.com

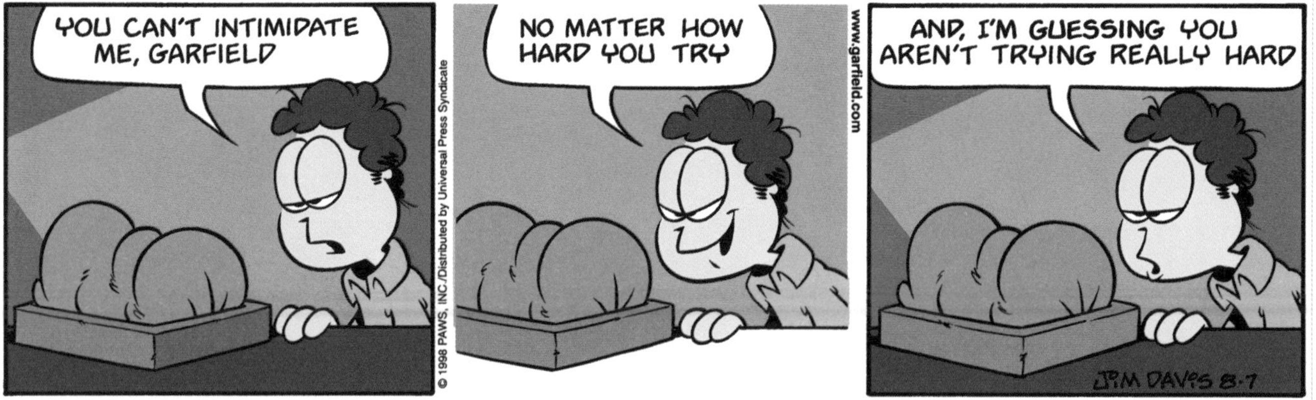
YOU CAN'T INTIMIDATE ME, GARFIELD
NO MATTER HOW HARD YOU TRY
AND, I'M GUESSING YOU AREN'T TRYING REALLY HARD
JIM DAVIS 8-7
© 1998 PAWS, INC./Distributed by Universal Press Syndicate
www.garfield.com

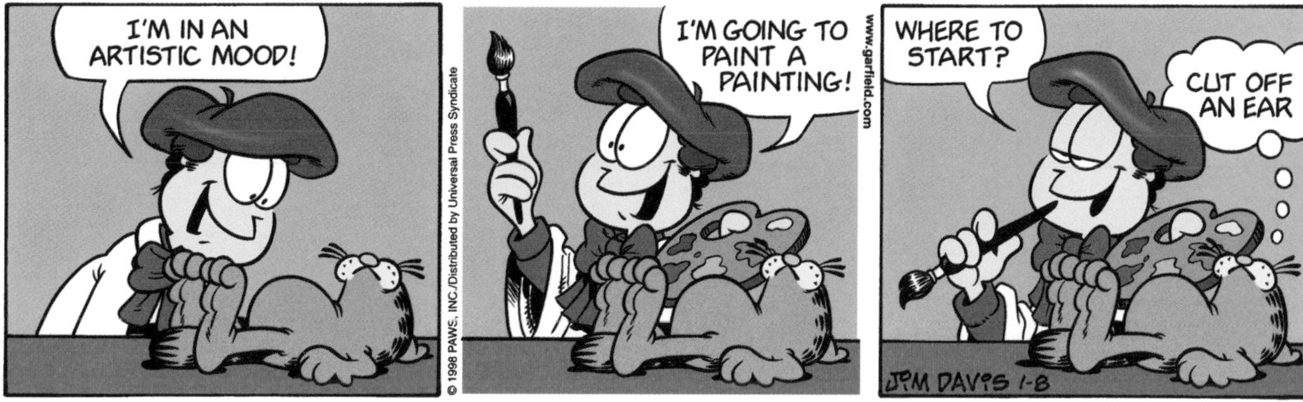
I'M IN AN ARTISTIC MOOD!
I'M GOING TO PAINT A PAINTING!
WHERE TO START?
CUT OFF AN EAR
JIM DAVIS 1-8
© 1998 PAWS, INC./Distributed by Universal Press Syndicate
www.garfield.com

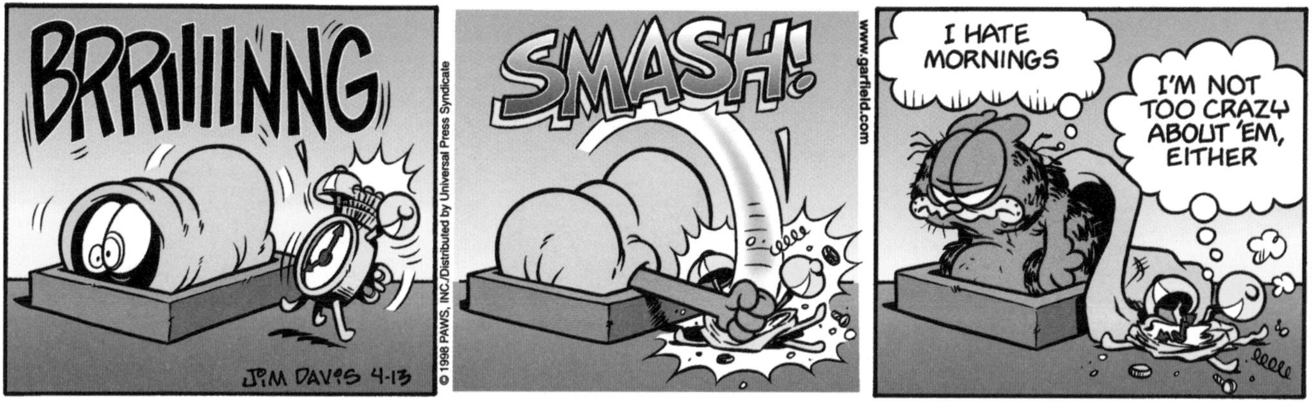
BRRIIIINNG
JIM DAVIS 4-13
SMASH!
I HATE MORNINGS
I'M NOT TOO CRAZY ABOUT 'EM, EITHER
© 1998 PAWS, INC./Distributed by Universal Press Syndicate
www.garfield.com

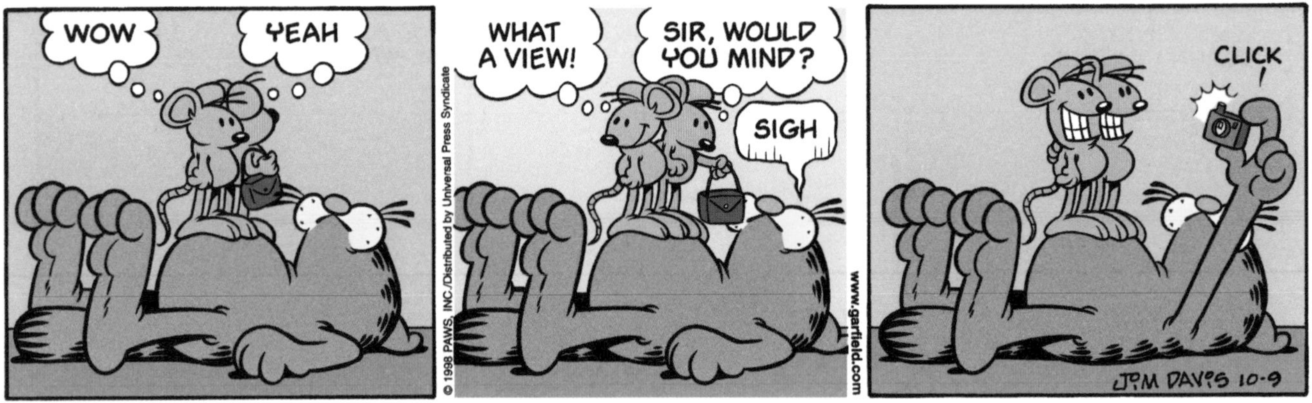
WOW
YEAH
WHAT A VIEW!
SIR, WOULD YOU MIND?
SIGH
CLICK
JIM DAVIS 10-9
© 1998 PAWS, INC./Distributed by Universal Press Syndicate
www.garfield.com

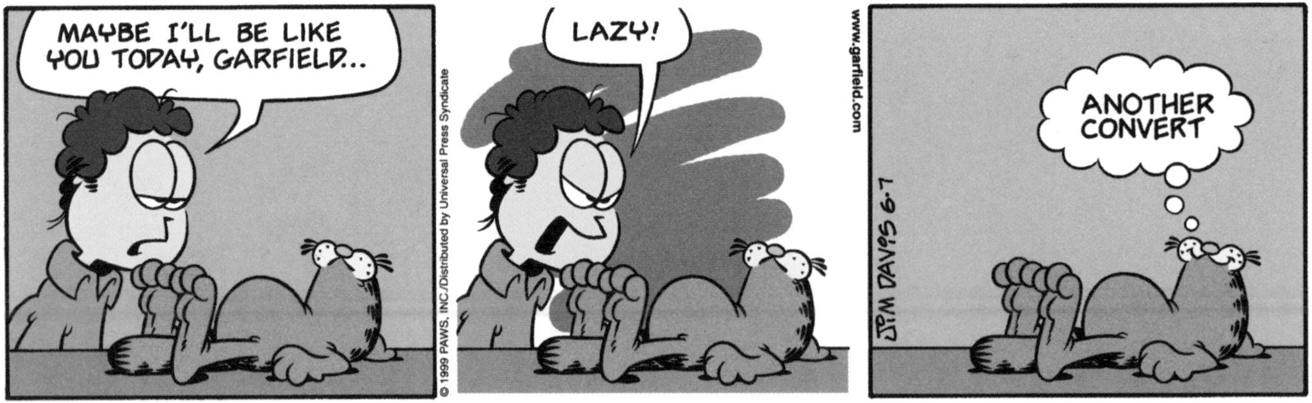
MAYBE I'LL BE LIKE YOU TODAY, GARFIELD...
LAZY!
ANOTHER CONVERT
JIM DAVIS 6-7
© 1999 PAWS, INC./Distributed by Universal Press Syndicate
www.garfield.com

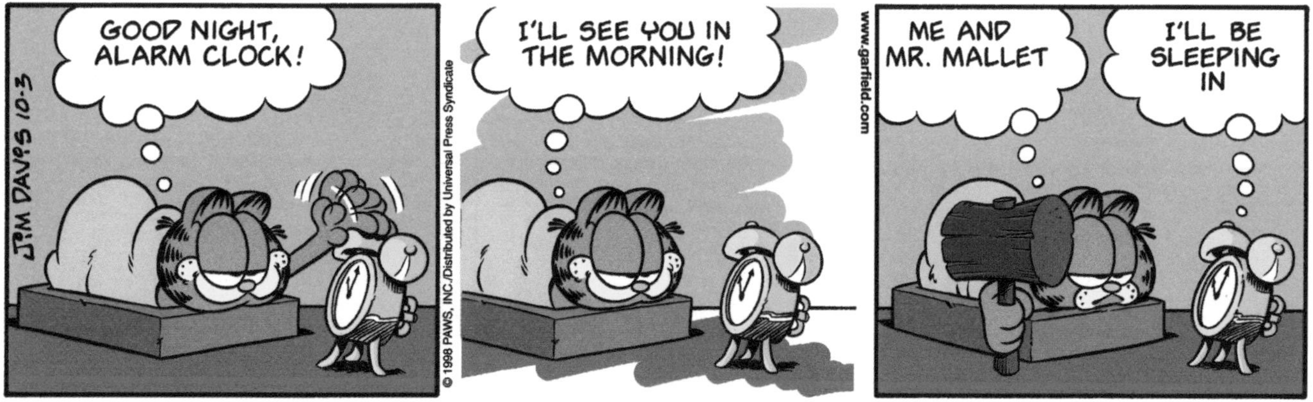
GOOD NIGHT, ALARM CLOCK!
JIM DAVIS 10-3
© 1998 PAWS, INC./Distributed by Universal Press Syndicate
I'LL SEE YOU IN THE MORNING!
www.garfield.com
ME AND MR. MALLET
I'LL BE SLEEPING IN

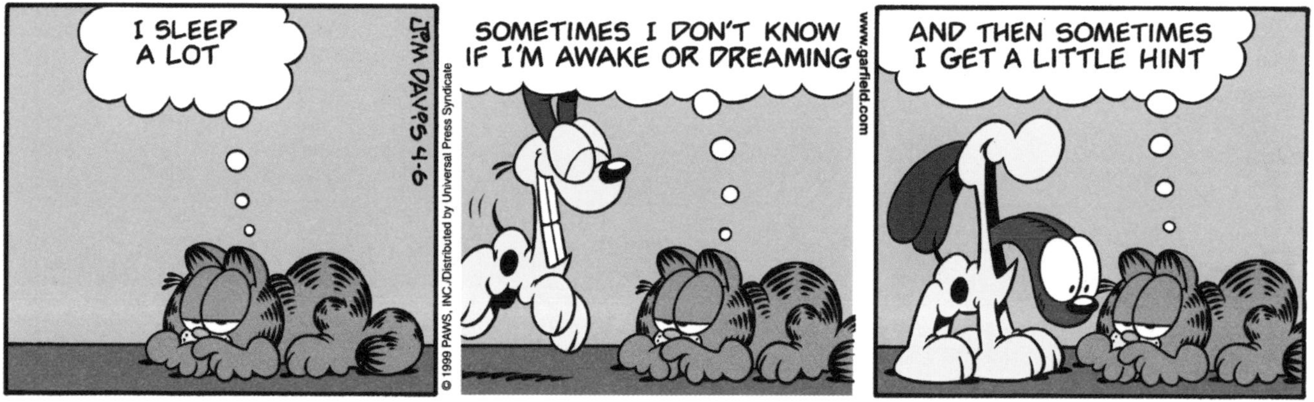
I SLEEP A LOT
JIM DAVIS 4-6
© 1999 PAWS, INC./Distributed by Universal Press Syndicate
SOMETIMES I DON'T KNOW IF I'M AWAKE OR DREAMING
www.garfield.com
AND THEN SOMETIMES I GET A LITTLE HINT

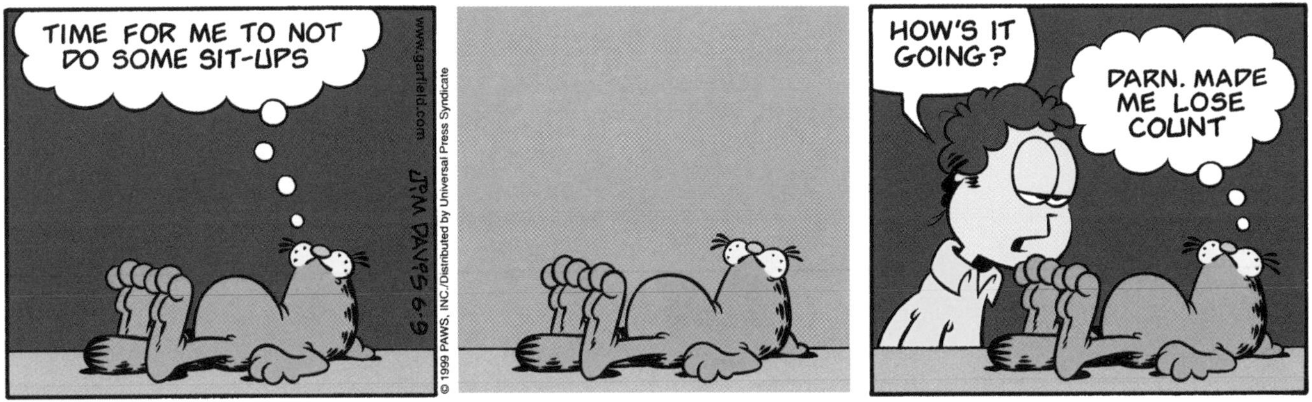
TIME FOR ME TO NOT DO SOME SIT-UPS
www.garfield.com
JPM DAVIS 6-9
© 1999 PAWS, INC./Distributed by Universal Press Syndicate
HOW'S IT GOING?
DARN. MADE ME LOSE COUNT

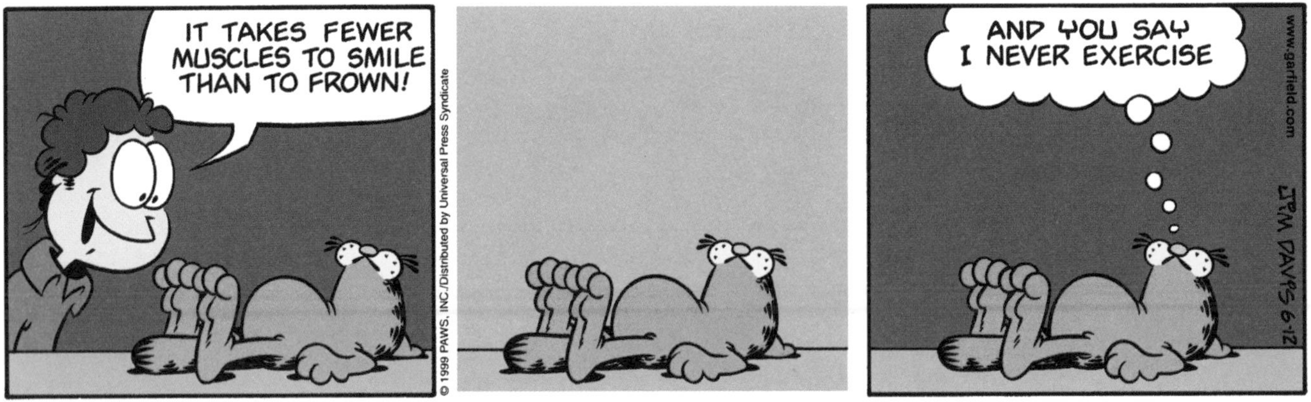
IT TAKES FEWER MUSCLES TO SMILE THAN TO FROWN!
© 1999 PAWS, INC./Distributed by Universal Press Syndicate
AND YOU SAY I NEVER EXERCISE
www.garfield.com
JPM DAVIS 6-12

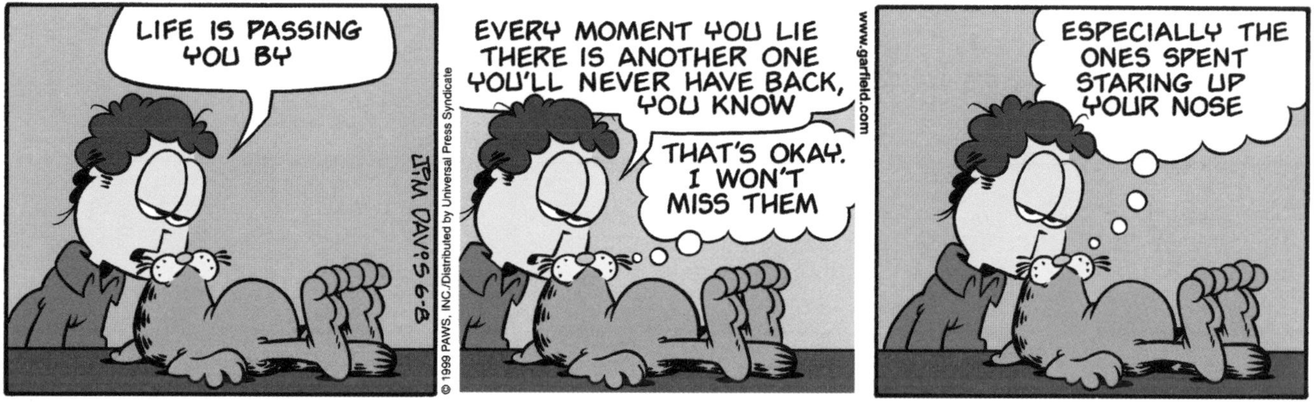
LIFE IS PASSING YOU BY
JPM DAVPS 6-8
© 1999 PAWS, INC./Distributed by Universal Press Syndicate
EVERY MOMENT YOU LIE THERE IS ANOTHER ONE YOU'LL NEVER HAVE BACK, YOU KNOW
THAT'S OKAY. I WON'T MISS THEM
www.garfield.com
ESPECIALLY THE ONES SPENT STARING UP YOUR NOSE

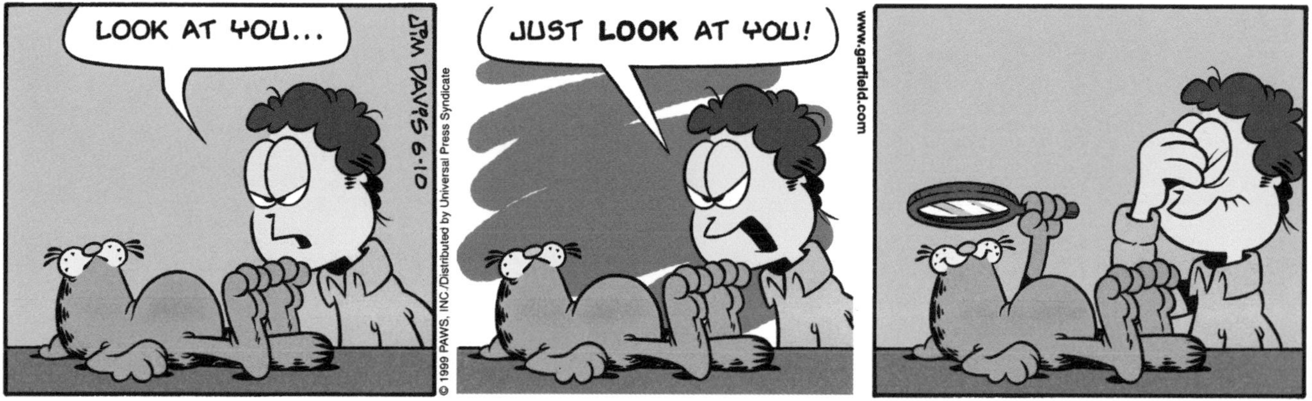
LOOK AT YOU...
JPM DAVPS 6-10
© 1999 PAWS, INC./Distributed by Universal Press Syndicate
JUST **LOOK** AT YOU!
www.garfield.com

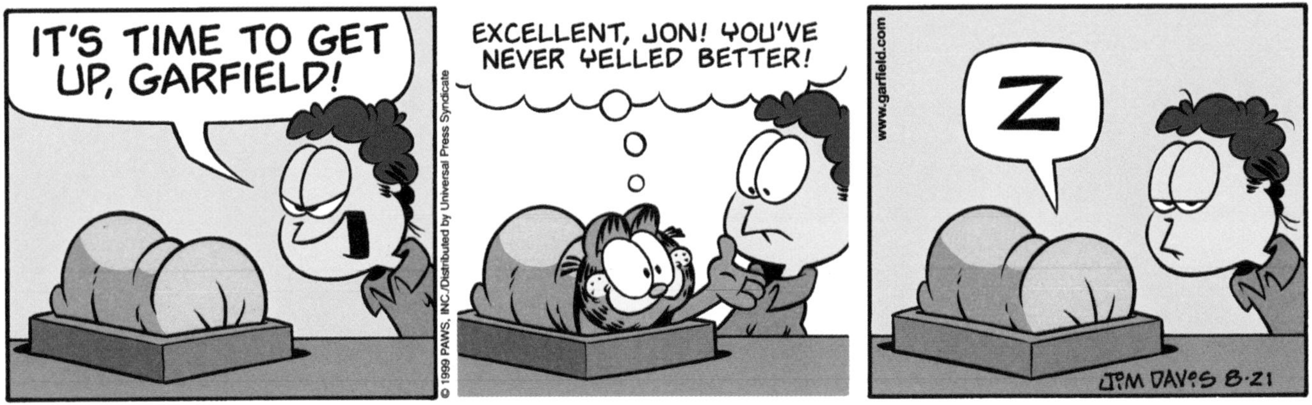
IT'S TIME TO GET UP, GARFIELD!
© 1999 PAWS, INC./Distributed by Universal Press Syndicate
EXCELLENT, JON! YOU'VE NEVER YELLED BETTER!
www.garfield.com
Z
JIM DAVIS 8-21

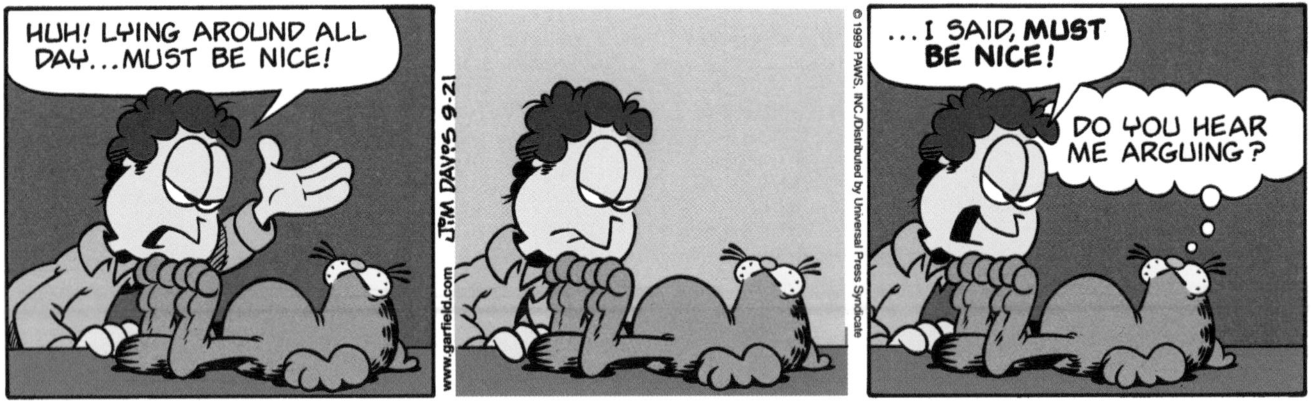
HUH! LYING AROUND ALL DAY...MUST BE NICE!
JIM DAVIS 9-21
www.garfield.com
© 1999 PAWS, INC./Distributed by Universal Press Syndicate
...I SAID, **MUST BE NICE!**
DO YOU HEAR ME ARGUING?

Other GARFIELD titles published by Ravette ...

Pocket Books

	ISBN	Price
Below Par	1 84161 152 2	£3.50
Bon Appetit	1 84161 038 0	£3.50
Compute This!	1 84161 194 8	£3.50
Double Trouble	1 84161 008 9	£3.50
Eat My Dust	1 84161 098 4	£3.50
Fun in the Sun	1 84161 097 6	£3.50
Goooooal!	1 84161 037 2	£3.50
Great Impressions	1 85304 191 2	£3.50
I Don't Do Perky	1 84161 195 6	£3.50
In Training	1 85304 785 6	£3.50
Light Of My Life	1 85304 353 2	£3.50
On The Right Track	1 85304 907 7	£3.50
Pop Star	1 84161 151 4	£3.50
To Eat, Or Not To Eat?	1 85304 991 3	£3.50
With Love From Me To You	1 85304 392 3	£3.50

Theme Books

		ISBN	Price
Behaving Badly		1 85304 892 5	£4.50
Cat Napping		1 84161 087 9	£4.50
Coffee Mornings		1 84161 086 0	£4.50
Creatures Great & Small		1 85304 998 0	£3.99
Healthy Living		1 85304 972 7	£3.99
Pigging Out		1 85304 893 3	£4.50
Successful Living		1 85304 973 5	£3.99
The Seasons		1 85304 999 9	£3.99
Entertains You	(new)	1 84161 221 9	£4.50
Slam Dunk!	(new)	1 84161 222 7	£4.50

2-in-1 Theme Books

		ISBN	Price
Easy Does It		1 84161 191 3	£6.99
Licensed to Thrill		1 84161 192 1	£6.99
Out For The Couch		1 84161 144 1	£6.99
The Gruesome Twosome		1 84161 143 3	£6.99
All In Good Taste	(new)	1 84161 209 X	£6.99

Classic Collections

		ISBN	Price
Volume One		1 85304 970 0	£5.99
Volume Two		1 85304 971 9	£5.99
Volume Three		1 85304 996 4	£5.99
Volume Four		1 85304 997 2	£5.99
Volume Five		1 84161 022 4	£5.99
Volume Six		1 84161 023 2	£5.99
Volume Seven		1 84161 088 7	£5.99
Volume Eight		1 84161 089 5	£5.99
Volume Nine		1 84161 149 2	£5.99
Volume Ten		1 84161 150 6	£5.99
Volume Eleven		1 84161 175 1	£5.99
Volume Twelve		1 84161 176 X	£5.99
Volume Thirteen	(new)	1 84161 206 5	£5.99
Volume Fourteen	(new)	1 84161 207 3	£5.99

Little Books

	ISBN	Price
C-c-c-caffeine	1 84161 183 2	£2.50
Food 'n' Fitness	1 84161 145 X	£2.50
Laughs	1 84161 146 8	£2.50
Love 'n' Stuff	1 84161 147 6	£2.50
Surf 'n' Sun	1 84161 186 7	£2.50
The Office	1 84161 184 0	£2.50
Wit 'n' Wisdom	1 84161 148 4	£2.50
Zzzzzzz	1 84161 185 9	£2.50

Miscellaneous

		ISBN	Price
Garfield The Movie	(new)	1 84161 205 7	£7.99
Garfield 25 years of me!		1 84161 173 5	£7.99
Treasury 5	(new)	1 84161 198 0	£10.99
Treasury 4		1 84161 180 8	£10.99
Treasury 3		1 84161 142 5	£9.99

All Garfield books are available at your local bookshop or from the publisher at the address below. Just tick the titles required and send the form with your payment and name and address details to:-

RAVETTE PUBLISHING, Unit 3, Tristar Centre, Star Road, Partridge Green, West Sussex RH13 8RA

Prices and availability are subject to change without prior notice.

Please enclose a cheque or postal order made payable to Ravette Publishing to the value of the cover price of the book and allow the following for UK p&p:-

60p for the first book + 30p for each additional book, except *Garfield Treasuries*, when please add £3.00 per copy.